# The Feminist Bestseller

From *Sex and the Single Girl* to *Sex and the City*

Imelda Whelehan

palgrave
macmillan

First published 2005 by
PALGRAVE MACMILLAN
Houndmills, Basingstoke, Hampshire RG21 6XS and
175 Fifth Avenue, New York, N.Y. 10010
Companies and representatives throughout the world

PALGRAVE MACMILLAN is the global academic imprint of the Palgrave Macmillan division of St. Martin's Press, LLC and of Palgrave Macmillan Ltd. Macmillan® is a registered trademark in the United States, United Kingdom and other countries. Palgrave is a registered trademark in the European Union and other countries.

ISBN-13: 978–1–4039–1121–6  hardback
ISBN-10: 1–4039–1121–5      hardback
ISBN-13: 978–1–4039–1122–3  paperback
ISBN-10: 1–4039–1122–3      paperback

This book is printed on paper suitable for recycling and made from fully managed and sustained forest sources.

A catalogue record for this book is available from the British Library.

A catalog record for this book is available from the Library of Congress

10   9   8   7   6   5   4   3   2   1
14  13  12  11  10  09  08  07  06  05

Printed in China

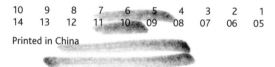

THE FEMINIST BESTSELLER

*Related titles from Palgrave Macmillan*

Peter Childs, *Contemporary Novelists: British Fiction since 1970*
Merja Makinen, *Feminist Popular Fiction*

Dedicated with love to the memory of Thomas
Joseph Whelehan (1921–2000)

# Contents

# Acknowledgements

My greatest debt of thanks is to the Leverhulme Trust for awarding me a Research Fellowship during 2001–2002. This period of leave allowed me to do the remainder of the research for this project and gave me space to think it through for the first time in nearly a decade. I thank you not only for allowing me to complete this project, but also for significantly enhancing my research life since.

Thanks also to Helena Wahlström, whom I met at a conference in 2001 and who very kindly sent me her PhD thesis when she learned that we had similar interests. Kathleen Bell is always willing to share her experiences as one who remembers reading the feminist bestsellers in the 1970s and I'm eternally grateful to her for her opinions and observations on these and so many other things. Mary Joannou collaborated with me on a chapter for *The Feminist Seventies* (2003), which helped focus my mind at an early stage of research for this book. Thanks to Deborah Cartmell for helping me to balance teaching and research and to all colleagues at De Montfort University who have slipped articles into my pigeonhole over the years. Esther Sonnet gave me signed first editions of *Kinflicks* and *Sexual Politics*, which I treasure. Carol Edwards is a great friend to have. John and Loreen literally kept things in order and prevented me from becoming a mad housewife.

Thank you Palgrave Macmillan – especially to Anna Sandeman for taking on the book and latterly to Kate Wallis and Sonya Barker for seeing it through and waiting the extra year. Sorry for being the typical author and holding things up.

David Sadler endures the fits and starts, the bad tempers and the reckless enthusiasm, and for that I thank him. Sorry for all the inconvenience (is there ever a good time to write a book?) and for needing to write this on the kitchen table. Did I prove that I am Superwoman?

Thanks to all my students, past and present, who always provide the most incisive and provocative criticisms.

# Introduction

I have been wanting to write a book about feminist bestsellers for years. In fact, when my PhD was nearing completion and I had my first meeting with an academic publisher, I pitched two proposals – one on Second Wave thought and one on the relationship between the Women's Movement and novels such as Erica Jong's *Fear of Flying* (1973), Lisa Alther's *Kinflicks* (1976), and Marilyn French's *The Women's Room* (1977). The publisher plumped for the first proposal,[1] which was probably very sensible since at the time I had no clear overall plan for the other project; just a sense that these writers were engaging in a dialogue with the Women's Movement without getting much of a response. There was little work on these writers at the time (the early 1990s) and feminist critics were only really beginning to take a broad interest in popular women's fiction at all. By the time I finished my first book, other, more achievable, projects came along and the original proposal lay in its buff folder until the turn of the new century. By then other critics had written on this and related topics and in writing this book I am grateful to be able to draw on the assiduous research and insightful thinking of Maria Lauret and Lisa Maria Hogeland, who both produced books covering many of the issues which had sparked my interest in this topic, not to mention other critics, such as Maroula Joannou, Gayle Greene, and Lorna Sage, whose work was also of direct relevance to me. Collectively their work allows me to move the debate forwards in a new direction, since there is certainly no need to write a book which covers much of the same ground.

The term 'feminist bestseller' only comfortably covers the novels I write about in chapters 3 to 5 of this book; and not necessarily all of these, if this means that the writer of each book must have seen action in the Women's Movement to be an authentic feminist. All of these books owe their success to their women readers who bought them, discussed them, and passed them on so that some, like *Rubyfruit Jungle* (1973), became a bestseller by word of mouth. Their content and the issues raised were unmistakably feminist: some seemed a rehearsal of problems foregrounded in other non-fiction texts such as Betty Friedan's *The Feminine Mystique* (1963) or Kate Millett's *Sexual Politics* (1970), themselves feminist bestsellers. Sue Kaufman's *Diary of a Mad Housewife* (1967) has remarkable echoes of Friedan's groundbreaking book and Bettina Balser, its central figure, is definitely a victim of the 'problem that has no name' (which I shall briefly explicate in chapter 1). Other epithets could also suit this clutch of writings that do not actually acknowledge each other's existence or seem to draw anything from each other. The earlier novels which closely followed the themes explored by Kaufman might be collectively dubbed 'mad housewife' novels (for reasons which will become clear in chapter 3) and those which were published after the mid-1970s and which have remained internationally renowned, such as *The Women's Room*, have been variously termed consciousness-raising or liberation novels for their much more direct engagement with the discourses of Second Wave feminism. I find the term 'consciousness-raising novel' particularly useful, as will become clear through the course of this book. However, generically 'feminist bestseller' suits my purposes extremely well, not least because it allows me to problematize the linkage of the two terms. The phrase feels awkward, even treacherous, particularly when we apply it to groundbreaking non-fiction texts such as Kate Millett's *Sexual Politics* or Germaine Greer's *The Female Eunuch* (1970), because the fact that individual women could make a great deal of money out of their feminist convictions caused controversy within the Women's Movement at the time.

Towards those feminist writers not visibly active in women's groups in Britain or the US, such as Greer, there was only suspicion: 'the whole tone of *The Female Eunuch* is shallow, anti-woman, regressive, three steps backward to the world of false sexual liberation from which so many young women have fled' (Dreifus 1973: 359). The Women's Liberation Movement (as the radical wing of the Second Wave of feminism came to be known) was a movement based on collectivity. Early activists went out of their way to avoid the media's selecting a 'star' from their midst to act as a spokesperson; and the idea that someone might make their living out of producing feminist ideas was unpalatable in the extreme. But such was the interest in feminism, and the thirst for knowledge about what it meant for individual women to be feminists, that these early publications flew off the shelves and individuals made money whether they had intended to or not. Those novelists who incorporated feminism into their fiction were also likely to receive similar opprobrium. Yet their work tapped into a mass readership and actually succeeded in communicating core feminist ideas simply and effectively. At this time, feminist criticism was developing a methodology of reading women's literature from the past and rescuing it from patriarchal obscurity, but it had no real interest in popular fiction and very little in contemporary literary fiction. Examples from popular culture were generally used to make a point about the preponderance of female stereotypes, the uses to which they are put, and their effect on an oppressed female population. There was little work being done on the ways popular fiction might be a useful medium of communication because of the contradictions involved in concealing a feminist message within a formula that was necessarily deemed conservative.

No matter how accessible some of the non-fiction feminist bestsellers were, the fiction was easier to read and had all the qualities of good popular fiction – page-turning incidents, engaging central characters – and if there was a political message, the pill was appropriately sugared. These were books that brought all the difficulties of calling yourself a feminist to life: they dramatized the pulls of relationships and family ties even while they exposed the soft sell of romantic love, and women devoured them hungrily and found them life-changing. Needless to say this success also suited the publishers, who thus found a way to brand modern feminism without having to endorse its politics. They were consciously selling a feminist identity to women who might never pluck up the courage or find the political conviction to join a women's group, and women bought it willingly.

When I returned to my original proposal I had just finished a book, *Overloaded*, which touched on the fate of feminism in contemporary Britain – an era wherein images of women as objects of desire again proliferate, set against the supposed fact that women have never had it so good in material terms. In *Overloaded* I argue, 'we have passed into a an era of "retro-sexism" – nostalgia for a lost, uncomplicated past peopled by "real" women and humorous cheeky chappies, where the battle of the sexes is most fondly remembered as being played out as if in a situation comedy such as *Man About the House* or *Butterflies'*[2] (Whelehan 2000: 11). It seemed entirely natural to include a discussion of Helen Fielding's *Bridget Jones's Diary* (1996) as also evoking a similar nostalgia for the battle of the sexes, and I observed then that 'Bridget neatly expressed the tensions of a woman who recognises the rhetoric of feminism and empowerment, but isn't always able to relate this to her fulsome desire for a hero from a Jane Austen novel' (Whelehan 2000: 136). My discussion of *Bridget Jones* and chick lit in general in this book was of necessity brief, and once I had finished it I knew I hadn't finished with Bridget. I was fascinated increasingly by the things being said about this book in the media and on the academic conference circuit, and by the seemingly endless proliferation of Bridget clones caught between the pastel soft covers that were to become the trademark of chick lit. It occurred to me that there might be some merit in looking at the impact of 1970s American feminist fiction on British chick lit since the mid 1990s through the lens of contemporary feminist debates.

On first glance there is little to connect the two groups of fiction – where feminist fiction takes its heroines out of marriage into singledom, chick lit moves in the opposite direction – but there is something about the reception of each which created a small quake in publishing history as well as generating a flurry of either angry or passionately defensive reviews. It is well known that early editions of *The Women's Room* were flagged, 'this book changes lives', and that this not only became a deft piece of niche marketing, but also seemed to reflect the experiences of many of its readers, prompted to view their own domestic lives afresh. For thousands of women the experience of reading *Bridget Jones's Diary* might not have been life-changing, but it facilitated a shift in the way contemporary young women's lives were discussed and described. Here was the generation who should be profiting from the activism of their feminist mothers, lamenting an excess of freedom and stumbling under the burden of choice and autonomy. It seemed that *Bridget Jones's Diary* revealed an anxiety about the legacy of the Women's Movement in the 1990s and spoke to a new generation of women about the complexities of their lives. On the face of it, this is accomplished through the irony which characterizes the style of the book's humour, but actually many readers chose to respond to Bridget in a much more direct way, seeing her as representing the plight of the modern 'singleton'. The form of the diary suggested a link to the writing of the 1970s which often used, if not always the diary, a confessional form of expression, and this form of narrative intimacy better communicated the themes and issues at the forefront of women's lives in both the 1970s and 1990s.

This book is therefore founded on the contention that both feminist bestsellers of the 1970s and the bestselling genre loosely known as chick lit are in dialogue with feminism, the former directly – often through the avowed feminism of its heroines – and the latter more obliquely by the way its heroines often seem to be wrestling with a nascent feminist consciousness set against their quest for The One. Both groups of books tell us something about their contemporary cultural context and both suggest that, much as feminism of the Second Wave was truly life-changing in the impact it has had on social policy, the law, and politics over the years, there were mistakes and deficiencies which left certain women out in the cold. The feminist bestsellers of the 1970s not only reflect the concerns of the Women's Movement and Second Wave feminism, but they also expose deficiencies and points of friction that have not always been explicitly addressed in the Movement writings. Moreover, they can sometimes echo absences in the political discourse of feminism, and nowhere is this more apparent than in the open endings of the novels where the central character may find herself alone, or on the threshold of decisions, always looking back. Thirty more years down the line, the gaps within feminism have become chasms in the social experience of women, where feminism, instead of being regarded as a means to self-determination and political knowledge, is popularly seen as tyrannical, shrill, and, worst of all, off-putting to eligible men.

It might seem on the face of it that novels such as *Fear of Flying* have nothing to say to the Bridget Jones generation for whom the home and family are places they see as a destination rather than as a point of departure, but I hope to show through the course of this book that the problems which beset the heroines of the 1970s classics were never resolved. It seems at first glance as if the chick litters of the nineties to the noughties have redirected their gaze away from the personal being political, but you do not have to read many of these texts to observe a shared note of anxiety about the fate of femininity after feminism and the culture of achievement it has seemed to breed. Chick lit speaks to those afraid that they won't make the cut and thrust of high female achievement and it repackages the classic romance formula found in Mills & Boon and Harlequin so that courtship no longer takes place in a vacuum,[3] but rather plots an uneven course through the chaotic lives of these women aged from twenty to thirty-something. Both feminist bestsellers and chick lit were publishing successes and drew on a huge community of readers, who not only loved them but identified closely with the main characters. In both cases the form of realism used encourages such close identification, just as it also prompts accusations of naïve writing and structureless narrative, and criticisms that both forms lack literary sophistication. Both created a media sensation through a word or phrase found in one of the best-known novels – in the 1970s it was the 'zipless fuck' coined by Erica Jong and in the 1990s it was a cluster of evocative words and phrases devised by Bridget and her friends to conceptualize the embattled world of the single woman, including 'singleton', 'smug marrieds', and 'emotional fuckwits'.

Jong's novel provides, through the life of Isadora, an account of the cultural life of white Western heterosexual women of a whole generation and declares the impossibility of being single or having significant life ambitions beyond that of marriage and the family. Feminism failed to encourage fully a more inclusive view of womankind, and chick lit demonstrates that 'everywoman' is still white, straight, reasonably well off, and able to fit into a size 12/14 dress. Within this highly restrictive viewpoint, writers such as Helen Fielding offered a view of women crippled by choice and seeing the relative freedoms their generation inherited as themselves a tyranny. What becomes foregrounded instead are questions about how one conducts intimate relationships in a world where the 'rules' have been swept away along with the logic of gender roles of the past. Both feminist bestsellers and chick lit have been sent up by commentators offering snappy descriptions listing their essential qualities (and, having discovered the 'formula', peremptorily dismissing them as mere disposable trash). Some of these snappy summaries are illuminating primarily because of what they say about the critics who pen them. Rosalind Coward's working definition of the feminist bestseller has been immensely influential to the way these books have been read. She depicts them (and sends them up) thus:

> in these novels where women's experience is highlighted, it has become a standing joke that we are to expect the first period, first kiss, first (fumbled) intercourse, first (disastrous) marriage, lesbian affair and usually lonely resolution. The end product is normally that the protagonist feels she has 'become her own person'. The disingenuous construction of an adolescent world derives precisely from the novel's attempt to create a higher realism. The complex family history and interrelations, the anecdotes presented as if passed from generation to generation, the eccentric view of the world, are all practices aimed at creating the sense of the autobiographical. This is something which is often reinforced by the way in which the central characters . . . are themselves writers or novelists (Coward 1984: 181–2).

I shall go on to discuss the impact of Coward's views on the feminist bestseller for subsequent feminist critics in chapter 3. For now it is worth noting that although this account does not by any means fit all of the novels I am going to discuss in this category, there are shared elements that recur often enough – particularly, the inclusion of an account of the main character's adolescence or young adulthood, the detailed description of unhappy marriages or suffocating relationships with men and the sense that at the end these women have chosen a different path for themselves. I would also add that very often these novels include heart-rending and graphic accounts of unwanted pregnancies and abortions, and of sexual experiences beset by ignorance and disappointment. That the women quite often are frustrated artists, writers, or would-be intellectuals makes the point that it is the life of the mind which domestic quietude so often quashes. Creative energies become symbolic of the power of self-determination; and in the more sophisticated accounts the woman as artist is shown as needing to break down the norms of what art can be in order to show its gendered foundations.

Lisa Maria Hogeland dubs this grouping of novels 'consciousness raising' (CR) novels to emphasize their link to the practices of Second Wave feminism, which placed a high degree of importance on the process of consciousness raising. As Hogeland remarks,

> What novels could provide was more personal narratives, more and more extended versions of the testimony that women provided in the face-to-face group meetings which were the basis of CR. Like the personal essays that were a staple of feminist periodicals in the 1970s – the 'click!' letters to *Ms.*, for example, in which women described some small experience that crystallized their understandings of women's oppression – the novels were to function as testimony of the absent member (Hogeland 1998: 24).

The narrational style of these novels draws the reader in, encouraging us to feel that we share these experiences rather than viewing them from a distance. Just as in consciousness raising sessions where a small group of women regularly met to share experiences, so, it is argued, the process continues in these works of fiction. In such groups women were encouraged not just to review their current lives, but also to look back at their relationships with their family, their upbringing, and their education, in an attempt to account for the numerous ways women are socialized into femininity and differing modes of behaviour and attitudes. For feminists of the Second Wave most attributes described as either masculine and feminine needed to be critically scrutinized to see where such categories spring from, and it was agreed that within family life and education lay many of the seeds of such assumptions about the way gender affects people, to the point that such assumptions can critically modify behaviour. The CR groups were deemed by many feminists to be essential for women to review the unconscious processes by which such assumptions are perpetuated because, as feminists observed, the power of the masculine/feminine binary was in the way it had become entrenched in common-sense thinking, to the point where one had to look twice and learn to scrutinize one's behaviour and unthinking prejudices.

The importance of consciousness raising as a precept underpinning modern feminism cannot be overstated. In many ways it is this process of using small 'rap' groups of women to develop a politicized awareness of women's lives which defined a new energy in modern feminism. The tradition of liberal feminism represented by writers such as Betty Friedan in her work *The Feminine Mystique* was sustained by the belief that once awareness of injustice was raised, the democratic processes could be tweaked to recognize women's special case. For radical feminists emerging in the mid-1960s, however, the idea was that if women could get together to 'tell it like it is', they would recognize the means of their own oppression as women, the ways in which this is a shared experience among women, with a view to eventually using this knowledge to frame their own political action towards a revolution in consciousness of gender. Although there are multifarious accounts of the CR process – the point being that each consciousness-raising group defines its own parameters – it was generally accepted that such groups should be small enough to allow all members a voice and that, once established, they should close their doors to newcomers in order to cultivate the trust, loyalty, and intimacy of existing members. The risks associated with using CR as a basis for developing political activism have been well documented by writers from the Movement (for example, Payne 1973: 283), not least the risk that CR may result in extended self-help therapy sessions, which may help the group bond at a personal level but may not necessarily become realized in political initiatives. Nonetheless, many feminists would find the process in itself illuminating and might communicate their new-found awareness less formally to other friends. This might not bring new members to a particular women's liberation group, but would contribute to a mass understanding of the basic principles and aims of modern feminism. These less formal aspects of CR and their happier side effects seem to mimic the CR potential of the feminist bestseller, with their tendency towards the first-person narrative voice and its direct address to an implied woman reader. This suggests that CR had far-reaching indirect benefits for women of the time, and for feminism, that have yet to be calculated. A key aim of this book is to show how the CR dimension of the feminist novels of the 1970s may have come through popular fiction to be still recognizable, but changed in emphasis in popular women's fiction of the 1990s and at the time of writing.

The lives of women narrated between the pages of these powerful novels of the late 1960s and 1970s offer the beginnings of a 'political' revelation in the sense of recognizing a problem shared. In the often explicit descriptions of sexual relationships, abortion, and mothering, both taboo subjects and the essentially mundane features of life were revisited and a challenge was made not only to the normative discourses of sex and femininity found in medicine and psychoanalysis, but also to the platitudes found in the popular women's magazines of the day. The seemingly naïve realism of the texts in a time when literary experimentation was becoming more prevalent suggests that they comprise an organic form for someone who wants to be seen to tell the simple truth of a situation, as it leads to a tendency for thematic rather than symbolic readings. Writers, drawing on the work of their peers, seemed content in part to repeat key issues and dwell on primal scenes of feminine identity formation, which suggests the rapid development of a popular feminist aesthetic eschewing that which obscures in favour of direct and hard-hitting prose. This was, of course, compatible with the political writings emerging from the Movement; and even Erica Jong, one of the more 'literary' of these writers, whose *Fear of Flying* is peppered with literary references and shows an indebtedness to the eighteenth-century picaresque writings of Henry Fielding and others, can be read with comprehension without any such background knowledge on the part of the reader. Her final scene in this novel, which has Isadora in the bathroom of her husband's hotel room, resonates with the final chapter of James Joyce's *Ulysses*, which depicts Molly Bloom (whose period has just started, signifying, as it does for Isadora, that she has not been made pregnant by her lover) on the pot begging the author to get her out of here. Jong and her readers know that, for the time being at least, Isadora is torn between returning to her husband (who is certainly no worse than the lover she left him for) and beginning again on her own. The unresolved ending of this and other novels I shall go on to discuss can be frustrating, but some form of open ending is essential to allow for the creative processes of the reader's own mind. Just as CR was supposed to clear the way for political action, so the novels demand a response – and even action – from their readers, who are strategically denied an ending which answers the questions for them. The use of literary realism also allows the starkness of some of the situations these writers were trying to convey to come through. It is difficult to remember in these times, when feminism has developed a whole panoply of conceptual jargon for itself, that early feminists sought means to represent that which had no customary language or means of representation – that was, quite literally, the 'problem that has no name' (Friedan 1982: 13–29). Feminists like Sheila Rowbotham remind us of the power of language and the importance of developing a feminist frame of reference when recalling that at the time it felt revolutionary to describe housework as 'work' (Rowbotham 1989: 37–58).

The problems raised by these novels, far from being surmounted or superseded by new directions in feminist politics, actually pinpoint gaps and silences within contemporary feminist thought. It is strange that until recently such texts were often overlooked by feminist critics, even those who had admirably reassessed the most conservative of fictional genres, such as romance. Were they too hot to handle, or simply so much a part of the everyday reading patterns of feminists, being so familiar and so close to hand, that there seemed no need for further comment or any concern about their place in a future feminist re-evaluation of the fictional scene? Criticism of popular romance and women's magazines provides one model for approaching the feminist bestseller because it recognizes the importance of analysing women's consumption habits and understanding how these products fitted in with their lives, rather than making quality judgements about their appropriateness and therefore condemning readers out of hand for their manifest 'bad faith' or trashy reading habits. However many volumes of *Sexual Politics* were sold, it cannot match the sales for novels such as *Fear of Flying;*

if feminists themselves were slow to capitalize on the power of popular literature to deliver a political punch, its success told another story. Fiction, more freely than political writings, can take opposing sides and study conflicted opinions and ambiguity, and is therefore far more likely to chime with the uncertainties of women attracted to feminism but confused by the mess of emotions generated by their own personal lives. Feminist bestsellers could actively address and debate the feelings of emptiness and loss of identity felt by women after marriage without recourse to a tortured description of the foundations of patriarchy. Instead, crucial feminist issues were explored by simply having the heroine look back and slowly reflect on the incidents in her own life from childhood to the present day. Novels, always so important a means of expression of the quotidian and of intimate relationships, remind us that love, whether viewed as a dangerous patriarchal construction or an essential expression of the human being, is an emotion that confuses the most sacredly held precepts, and each of the heroines found in these texts discovers that their feelings prey upon them (to paraphrase one of Jane Austen's most engaging heroines, Anne Elliot[4]).

What is fascinating, looking back at feminist publications produced at the time of feminism's heyday, is the way discussions of gender encouraged people to read widely across numerous topics and to pick up both fiction or non-fiction as new books emerged from feminist and pro-feminist presses. During the writing of this book a number of people have remarked anecdotally to me that women with feminist interests at this time would read anything and everything that came out on women's issues, so might well be reading The Boston Women's Health Collective's *Our Bodies Ourselves* (1973) at the same time as *Fear of Flying*. This recognition that feminist thinking potentially transformed every avenue of knowledge was exhilarating for women and perhaps for the first time many were reflecting on areas of experience about which they would have previously considered themselves unqualified to comment. For such women, if the anecdotal reports I received are in any way representative, the texts they devoured would represent some kind of a dialogue as well as comprising in a few short years a huge bank of oppositional knowledge with which to challenge some of the most dogged common wisdoms about women's behaviour and the nature of their lives. Never before had women had such resources to reflect upon their own lives: the confessional novels encouraged further personal reflection and added weight to a feeling that at last meaningful truths about women's lives were being shared.

One of the academic by-products of feminist politics was feminist literary criticism – partly an accident, a result of so many women being clustered in a subject that had traditionally been seen as eminently suitable for female study. Critics were interested in this emergence of new expressive writing, but, perhaps understandably, still felt better able to assess and debate the value of texts from bygone eras. At many levels these bestselling novels did lack sophistication: they were anachronistic in an era when experimental writing was becoming *de rigueur*. Hidden meanings and suppressed anger need not be unearthed (as with much nineteenth-century women's writing), because the anger and the accusations were there on the surface in the feminist bestseller. They were energetic testament to the contemporary health of feminist debate, but did not fit in with the broader project of literary rediscovery. The relationship of the feminist bestseller to literature was tangential: they were written and marketed in such a way to suggest naked commercialism and feminists were inclined to remain suspicious of texts which might understandably be viewed as selling out to the capitalist 'malestream'. Elizabeth Cowie portrays them in this fashion:

> The last decade has seen a revival of the women's novel as a first person realistic narrative, a form which is ideologically appropriate to feminism; authors see it as a way of telling women's story for the first time in an undisguised voice. The result has been an identification of author with protagonist, and of both with 'woman', a result emphasised when commercial publishers use it as a marketing device, selling women's writing as subversive, sexual autobiography – the autobiography of gender (Cowie in Feminist Anthology Collective 1981: 242).

What Cowie hints at here – that a successful literary form becomes merely a formula to be copied, reproduced, and packaged appropriately – obviously occurs to some extent as a result of the runaway success of writers such as Jong, Alther, and French. But this success is also beneficial to feminism, because so many women can potentially come to feminism via these novels. Outspoken, humorous, sexually candid and all about the contemporary, these novels on the whole make for a breathtaking read. They are accessible and women may understand them by simply looking to the resources of their own lives; they appear to strike a new chord of honesty which can be seductive as well as provocative.

The question of whether these books and their writers are 'selling out' is a difficult one to answer. Commercial success clearly brings with it celebrity and wealth and in any case well-known authors become fetishized individuals. Radical feminists from the Women's Liberation Movement had favoured articles and pamphlets written collectively, perhaps even anonymously, to reinforce the view that feminism was a mass movement owned by all women and developed to support and liberate all women. Spokespeople, so dearly loved by the media, were frowned upon by feminists and those who stood out from the crowd, whether by accident or design, were seen as self-aggrandizing. Authors of successful books will necessarily be individuated from other feminists and their alienation from the Movement became a self-fulfilling prophecy. Their stardom was going to be unpalatable to other feminists and their feminist credentials, fairly or not, criticized.

Writers such as Maria Lauret in *Liberating Literature* (1994) identify these tensions between the Movement and the writers inspired by it; in addition, Lauret's book is important in really establishing re-readings of these novels as a corrective to past interpretations which often expose deep prejudices about popular fiction as well as necessarily associating the confessional with artlessness. By providing a strong historical and political context for these writings, Lauret reinforces the sense that women's daily occupations and pleasures would be refracted through the lens of feminism and that this lens itself never offered total clarity of focus, because of the well-documented chasms and conflicts within Second Wave feminism from its very origins. Rosalind Coward is one of many critics to problematize what a 'feminist text' or a 'feminist reading' can mean, and this concern with labels and categories and agonizing over what can be titled 'feminist' and what may simply become 'feminist' by the way we read it will obviously become a feature of my own analysis. I will also attempt to show that there is a common thread between some writers, regardless of whether or not they were active in the movement or whether or not they have professed their commitment to feminism since, which marks out the 'consciousness-raising' novel as an important contribution to the popular understanding of modern feminism. As Lauret said of the CR novel:

> Here was a body of texts which took feminism seriously, which spoke to women's contemporary concerns, voiced their discontents and envisioned their dreams. Here also was a mode of writing which reinserted women into the literary domain and demanded that they be taken seriously as imaginative and political writers (Lauret 1994: 1).

It seems to me that Lauret's summary is entirely accurate here, but definitions of feminist fiction are so tricky that one has to accept there is no agreement on what this might be. Patricia Duncker, for instance, is clear that 'the women who write feminist fiction propose and imagine a revolution' (Duncker 1985: 41), but she is also certain that there remain clear demarcations between literature and its other. For her, Marilyn French's *The Women's Room* is 'as American blockbuster, the feminist fictional equivalent of fast food, is not concerned to engage with any kind of literary tradition, masculine or otherwise. Her book is a fist in the face, agit-prop fiction' (Duncker 1985: 42).

This description of French's novel actually suggests a fundamental compatibility between the radical feminism of the Women's Movement and the work of these writers, and it remains surprising that they haven't received greater critical attention over the past thirty years. The key aim of the first part of this book is to negotiate the terms of the relationship between a selection of these novels with the Women's Liberation Movement as well as to bring these novels to the attention of a new generation of women readers. I also recognize that many readers, even those studying gender in an academic environment, may not have a clear understanding of the fundamental tenets of feminism's Second Wave. Chapter 2 is intended as a brief summary of the Movement and deliberately contains references to material not widely available to supplement the readers and anthologies that have done much to preserve the best of feminist scholarship over the years. There are references to journals and Women's Liberation newsletters from the US and the UK which are used to gauge the ways in which these grass-roots feminists, with no pretensions to theory or academic writing, were communicating. The novels are themselves not purely a product of the Women's Movement but have important predecessors, both in fiction and non-fiction, and chapter 1 will explore some of these landmark texts, which will also serve to better situate the work of later writers of the 1980s and 1990s and their own thematic concerns. Chapters 3, 4, and 5 focus on these bestselling novels and their legacy, from the 'mad housewife' writings at the end of the 1960s to the global bestsellers of the 1970s. I look at them comparatively, in relation to how they were received at the time and also in the light of critical commentaries that have paused to consider them since. Chapters 6 and 7 look at the changing face of fiction and feminism in the 1980s and 1990s, while chapters 8 and 9 reflect upon the genre of chick lit and consider whether within these novels we find the germ of the legacy of the consciousness-raising novel.

This is a long journey to travel and at times I may seem to be stretching the reader's credulity in the connections I wish to make. I would just say that it is the easiest thing in the world to dismiss chick lit as Beryl Bainbridge did, as 'froth', and move on to more 'serious' evocations of women's lives in the 1990s and into the millennium. In previous publications I have found myself being more dismissive about these works, since it is so easy to classify them as retroactive and merely souped-up, sexed-up versions of the classic Mills & Boon romance. They are all these things, but in a very different way, these novels invite female readers to appraise their own lives while reading fictional accounts of contemporary women. Their impact on publishing has been formidable and while there are endless prophecies of the demise of chick lit, there still seems to be plenty in evidence on booksellers' shelves, distinctively wrapped in their trademark covers. Some chick lit writers, for all their assertions of writing disposable fun fiction, are keen to act as advocates for the genre, and websites and fan bases are regularly springing up. Looking at the diversity of chick lit available today, it would be fair to say that it becomes more difficult to identify the core formula and claim that the women depicted are all latter-day Bridget Joneses.

It is difficult for me to determine whether I actually like reading chick lit; as with many readers with whom I've discussed the genre, I find that the experience is short-lived and the situations do tend to blur into each other. One quickly notes distinctive author trademarks, so for instance the work of Marian Keyes has a darker tinge than, say, Lisa Jewell; and Adele Parks seems more preoccupied with the craft of writing than some of the others. I still find popular fiction very difficult to write about in academic terms, because the act of reading can seem so transient, so effortless. For me, the experience of reading these books has always been to do with my work – about reflecting on the fate of feminism in the millennium and wondering whether a new wave of feminism, necessarily more at home with popular culture than its predecessors, might itself be engaging in a much more meaningful dialogue about contemporary women's lives than is first apparent. The key point is, as with feminist bestsellers of the 1970s, that women read them and that they read them by the truckload. Readers may well be dismissive of this consumption for much the same reason as for years women have casually admitted to their consumption of glossy magazines, regarding their content as mere distraction; but both media declare powerfully a gendered community of interests.

Newer critical perspectives have examined the guilty pleasures of women's lives and have asked why genres such as romance endure and might well be ripe for reinvention. The fact that it is now trendy to declare these guilty pleasures (and devote whole feminist conferences to them) suggests that this is just one more area that Second Wave feminism left undiscussed. In a sense this book is an account of my own guilty pleasure when first encountering feminist bestsellers and knowing that in some key way they were sacrilegious combined with my own desire to know more about the origins of modern feminism, its failings as well as its successes.

It is perhaps useful to end this Introduction by confirming what is probably already clear to the reader – that is, that feminist bestsellers and chick lit are predominantly the work of white, middle-class, heterosexual women. I considered trying to 'import' black writings which had been life-changing in their own ways (and the confessional epistolary element of Alice Walker's *The Color Purple* would have been fascinating in this respect), but ultimately decided that I would merely be further stretching and blurring quite unwieldy categories to produce something rather unsatisfactory and at best tokenistic. I do not know of any black women writers who have produced work that fits into the broad category of the feminist bestseller in this way, but would be delighted to know of any whom I have missed and would accept full responsibility for the consequences of this omission. In the genre of chick lit I have so far discovered one black British writer, Dorothy Koomson (whose first novel, *The Cupid Effect*, was published in 2002), and very much hope that a form so popular with young women readers will attract more black writers to it. Had I the time, space, and resources, it would have been fascinating to look more closely at the multitude of ways in which the US equivalent of chick lit has matured since the publication of texts such as *Sex and the City* (1996); and how other strands of women's popular fiction such as 'Buppie' (Black, urban, professional) literature – for example Terry McMillan's *Waiting to Exhale* (1992) – offer a host of further challenges to how mainstream culture perpetuates a favoured view of white femininity as at the heart of western notions of beauty. Popular culture is often the least inclusive of forms, playing as it does to quite narrow perceptions of mass demand, a feature unfortunately replicated by recurring blind spots in modern feminism.

# Part 1
# The Second Wave

# 1

# Sex and the Single Girl

Before I embark upon an evaluation of the emergence of Second Wave feminism and consider the relationship of feminist bestsellers to feminist politics, it is worth considering the legacy of some earlier works of popular fiction and non-fiction which give some insight into an informal 'tradition' that later women writers draw upon. As shocking as some of the material in the feminist bestsellers was, it is apparent that they were able to follow the success of earlier women writers whose work similarly caused consternation in its time, but was devoured hungrily – especially by women readers. These books are remembered mainly for being scandalous – usually for elements of sexual explicitness in their content – but looking back, they are inevitably a commentary on their time, containing some profound insights into women's lives. It is reasonable to assume that the act of reading these texts might have been found liberating if these books were able to confirm personal insights normally concealed or obscured in the more sedate literary publications of the time. These kinds of books were sometimes banned and were always censured for their immoral content; yet it is certain that even where they were disapproved of, they were passed between friends and perhaps more clandestinely by girls who might use these novels to try to obtain insights reserved for married women.

In 1944 Kathleen Winsor published her bestselling *Forever Amber* in the US and shortly after it was made into a film directed by Otto Preminger (1947). Epic in scope and deliciously melodramatic, this historical romance set in seventeenth-century England itself owed a debt to Margaret Mitchell's *Gone with the Wind* (1936). Winsor's novel was an international bestseller and clearly a 'women's novel' in its depiction of a headstrong and powerful young woman who, despite establishing her wealth and position in society through marriage, is most notable as someone who survives alone much of the time while in pursuit of her one true love. Published during the last year of the Second World War, it is both a commentary on the secondary social position women continued to inhabit in Winsor's contemporary society and a celebration of the strong, self-determined female who, like the numerous women taking war-related jobs at this time, was a survivor. Amber St Clare journeys from being an impoverished teenage country girl, abandoned by her lover in the streets of London, to being the mistress of King Charles II. This 800-page blockbuster weaves a romance plot into the backdrop of seventeenth-century history, taking Amber through some fairly improbable experiences – such as surviving, and nursing her lover, through the Great Plague – to end up on the verge of departure for America in pursuit of Lord Carlton, the love of her life.

The circumstances surrounding Amber's birth during the English Civil War is symptomatic of the tensions of her time, with her mother's family declaring as Royalists and her father's as Parliamentarians. At the time of the outbreak of the Civil War, their marriage is prevented and her mother runs away with her father but dies in childbirth. Amber's true noble background is concealed from her, but from the start she is marked out as different from her village friends, so that her upward social climb is seen in some sense as natural justice, reflecting her own aristocratic roots. Lord Carlton's companion Almsbury's first words to her suggest that her aristocratic background shows through: 'What are you? Some nobleman's bastard put out to suck with a cottager's wife and forgotten these fifteen years?' (Winsor 1991: 21) She peremptorily loses her virginity to Carlton and persuades him to take her to London. The sex is nowhere explicit but her serial extra-marital relationships, mercenary attitude to marriage, neglect of her children, and procuring of abortions made the book enormously scandalous in its day. Moreover, sex is depicted in two disparate ways, as the affirmation of her deep love for Carlton, but as primarily a means to an end for women – Amber is just one of many women at court who barters her body for patronage and other favours. The London described is intriguing, not least because the author is American, writing from a geographical as well as historical distance. The city itself remains a convincing central character in the narration, described in such a way as to emphasize its teeming humanity and the moral hypocrisy of the ruling classes: 'London – stinking, dirty, noisy, brawling, colourful – was the heart of England, and its citizens ruled the nation' (Winsor 1991: 42). At the end of the novel Amber's enemies have seemingly got the better of her, sending her off on the long and treacherous voyage to the New World by falsely informing her that Carlton's wife is dead. But while the romance is a permanent and sometimes improbable strand throughout the novel, what is memorable is Amber's hard-headed approach to society and her willingness to exploit every possibility that presents itself to her regardless of its moral implications. It is this heedless amorality which adds to the shock value of the text, as well as Amber's sheer force of character.

In many ways the scandalous edge of *Forever Amber* could be blunted by the fact that it is a historical romance set in a period which people associated with sexual licence and corruption. Readers could enjoy the immense spectacle and even identify with Amber's personality, without having to reflect too closely on their own lives. The reception of Grace Metalious's *Peyton Place*, published in 1956, would be quite a different matter because, in the spirit of Theodore Dreiser, she turns her gaze on the intimate lives and secrets of small-town America, offering a particularly unflattering reflection of her times. The novel was a true blockbuster, selling 60,000 copies within the first ten days of its release, and it stayed at the top of the *New York Times* bestseller list for over a year (Cameron in Metalious 2002: viii–ix). As Ardis Cameron makes clear in the introduction to the new Virago edition of the novel, '*Peyton Place* turned the "private" into the political. By reinterpreting incest, wife beating, and poverty as signs of social as well as individual failure, Metalious turned "trash" into a powerful political commentary on gender relations and class privilege' (Cameron in Metalious 2002: xv). Metalious, of French-Canadian origin and born in New Hampshire, might have enjoyed the irony that her book was promptly banned in Canada. Ironically, its scandalousness engendered a Hollywood film a year after publication and an extremely successful television serialization by 1964, both of which severely bowdlerized the original text; unfortunately, it is through these screen versions that the novel is widely remembered today. These adaptations took away the novel's woman-centred focus and, with a complete disregard for the social critique implicit in Metalious's book, reinstituted a moral core. It was not uncommon for runaway bestsellers to be rapidly transformed to the screen in this way, as was also the case with *Forever Amber*, but censorship remained much tighter in both film and popular television at this time and inevitably fiction of the period was better able to take risks. If only for this reason, the novels bear re-examination today.

Set in a sleepy New England town of Peyton Place, the novel focuses on the lives of three women: Allison MacKenzie, who wants to be a writer and in many ways becomes the central voice of the novel; her mother Constance, who pretends to be widowed rather than reveal that her daughter is the result of a long-finished extramarital affair; and Selena Cross, who lives on the wrong side of the tracks and is sexually abused and impregnated by her stepfather, whom she finally kills. From the start of the novel Metalious's preference for lush evocative description also suggests its nascent eroticism: 'Indian summer is like a woman. Ripe, hotly passionate, but fickle, she comes and goes as she pleases so that one is never sure whether she will come at all, nor for how long she will stay' (Metalious 2002: 3). There are descriptions of Allison's caressing her own body as she goes through the changes of adolescence as well as less savoury descriptions of the couplings of Lucas Cross and his wife, the drunken antics of some of the men in the community, and the graphic description of the loss of Allison's friend Kathy Ellsworth's hand in a fairground accident. There is also a rather unpleasant scene which demonstrates how far we've moved on in the description of female sexual desire. Intended to show the sexual reawakening of Allison's mother Constance, it describes the new headmaster Tomas Makris' forcing her to bed with a violent slap, after which 'she felt the first red gush of shamed pleasure' (Metalious 2002: 196).

While Allison might be the narrative heart of the book, Doc Swain the local medic seems to be the moral core. With his hatred of death, venereal disease, and organized religion, he makes a huge decision which provides one of the more shocking moments in the book when he gives Selena Cross an abortion, knowing that it is her stepfather's child and that keeping it will ruin her life. In doing this he wrestles with his hatred of death, but more importantly utters a justification that proved so important to the Women's Movement just over a decade later and what Emily Toth sees, perhaps overstating the case, as 'one of the strongest defenses of abortion – or woman's right to choose – in literature' (Toth 1981: 31). As he agonizes over confronting his own fear of death, he asserts, 'I *am* protecting life, *this* life, the one already being lived by Selena Cross' (Metalious 2002: 189). After the grittiness of incident throughout the book, the ending may seem overly romanticized, even mawkish, when Allison's New York admirer comes to Peyton Place to find her, but in the closing scenes there is a sense of both entrapment and endurance. Selena Cross goes to trial for the murder of her stepfather but Doc Swain testifies about the baby, thereby owning up to his own role as abortionist. From being a town of deceit and buried secrets, truths have been slowly unravelled (so Allison, for instance, is told the truth about the fact she is the bastard daughter of a married man) and the Indian summers come and go, suggesting in true naturalist fashion that these people are as much a product of their environment as their life's decisions.

Helen Gurley Brown published *Sex and the Single Girl* in 1962 at the age of 40 – three years after her marriage to the movie producer David Brown. She credits her husband with having the idea of writing the book in the first place, which stayed on the bestseller list for seven months from July 1962 and earned her the biggest movie rights sum ever paid out for a non-fiction work at that time (the film of *Sex and the Single Girl* was released in 1964, directed by Richard Quine and starring Natalie Wood). The opening sentences of the book set the tone for the rest: 'I married for the first time at thirty-seven. I got the man I wanted. It *could* be construed as something of a miracle considering how old *I* was and how eligible *he* was' (Brown 1962: 3). She makes it clear to her reader that her success both in marriage and in her career was not a matter of luck or amazing good fortune, but was ultimately due to working extraordinarily hard at transforming herself from a 'mouseburger' from Arkansas (as she describes herself) to a sophisticated career woman. The book is essentially a self-help manual and throughout she doles out advice which would floor all but the most determined, not only prescribing a strict diet and exercise regime, but also giving suggestions for how to live on a budget and divert one's energies to the essential – the man in your life and your career. The whole thrust of the book seems to be towards getting married, not least because she starts by telling us of her own successful match, but Brown claims it is 'not a study on how to get married but how to stay single – in superlative style' (Brown 1962: 11). Certainly her vision of the single young woman is compelling: 'She is engaging because she lives by her wits. She supports herself. She has had to sharpen her personality and mental resources to a glitter in order to survive in a competitive world and the sharpening looks good. Economically she is a dream. She is not a parasite, a dependent, a scrounger, a sponger or a bum. She is a giver, not a taker, a winner and not a loser' (Brown 1962: 5–6). Whether one believes this or not, coupledom emerges as infinitely preferable to singledom and even singles have to be constantly alert to the attentions of men. In this resolute focus on heterosexual attraction – above and beyond friendships and family ties – Brown echoes the contradictions that beset young women in the 1960s: while directing the energies of the single 'girl' towards her future married state she criticizes the stigma attached to the spinster, claiming the right for full 'adult' status for the single girl in both social and sexual terms. For this reason she asserts that the essential accessory for the single girl is a room of her own – 'roommates are for sorority girls' (Brown 1962: 10) – and that all the other attributes of the successful woman, that is, fashion sense, social skills, and a good body, are to be learned by sheer hard work and sacrifice.

This is a self-help manual written by someone with uncompromising views and enormous self-belief; one of the things which makes it compelling is that Brown offers herself and her own struggles as inspiration to the reader, insisting all along that the raw material she had to work on was, at best, mediocre. Strikingly for her time Brown expresses surprisingly forthright views about single female sexuality and suspends all moral judgements on issues such as having affairs with married men. In fact, through her defence of premarital sex, Brown is questioning the normal economy of heterosexual relations at the time and foregrounding women's right to pleasure, among other things. Although her own life story offers the possibility of a fairy-tale ending – marriage to a rich man and fame and fortune as a top magazine editor – her book is relentlessly unromantic. She believes that her readers should be realistic in the qualities they expect to find in their ideal man, and accept that there are no rewards without hard work – and she does indeed make the business of snaring a man sound like very hard work: no dates should be passed up and all men and women friends are good sources of other possibly eligible men. In all this, however, Brown, contradictory as ever, is clear that the woman's own body is an object of exchange whose assets must be guarded and which, moreover, should be used as a bargaining chip in the game of courtship: 'A single woman who doesn't deny her body regularly and often to get what she wants, i.e. married or more equitable treatment from her boy friend, is an idiot' (Brown 1962: 70). For Brown, sexuality is the route to female empowerment and sex appeal should be used in the workplace, in social settings, and in the bedroom to gain all the glittering prizes, whether they be promotion, friendship, status, or marriage. This is a regime rather than a lifestyle, requiring dedication and endless self-sacrifice because discipline in matters of diet, exercise, social stratagems, and even interior design and style, are all equally important.

What is compelling about this book, as I read it over forty years later, is that Brown's regimen explodes the myth of natural, effortless sex appeal, replacing it with the notion that femininity is treasured because it is an asset hard won and bolstered by being aware of one's strong points and knowing how to apply cosmetics and wear the appropriately styled clothing. The ideal single girl is an artist whose most treasured creation is herself and because of this she is always 'being' that creation, always ready to impress and capitalize on these assets. It's a fascinating book to read in retrospect because it offers a 'lifestyle' before such a term arrived in common parlance, packed as it is with practical home decorating tips and even recipes. It has the romance of a 'rags to riches' story because of Brown's meteoric rise to fame as Editor-in-Chief for *Cosmopolitan* and her corresponding role in shaping the ambitions and aspirations of the modern young woman from the mid-1960s right through to the 1990s. It is a romance with a happy ending, but it is also a document which exposes the underbelly of romance, where we begin to question the possibility of effortless femininity and natural beauty, and Brown encourages us to do this. The book has a winning style because of the fact it is underpinned by Brown's own confessions – she imparts knowledge with the air of someone who has decided to admit you to her charmed circle and share all her secrets, borrowing from her own struggles as a mouseburger from Arkansas who overcame the tragedies of the early death of her father and the needs of a disabled sister to become one of the most influential women of the 1970s and 1980s.

This element of sharing, the use of the comfortable first person and constant anecdotes about the problems and triumphs of friends, reminds us of the honeyed hectoring provided by contemporary women's glossy magazines and the fact that Brown turned round the fortunes of the previously failing magazine *Cosmopolitan* when she took it on in 1965. Through this magazine and the way it became the byword for all glossy women's magazines, Brown made an indelible mark on the lives of contemporary women. The whole product was conceived as a paean to the freedoms of the young working woman – and after her long climb up the career ladder, Brown knew more than most about the struggles and the pitfalls. The germs of the *Cosmopolitan* philosophy can easily be found in Brown's book, which celebrated the relative freedoms opening up for the modern career girl while at the same time keeping a weather eye on the goal of marriage and romance. Brown herself latterly described *Cosmopolitan* as 'a bible for young women who want to do better' (Schuch 1998) and later this will for self-improvement came to be sent up by Helen Fielding in her *Bridget Jones's Diary*. Even with this, the project which was to make Brown a global name, she typically credits her husband David Brown with one of the most innovative and memorable aspects of the magazines – the catchy cover strap-lines which he was to write for the next few decades (Brown 1983: 59).

*Cosmopolitan*'s relationship with political feminism became an uneasy one. Perhaps *Cosmo*, like its editor, was more a child of the Sexual Revolution – and even today in 2005, many people are more likely to cite the Pill as the chief contributor to women's emancipation than the epoch-changing demands of feminism. In any case, the magazine's commercial success depended on a more disingenuous promotion of feminine wiles with its dependence for advertising revenue on the beauty and fashion industries.

Notwithstanding this, career girls were celebrated within this and other magazines, and young women's expectations about their futures were changing irrevocably. As Susan Douglas noted, for all that was backward-looking in Brown's work, 'we see some startling stirrings of female liberation. And for her, liberation came through sex, by throwing the double standard out the window' (Douglas 1995: 68). Rather than wanting to move beyond the identities of wife and mother, Brown accepts that marriage is deemed to be the 'norm', yet also radically suggests that singleness is a space for women to exploit their power. Brown's message, written in proto-*Cosmo* self-help speak, is hardly revolutionary, but its implications could be: she uttered the heresy that marriage was optional for women and that they should certainly have sex before they entered that institution, with whomever they chose. Although most of the advice in her handbook was about cultivating feminine wiles to snare the man and career of one's choice, there is a celebration of single life and even an argument to prolong this state for as long as possible, witnessed by the fact that she didn't marry until she was thirty-seven and that she asserted, years before it was commonly accepted, that women could quite easily have children well into their forties.

Brown is a pragmatist in her offered solutions to the palpable inequality of men and women's lives: her decision is to work around men rather than to identify them as the sole problem which women encounter in their struggle for self-definition. Her book was published a year before Friedan's pathfinding *The Feminine Mystique* and in a sense the two books spell out two different trajectories for women stultified by the promises of post-war prosperity which seemed to rely on women embracing the traditional roles of wife, mother, and homemaker. Friedan, while stopping short of suggesting radical alternatives to marriage, argues that women need more agency beyond the home, while Brown offers a more practical set of propositions around making the best of the feminine assets you have. Freedom for Brown comes with material wealth, career focus, and a judicious marriage; Friedan uncovered the baffling facts that women were failing to realize their personal potential at a time when more of them than ever were receiving higher education. In one of her chapters Friedan singles out women's magazines for attention and looks at the way they construct an image of ideal femininity, which is difficult for anyone to live up to, by creating powerful myths about the happy housewife and her centrality to social existence. Her work and De Beauvoir's *The Second Sex*, increasingly available in translation at this time, inform the key critical processes at work in Second Wave feminism and in a sense Brown's work as self-help guru and later as magazine editor suggests another undertow pulling at women's sense of their selves at this time of profound change. Brown herself has asserted, 'I was there before Betty Friedan and *The Feminine Mystique*. I was there saying, "You're your own person, go out there and be somebody . . ." You don't have to get your identity from being somebody's appendage' (de Bertodano 2003). The overwhelming irony is that the more you read *Sex and the Single Girl*, the more you realize that it simply could not have been written by a single woman. The book starts with the information that Brown finally managed to snag her man, and, for the book to work as a self-help manual, the writer and guru has to be one who has already arrived.

Brown's vision of the striving and glamorous career woman which informed the glossy magazines of the 1970s comprised the message Second Wave feminists were rejecting as the patriarchal soft sell, but it clearly informs the content of the so-called 'bonkbuster', the sex and shopping novels of the 1980s. In these books sexual liberty and revenge often supplant the domestic core of the CR novels – children are as likely to be abandoned or absent from the main space of the narrative while the heroine plays out her bid for ultimate power in whatever business empire she finds herself. It is clear that, despite her purely tangential relationship to organized feminism, Brown would regard herself as a feminist who leads by personal example, because feminism for her – in common with many women in the 1990s and beyond – is about individual female empowerment. It is interesting, therefore, that Brown's bestseller should be reissued in 2003 after being out of print for nearly twenty years; it is dated, but its core ideas are current enough to offer something to the Bridget Jones generation (in her later book, *Having it All*, published in 1982, she repeatedly mentions Dr Atkins and his revolutionary diet).

Both Brown's and Friedan's bestsellers are landmarks for the changing face of modern woman and there are some similarities between them. Both emphasize individual transformation over and above social transformation, but Friedan's picture of the suburbs would have been alien to Brown, who set out for the city to seek her fortune rather than seek marriage and motherhood in Arkansas. Friedan wrote about the sense of futility experienced by middle-class highly educated women with young families throughout the American suburbs of the 1950s and 1960s, swamped in domestic drudgery, calling it 'the problem that has no name'. On the back of the extraordinary success of this book Friedan helped found the National Organisation for Women (NOW) in the US in 1966; her book would also be one of the inspirations behind the more radical feminism of the Women's Liberation Movement, which, unlike NOW, sought revolutionary changes in the basic fabric of the relationships between men and women. Friedan, in common with Brown, used personal testimony in *The Feminine Mystique* to drive home her argument, citing many of her lengthy interviews with housewives across America, but she also uses her own experiences and casts herself most definitely as one of those who left a promising future in higher education to start a family and, as a mother with small children, now wonders if this is all there is. The power of Friedan's book lies in how much she is alive to the political realities of being a woman in the 1960s: there is a recognition of the role of advertising, popular psychoanalysis, education, and economics in forming the state of femininity which comes to define the modern woman. Her interviews with ordinary women and with magazine editors and journalists demonstrated that this anxiety created about maintaining one's femininity and allowing the husband to be the 'man about the house' was a response to a real sense of guilt which tied in with changing social realities for women in the postwar era, when the return of the male workforce and an economic boom put pressure on them to stay at home. There was no organized conspiracy to return women to their 'rightful' places, but the effect was powerful at an ideological level through education, medicine, and the popular culture of the time, prompting Friedan to observe that 'our culture does not permit women to accept or gratify their basic need to grow and fulfil their potentialities as human beings, a need which is not solely defined by their sexual role' (Friedan 1982: 68).

Perhaps Friedan was so vital to budding radical feminists because part of her book remembers the legacy of feminism's First Wave and laments the demise of this powerful voice in politics which resulted in women's seeming to have lost their way by the Second World War. Friedan claimed that there had been a noticeable shift in women's ambitions and the way they perceived their lives since the 1930s and she charted this by looking at back issues of women's magazines, noting that in the stories published in these magazines happy, adventurous career women of the 1930s with their supportive and equally intrepid young men had given way to the selfless homebodies of the 1950s. Of the fiction of the 1930s, Friedan notes that even though the focus of each story was the romance between the central characters, 'very often this was not the major theme of the story. These heroines were usually marching towards some goal or vision of their own, struggling with some problem of work or the world, when they found their man' (Friedan 1982: 34). She notes that the thematic shift begins in 1949 and that by 1959, in the fiction, 'only one in a hundred heroines had a job; even the young unmarried heroines no longer worked except at snaring a husband' (Friedan 1982: 39). One of the reasons for this shift, Friedan discovers, is, 'the old image of the spirited career girl was largely created by writers and editors who were women ... The new image of woman as housewife–mother has been largely created by writers and editors who are men' (Friedan 1982: 47), suggesting that the movement of men back in to the workforce had literally affected the scope and voice of women's magazine publishing.

Friedan talks extensively about the image of the happy housewife and the way it features as a chief character in newspaper articles and magazine fiction, admitting that as a journalist,

I helped create this image. I have watched American women for fifteen years try to conform to it. But I can no longer deny my own knowledge of its terrible implications. It is not a harmless image. There may be no psychological terms for this harm it is doing. But what happens when women try to live according to an image that makes them deny their minds? What happens when women grow up in an image that makes them deny the reality of the changing world? (Friedan 1982: 59).

Looking back, the women addressed in this book make for a large, but clearly defined constituency – they are white, married with children and comfortably middle-class – but yet still this book touched many people beyond that category. The key to its success lies in Friedan's analysis of the myth of the happy housewife and her acknowledgement that this is purely an image set up for women to aspire to, being impossible to live up to. In this approach she anticipates some of the key ideas of the early Women's Liberation Movement, which looked closely at how the images of women used in popular advertising, in the movies, and on television constantly reinvented this myth of unimpeachable femininity. For Susan Brownmiller, an important feminist voice from the late 1960s and someone who would write extensively on the construct of the feminine, 'I'd seen myself on every page. *The Feminine Mystique* changed my life' (Brownmiller 2000: 3).

Helen Gurley Brown's book is of course alive to the realities of the male-dominated workplace and the seeming unnaturalness of the career woman. Her own personal narrative of her struggle for success shows a recognition of the odds against which she is working in a man's world, even though with relentless (and perhaps misguided?) optimism, she takes the view that the success or failure of individual women to change their own lives is very much their responsibility. Indeed, Brown's philosophy is based on an acceptance that it is a man's world and that men behave differently from women – perhaps this is why her book has endured for so long, because it encourages women to fight their corner as individuals rather than encourage any more radical social challenges. Men may come out of this formulation as dupes of the stratagems of women so that women perversely are portrayed as actually more superior, but this will do nothing to disturb the *status quo*, as Brown suggests that the knowing possession of feminine wiles is positively radical! The conclusions of both texts brought Brown and Friedan together closer than was comfortable in retrospect, epitomized by the title of Brown's follow-up book, *Having it All*, in that even in Friedan's frank exposé of women's lives in the US, her subjects were assumed to lose little of the baggage of domesticity in their pursuit of individual self-improvement. Radical feminists would have less and less in common with either of these women as they proposed a change in consciousness which would dismantle patriarchy as both a system of ideas and a material and economic system.

The fiction of this period, however, sharply echoed some of the themes raised by Betty Friedan, suggesting that these ideas had been in circulation for some time before being developed into a more polished feminist critique. Mary McCarthy's *The Group* (1963) focuses on eight girls who graduated from Vassar in the 1930s, starting with Kay Petersen's wedding and ending with her tragic death and funeral some years later; her death may or may not be interpreted as suicide. The girls, ranging from upper to lower middle class, struggle through a representative sample of the ups and downs of a woman's life. Those who marry suffer the disillusionment resulting from their husband's extramarital affairs or the isolation brought about by childbirth; those who are single struggle with their ignorance about sex and the demands of more sophisticated men. This novel, though set in the 1930s and 1940s, anticipates the dawning of the Sexual Revolution of the 1960s, and already there is a feeling that this is a revolution in which women will remain bystanders, duped by the promises of freedom yet to be delivered. According to commentators such as Barbara Ehrenreich, Elizabeth Hess, and Gloria Jacobs, the Sexual Revolution was inevitable, not just because of emerging feminist treatises such as Betty Friedan's, but because it 'initially represented the aspirations of the "new woman" – urban, single, educated – who had overcome both the Puritanism of small-town America and the smothering conformity of suburban married life' (Ehrenreich et al. 1987: 40). Interviewed as early as 1961, while working on the novel, McCarthy describes *The Group* thus:

It was conceived as a kind of mock-chronicle novel. It's a

novel about the idea of progress, really. The idea of progress seen in the female sphere, the feminine sphere. You know, home economics, architecture, domestic technology, contraception, childbearing; the study of technology in the home, in the play-pen, in the bed' (Plimpton 1989: 173–4).

This novel did not provide the shocks that *Peyton Place* or *Forever Amber* had, but it did contain some controversial elements, such as the character of Lakey, who openly identifies herself as a lesbian, reappearing late in the novel after years of exile in Europe: 'within a month some of the girls found themselves talking of "having Lakey and Maria to dinner", just as they might speak of a normal couple' (McCarthy 1966: 344). Other novels of ideas that particularly struck a chord with the Women's Movement included Doris Lessing's *The Golden Notebook* (1962), even though Lessing herself declared that 'this novel was not a trumpet for Women's Liberation' (Lessing 1993: 8). She experiments with the expression of subjectivity in this novel and encounters similar concerns to those writing conciousness-raising novels a few years later: 'Writing about oneself, one is writing about others, since your problems, pains, pleasures, emotions – and your extraordinary and remarkable ideas – can't be yours alone' (Lessing 1993: 13).

It is clear to see why women loved *The Golden Notebook* and found in its female characters aspects that chimed with their own lives, just as one can understand how frustrating it must have been for Lessing to have her work untangled, reassembled, and read thematically with less regard for her experiments with its overarching structure. But there are moments while reading the novel when her work clearly chimes with Friedan's observations, so that it is difficult not to identify some narrative continuity between them, even though this is simply the accident of synchronicity as they are writing at much the same time. In the Red Notebook, Anna Wulf is talking about the women she encounters when canvassing for the Communist Party and describes '[f]ive lonely women going mad quietly by themselves, in spite of husband and children or rather because of them. The quality they had: self-doubt. A guilt because they were not happy. The phrase they all used: "There must be something wrong with me" ' (Lessing 1993: 161).

Sylvia Plath's *The Bell Jar*, published (originally under the pseudonym Victoria Lucas) in 1963, a few weeks before she committed suicide, went on to become one of the most powerful novels of its generation. Esther Greenwood, like the women in *The Group*, is considering all the possibilities open to her as a straight 'A' student having won a prize to work at *Mademoiselle* magazine in New York. Unlike the women in *The Group*, who gradually find the gloss peeling off the lives they dreamed of, Esther descends into sudden mental depression, seemingly at the infidelity of her boyfriend Buddy Willard, which is telescoped into a searing view of the gendered double standards at work in modern America. The use of the first person anticipates the tone of the later confessional feminist bestsellers and, like Esther, the reader becomes almost suffocated under the distorting bell jar of her illness, not because her illness seems mysterious and self-generated, but rather because the longer we look through her eyes the more we feel that society is sick. Esther's extreme reaction to marriage and childbirth is demonstrated through the grotesque descriptions of both her mother and the fecund mother-of-six Dodo Conway, not to mention the scene of childbirth which she witnesses on a visit to a hospital with Buddy. Although Esther at the end of this journey and after electrotherapy treatments is 'patched and retreaded' and sent back out into the world, we're haunted by her anxiety that 'someday – at college, in Europe, somewhere, anywhere – the bell jar, with its stifling disortions [would] descend again' (Plath 1967: 254). Certainly Esther's friends and the women she meets at *Mademoiselle* all seem to have swallowed the feminine mystique; and the only career women she encounters – her editor and one of her professors – are perceived to be mannish and plain or lesbian.

According to Marcia Cohen in her book *Sisterhood*, which charted the lives of some of the most visible women in the Women's Movement as perceived by the media – Betty Friedan, Kate Millett, Germaine Greer, and Gloria Steinem – Friedan met Helen Gurley Brown the year after the publication of *Sex and the Single Girl* and, despite their very different responses to contemporary women's lives at that time, it is said that they became friends (Cohen 1988: 98). Not only did Helen Gurley Brown draw the admiration of Betty Friedan, but she was also a friend of Jacqueline Susann, author of the blockbuster *Valley of the Dolls* (1966). They shared the same publisher and Helen admired her friend's famous, rather garish, showbiz costumes – 'It was sequins, it was chiffon, it was high heels and ankle straps and lots of jewelry and the beautiful dark hair. I adored her. She was like a role model, almost like a star' (Seaman 1996: 283). Susann, a frustrated movie star by all accounts, did indeed devote much of her life to acting the part and she was another important precursor to the Women's Movement because of the way women readers responded to her racy popular fiction. She came to fiction partly because of her failure as an actress and because she longed for fame and notoriety in one sphere of the creative arts. She encountered Grace Metalious on a television show on which she worked one evening and although she wasn't taken by Metalious as a person, she was attracted to her literary success and the type of novel she had written, something she felt she could do for herself (Seaman 1996: 239–41). And she did, when *Valley of the Dolls* went to number one on the *New York Times* bestseller list and stayed there for 28 weeks. Susann's heroine is a simple provincial girl who turns up in New York looking for office work and becomes independently wealthy while still working for theatrical attorney Henry Bellamy; later she becomes a television actress. Anne Welles has model good looks and is determined to marry for nothing but love. The novel follows her dream through to the promise of a romantic conclusion, only to deflate all her ideals at the end. My Corgi edition of the paperback has a testimony from Helen Gurley Brown in the inside cover, in which she says, 'I couldn't believe these weren't real girls because I *know* them. Maddeningly sexy. I wish I had written it' (Susann 1982: 3).

The book's central appeal lay in its fictionalized exposé of Hollywood in the 1950s, and it is said that one of Susann's characters, Neely, was a thinly disguised Judy Garland, whereas the depiction of the ageing actress Helen Lawson reflects Susann's troubled relationship with the actress Ethel Merman. This is a world of casting couch ethics, ageing women being usurped by younger, more biddable wannabes and predatory theatrical agents. Talent is figured as only one factor (and perhaps not the most important) in these women's lives and, while each undergoes her own tragedies, it is clear that the career comes first. Yet the women's very fragile hold on fame wrecks their personal lives and their relationships with their children, and sends them to the refuge of a cocktail of alcohol and prescription drugs. Initially it seems that Anne's story is one of hope among the human wreckage left behind in the quest for fame, in that she finally marries the love of her life (having in the process turned down two very rich and powerful men), but ineluctably she has to accept the fact of her own husband's continual infidelities, most shockingly with her friend Neely. She too is seen popping her pills (the 'dolls' of the title) as the novel draws to a close. There are moments in this novel which are strikingly reminiscent of key Hollywood films of the 1930s, 1940s, and 1950s, such as *The Women* (1939), *The Razor's Edge* (1946), *All About Eve* (1950), and *A Star is Born* (1954), but the glossier dominance of the romantic storylines in the films is replaced by sleaze, observed with a harsh naturalistic eye for detail. Hollywood is propelled by money and power and the men are seen as wielding it in ways that women can never hope to emulate. Sex is connected to all kinds of motivations, love being the least important among them; women can flirt with lesbian dalliances (although real lesbians are portrayed as 'freaks') and Susann can at her most risqué describe these interludes as deeply pleasurable without suggesting her characters are any less 'heterosexual'. The blurring of such boundaries suggests nonetheless a prevalence for polymorphous sexual expression, and whether or not this is supposed to contribute to the picture of corrupt Hollywood social mores there is also some tenderness and understanding expressed. Jennifer's relationship with Maria, whom she met at finishing school in Switzerland during the Second World War and whose lover she becomes, is described in some detail: 'Maria had been gentle, and very patient – taking more liberties each night, slowly teaching Jennifer to respond, erasing any embarrassment . . . until at last Jennifer found herself responding with equal ardour and reaching peaks of exaltation she never dreamed existed' (Susann 1982: 208).

Although the main narrative focus is on Anne Welles and it is with her arrival in New York that the novel starts in September 1945, the perspective variously shifts between three characters, to focus on Jennifer and Neely as well, until the closing scenes in 1965 when Anne overhears her husband talking intimately to a young actress at a New Year's Eve party, confirming her suspicion that he is serially unfaithful to her. Jennifer has killed herself, having learned that she needs a mastectomy after being diagnosed with breast cancer (the illness that Susann herself was later to die of, having lived with it for over a decade). She refuses an operation on her breasts - vaunted throughout the novel as her greatest asset - because she fears losing her husband. Neely is seen as moving through a cycle of self-destruction, which will result in a see-saw of retreats into drug dependence, obesity, breakdown and comebacks, while the novel ends with Anne wilfully maintaining the appearance of a normal loving relationship:

> She had Lyon, the beautiful apartment, the beautiful child, the nice career of her own, New York – everything she had ever wanted. And from now on she could never be hurt badly. She could always keep busy during the day, and at night – the lonely ones – there were always the beautiful dolls for company. She'd take two of them tonight. Why not? After all, it was New Year's Eve! (Susann 1982: 509).

This is a book which appears to be framed by its central romantic thread, the beautiful Anne Welles falling for the irresistible Lyon Burke, right up until the end. When Anne flees New England for New York she still has her mother's views on romantic love ringing in her ears – 'you'll only find that kind of love in cheap movies and novels' (Susann 1982: 15) – and this is largely borne out by all the characters' experiences. Part of Anne's education is to learn the difference between sex and love, and while the sexual content is not very explicit, Susann's rather salty language, particularly as uttered by Neely, contributed one of the more scandalous aspects of the text. On the whole, the sexual context is simply straightforward and down-to-earth and Anne's sexual dalliances with other men do not impinge on her romantic attachment to Lyon. Later in the book another young hopeful tells Anne that she had admired her when she was ten – and we're reminded of Anne's own first infatuation with Helen Lawson at the same age and how all the prophecies about women disappearing into oblivion once they age are beginning to come true for Anne, proving to her that womanhood is experienced in cycles and femininity as an ideal is actually the province of the young. In all cases as the women age and their sexual attractions wane they find themselves supplanted both professionally and in their personal relationships by a new generation of younger women. As Anne's first fiancé Allen Cooper remarks, '[t]his is a man's world – women only own it when they're very young' (Susann 1982: 173).

Beyond the Hollywood parties and intrigues there are also some touchingly evocative scenes of Neely in the private asylum after her breakdown. Here there are echoes of *The Bell Jar* with the well-heeled inmates representing nothing so much as a sorority house as they move from one ward to another, getting fat on sweets and treats to gradually earn more and more privileges before they get to be outpatients. Yet the *Valley of the Dolls* was by common consensus a trashy read and no one credited Susann with an ounce of creative originality. Don Preston, who extensively edited her manuscript and had her write a whole new scene, described Susann as a 'painfully dull, inept, clumsy, undisciplined, rambling and thoroughly amateurish writer whose every sentence, paragraph and scene cries for the hand of a pro' (Seaman 1996: 286). However, the book succeeded in drawing readers to it, particularly women who might aspirationally love to read about the doings of the rich, but were also drawn to it because these women suffered just because they were women. In addition to this, Jacqueline Susann had made sure that she was talked about, by appearing on television and by putting all her energies into author tours and book signings, even arriving at book warehouses at dawn to hand out Danish pastries to the truck drivers and sign copies of her book (Seaman 1996: 246).

There are always people who associate the confessional, especially sexual frankness, with vulgarity, suggesting it cheapens the value of true revelation and deeper insights provided by great literature. The more honest appraisals of the popular fiction of this time are hampered by this accusation of cheap vulgarity, Rosalind Miles being one such critic who argues that '[s]uch women writers as Grace Metalious and Jacqueline Susann, with their grossly vulgarised and degraded accounts of women's sexuality, are merely taking neo-pornographic advantage of freedoms won with all the serious purpose by others' (Miles 1974: 183). For Miles, it seems that sexual frankness expressed via popular fiction is the obvious result of exploitation of the themes used to higher purpose in literary fiction. But what is refreshing about Susann and Metalious is that they denounce the notion of a higher purpose and disturbingly, perhaps, present a view of modern human relationships as profoundly motivated by lesser emotions such as the will to power, jealousy, or revenge. These are motivations that will re-emerge as the governing principles for the 1980s bonkbuster or 'sex and shopping' novel, and Susann is obviously the precursor to the writings of Jackie Collins, Shirley Conran, Danielle Steel and Judith Krantz. Her next two novels also went straight to number one of the bestseller lists and estimates of global sales of her novels are from 20 to 30 million.

All the books discussed so far did, in their various ways, chart a changing world for women, but also suggested that women could resist the path traced out for them and enter a man's world, even while the men to a large extent controlled their destinies. They gave the frankest account yet of women's dissatisfaction with the limitations femininity supposedly imposed on them, and even while writing about romance they roundly debunked the most pervasive myths about true love. Just like the young women Brown addresses in *Sex and the Single Girl*, these fictional characters could experiment with sex before marriage and could mark out their own careers at the same time as having relationships. Women's popular fiction, as was shown by the scandals attached to Winsor, Metalious, and Susann in three respective decades, prompted social debate and created anxieties about the moral health of the nation. Following on from these examples the consciousness-raising novel would show that, unlikely as it would seem, books could change lives.

# 2

# Burnt Offerings: The Emergence of Radical Feminism

This chapter will concentrate on the early years of radical feminism in Britain and Europe from 1967 to around 1975. It wasn't that Second Wave feminism died in 1975 – in many ways it was just getting really established and becoming rooted in the popular consciousness and in academe – yet, nonetheless, the heady period of activism was on the wane and intra-feminist groupings were becoming more clearly demarcated than they had been. One chapter alone could not do justice to the history of radical feminism, even over these eight years; instead I intend to focus on what brought feminists together from other political movements and what they sought from a new kind of politics. The intention is to set up a context in which the fiction discussed in the following three chapters can be placed, and also to give a vivid enough snapshot of early Second Wave feminism even for those new to the topic. Second Wave feminism, as will rapidly become clear, emerged from the energies of small groups of women disaffected with their male peers in civil rights and New Left movements; the early writings are exploratory, often full of anger and incredibly bold in their identifications of the world's wrongs. In their generally iconoclastic fashion, the new militant women didn't obey the 'laws' of academic or political or psychoanalytical discourse and their work constituted a fascinating *mélange* of many types of writing. Academics were joined by those with less formal education and the emphasis of all their writings seemed to be on accessibility, which meant that some critics mistook the apparent simplicity of their work for naïvety or political ignorance.

What we now term 'Second Wave' feminism arrived in the public domain in the US around 1967, but the stirrings of a new political energy had been in evidence before then, since many feminists emerged from New Left politics and student Civil Rights groups, where they felt that their contributions were not perceived to be of equal worth because they were women. Many spoke of their sense that women were being used simply for their typing skills, to make the coffee, and for sex, and that there persisted an assumption that women simply weren't political animals. When such women tried to raise feminist issues within these groupings they were often marginalized or accused of diverting discussion from the main business of revolution. During the 1967 National Conference for New Politics in Chicago, Jo Freeman and Shulamith Firestone (both destined to become important voices within the early Women's Movement) put forward a resolution which demanded greater representation of women at the conference, condemned the images of women in the mass media, and demanded that women have control over their bodies through birth control and the legalization of abortion. In a move that many of the women felt was typical of Left men, this resolution was swept aside to give room for what was considered more important business. A number of women met to set up their own agenda and gradually women's groups were to spring up across America (Echols 1989: 46–9).

Feminists not only had the example of Left-wing and Civil Rights activism with which to structure their own protest movements, but they also embraced the work of lone feminist voices who were echoing some of their own sentiments. These included Simone de Beauvoir, Betty Friedan, and Juliet Mitchell, whose essay 'Women: The Longest Revolution' was published in the British *New Left Review* in 1966. These disparate groups of women trying to establish their own political voices from scratch were what would become the Women's Liberation Movement, and the nature of their formation makes it clear that Second Wave feminism would be fragmented from the start. These were exciting times for politically minded women, who found themselves disaffected with what male-dominated radical politics had to offer because this new

feminism had no pre-set rules and no central party dogma to
adhere to. During this period a new language was being
developed and its makers were striving, in theory at least, to
speak of women's lives as women perceived them, to accurately describe and evoke the ways in which gender oppression was experienced and perpetuated in order to encourage
the participation of as many women as possible.

Sara Evans's *Personal Politics* (1979) gives an excellent
historical introduction to the roots of US women's liberation
within Civil Rights and the New Left, and she makes the point
that one of the other defining features of this wave of Women's
Movement is that the majority of the active participants were
young, quite often students or those without the ties of childcare and careers:

> The young are prominent in most revolutions. In this case in
> particular it seemed logical and necessary that the initiative
> should come from young women who did not have
> marriages and financial security to risk or years invested in
> traditional roles to justify (Evans 1979: 22).

As I shall go on later to explore, the cross section of women
found in feminism at this time determined the shape and
structure of the later Movement as a whole and this in part
explains some of the notable gaps in their agenda. Suffice to
say for the moment that the constituency of these small groupings and the desire of the majority to take direct action and
expend their energies in following up on their own actions
might in part be attributed to a more freely available resource
of spare time. Freeman confirms Evans's view that most
members of the Women's Liberation Movement were under
thirty and that they saw themselves in clear contrast to the
centralized organization of the National Organisation for
Women. She observes that 'the younger branch of the movement prides itself on its lack of organisation. Eschewing structure and damning the idea of leadership, it has carried the
concept of "everyone doing their own thing" almost to its logi-
cal extreme' (Freeman 1971). Liberationists seemed to agree on
one thing, that their movement should not replicate the power
structures and petty hierarchies on the Left; nor did they want
the matriarchy that some regarded as typified by the organi-

zation of NOW. Nonetheless, a leaderless organization ironically takes some organizing and the costs of retaining this
principle were to be felt in later years.

In these early days the term 'Women's Liberation' was not
something universally used, the word 'liberation' being
thought too extreme by some groups who preferred just to call
themselves 'radical women'. However, in the US in March
1968 the first national newsletter was published entitled the
*Voice of the Women's Liberation Movement* and it is thought that
this helped popularize the term by the end of the year.[1] In this
early women's newsletter (at six pages long, little more than a
pamphlet) its editor (and Movement stalwart) Jo Freeman
writes, 'Women's liberation does not mean equality with men.
Mere equality is not enough. Equality in an unjust society is
meaningless. Inequality in a just society is a contradiction in
terms'. She continues, 'only women can define what it is to be
a woman in a liberated society and we cannot allow others, by
our inaction, to do this for us' (Freeman 1968: 1; 4). And action
is certainly one of the defining characteristics of the early years
of Women's Liberation, while separatism is another; having
found their cause women were anxious to make their voices
heard *as women* through demonstrations, direct action, and
street theatre. One of the early public demonstrations in
Atlantic City was to inflict upon feminists a label – bra-
burners – that was none too easy to deflect.

The Miss America Pageant held on 7 September 1968 was
considered a legitimate target for a protest and a group of
about 100 women travelled to Atlantic City to disrupt the
proceedings. Here is part of a memoir by Carol Hanisch, a
member of New York Radical Women, the protest organizers:

> We did some street theatre: crowning a live sheep Miss
> America; chaining ourselves to a large red, white, and blue
> Miss America dummy to point up how women are enslaved
> by beauty standards; and throwing what we termed 'instru-
> ments of female torture' into a Freedom Trash Can. It was
> the latter that brought about the 'bra-burner' moniker. It
> wasn't that we hadn't intended to burn bras – we had – but
> along with other 'instruments of female torture', including
> high heels, nylons, garter belts, girdles, hair curlers, false
> eyelashes, makeup, and *Playboy* and *Good Housekeeping*

magazines. One of the members of our group – a Yippie who was a bit of press hound – had quipped to a reporter that we were going to burn our bras, and the media had a field day. Everything else we were to burn was quickly forgotten. Atlantic City officials refused to let us have a fire on the boardwalk, anyway, so nothing in fact was even burned there, but 'bra-burner' made the action more than even many feminists wanted to own. Had the media called us 'girdle-burners', nearly every woman in the country would have rushed to join us (Du Plessis et al. 1998: 198–9).

The mixed messages that seemed to be transmitted during the course of this protest taught these activists an important lesson about the role of the media in gaining visibility. From the above remarks it is clear that these women felt such a moniker both made their causes unattractive to other women and trivialized the issues that Women's Liberation stood for. As clear as these feminists felt their motives for the demonstration to be, it was quickly interpreted as a jealous attack on the young glamorous contestants by a bunch of harridans who would never be Miss Americas themselves – an impression which is perhaps understandable given the songs they chanted outside the Pageant, such as:

Ain't she sweet
makin' profit off her meat,
Beauty sells she's told so she's out pluggin' it
ain't she sweet.

Ain't she quaint
with her face all full of paint.
After all how can she face reality,
ain't she sweet.
(*Voice of the Women's Liberation Movement* Oct 1968: 6)

As an article in the *Voice of the Women's Liberation Movement* makes clear, 'our purpose was not to put down Miss America but to attack the male chauvinism, commercialization of beauty, racism and oppression of women symbolized by the Pageant' (Duffett 1968: 5). Nonetheless, the fallout from events such as these left an indelible mark on the Women's

Movement and to some extent laid the path for their unhappy relationship with the media since. There was evident frustration at the ways in which the media could twist any event to create a sympathetic or unsympathetic reading, but there was also reluctance to court the media in order to stand a better chance of getting one's chosen message across. The media liked to deal with spokespeople and, given the power of the image on television and in newspapers, preferably an attractive or eloquent person; feminists were opposed to the development of a 'star system' within their ranks and insisted on a rota for media appearances. This neither satisfied the media nor did it always allow these groups to convey themselves in the best light when some of their representatives clearly lacked the experience to handle these encounters to their advantage. The media already had its stereotype of the shrill angry feminist, which had taken root in the popular consciousness, and such assumptions were hard to undercut. Given the hard realities of the political message feminists had to deliver, they *were* angry.

In the UK the impact of the Second Wave in America was rapidly felt from the late 1960s onward and by 1969 'Women's Lib' was well established, with the first publication of the magazine *Shrew* and the establishment of the Women's Liberation Workshop in London. *Spare Rib*, the magazine most popularly associated with feminism in the UK, and the nearest thing to a 'glossy' magazine, started in 1972.[2] The first major Women's Liberation Movement conference in the UK was held at Ruskin College, Oxford from 27 February to 1 March 1970, which more than 500 women attended. This was really the opportunity for disparate women's groups to meet and report on their own activities and political priorities though, as *Shrew* noted, the press were more interested in describing the squabbles, the graffiti on the walls, and the apparent influx of communist cells among the women, who in the *Observer*'s words were 'young, violent, radical, and very attractive with their long hair and maxi coats . . .' (quoted in Tufnell Park Women's Liberation Group 1970: 2).

While much of early British feminism's published work examined further the means by which the material position of women was governed by the ways in which they were perceived to be different, the demos and populist campaigns were very much to do with representations of women in the press, in magazine advertisements, on television and in films. Small wonder, then, that British feminists capitalized on the notoriety (if not unqualified success) of the Miss America demonstration by holding their own demo at the Miss World contest in London on 20 November 1970. This again was commonly taken to be an expression of rather unsisterly resentment against beautiful women, but to the organizers it was the 'first militant confrontation with the law by women since the suffragettes' (Anon. 1972: 254).

Each small feminist grouping, whether in Britain or the US, had its own unique political coloration and identity because of the determination to keep the Movement decentralized and let groups of women work it out for themselves, contributing to wider feminist knowledge as if it were the equivalent of some kind of giant patchwork quilt. At the heart of all of this energy and feverish production of pamphlets and newsletters was the will to communicate to as wide a constituency as possible, which meant huge disagreement over the register in which one should address other women. Many of the articles in newsletters and pamphlets at this time share the touching wish to be understood by all as well as demonstrating the impossibility of this aim when more erudite subjects such as Marxism and ideology or Freudian psychoanalysis are under discussion. What is also striking about these pieces of writing is their fragility and ephemerality; even at the time they were written they had limited circulation, and now their survival depends on the few anthologies published at the time, feminist archives in existence, digitized collections on the web, or on collectors who treasure such material.

In Britain the last massed Women's Liberation Movement conference was in 1978 and demonstrated the massive rifts that had sprung up in the Movement here and in the US by this point. In Britain, which had a stronger tradition of socialist feminism and where radical feminism was associated strongly with cultural feminism and the establishment of separatist activities and events, there were huge rifts between these and other groups. In fact, the attempt to create and maintain a national platform was seen to be part of the problem. In the British magazine *Red Rag*, anonymous authors suggested that what was needed was a greater regional identity for the WLM. The implication was that too much energy was diverted into the annual WLM conference, resulting in little free space on the agenda so that there was scant time for differing groups to reflect on their experiences or think about future plans (Anon. 1978: 18–19). In the face of all the infighting recorded on both sides of the Atlantic some activists were keen for the evolution of a more structured Movement core, where differences could be debated but where women searching for access to feminist politics might find a space for themselves. By the mid-1970s feminist themes were widely circulated and discussed in the popular press and key issues were feeding through to the mainstream in ways that were difficult to anticipate or control. The UK pro-feminist glossy young women's magazine, *Honey*, on one occasion ran a three-page article on the Women's Movement and consciousness raising groups, making such events seem a relatively normal part of an average woman's social life (Bowles 1975: 87–90). For obvious reasons, articles in magazines such as *Honey* weren't necessarily going to be greeted with wild enthusiasm from groups of feminists who recognized that any feminist content in such a publication was double-edged: after all, most of their revenue depended upon advertising products which were still selling women a version of the feminine mystique. Active feminists were still in the business of refining their politics; and their anger as more and more research exposed the inequities of a patriarchal system was not going to be appeased by the more dilute form of politics required to gain the attention of the mainstream media.

A common thread running between small Movement groupings from the beginnings of Women's Liberation would be their embracing of consciousness-raising or rap groups as one of the means to encourage women to politicize their personal lives, by sharing experiences with a small gathering of other women and therefore simultaneously learning about other women's experiences. Many groups found this process much more difficult than they envisaged, as so much depends on degrees of trust and discretion outside of the safe confines of the group: often interpersonal relations would go sour and the group would simply break up having achieved very little. Others persevered and found that the benefits were very much about self-realization and confidence-building, but that this helped the process of politicization and finding means to share in other ways with a group of women. For Sheila Rowbotham, looking back at this practice from the vantage point of the late 1980s, 'it transferred this familiar personal culture into politics – unfamiliar to most of the young women who became involved. In the process it introduced a different way of conceiving needs and writing about politics' (Rowbotham 1989: 6).

Consciousness-raising was one of the most fascinating and mysterious aspects of Second Wave feminism because the practices of such groups largely remained undocumented. This was the fundamental outreach work of the Movement, in that this was how small groups of women in local areas could politicize each other and develop their own interpretations of the key factors of a feminist politics. There are mentions of consciousness-raising as legitimate political practice in pamphlets everywhere, and mixed testimonies about whether it does or does not work, but the demand for guidance and structure was clearly enough for the groundbreaking American anthology *Radical Feminism* to include a worksheet taking readers through the basis steps of the consciousness raising process, with the emphasis that the guidelines are not prescriptive. This worksheet recommends that groups do not exceed 12 women and it reminds us of the intention that personal experiences are shared so that they 'are recognized as a result not of an individual's idiosyncratic history and behaviour, but of the system of sex-role stereotyping. That is, they are political, not personal, questions'.[3] With this in mind it is recommended that the first three to six months are devoted to talking and analysing personal experiences, and then projects are initiated: whether these be reading feminist texts, setting up childcare centres, or in other ways contributing to the dynamism of the Women's Movement, the reality is that without such localized groupings and campaigns the Women's Movement, as a social movement, would not exist.

The clash between political agendas and the sum of the experiences which made up the grass-roots base of Women's Liberation in consciousness-raising was never likely to be easily resolved. But the idea of a political core begged the question of whether there was any widespread consensus about what that might be. From Echols's point of view, '[f]rom the beginning the women's liberation movement was internally fractured. In fact, it is virtually impossible to understand radical feminism without referring to the movement's divided beginnings' (Echols 1989: 101). At this time, of course, such fracturation was regarded as a strength rather than an inherent weakness and was about determining one's group's own political strategies and priorities. Whether or not any of these Movement women, themselves often dissatisfied with the hierarchical structure of NOW for instance, felt the need for national or international agreement at this time, the special identity of each early group in the US was a cause for celebration of diversity and an indicator of dynamism. These groups were coming together at national events, not always without incident, but with a convincing show of strength as evidence that the popularity of the Movement was growing rapidly. The principle underlying such groups in the US and the UK was that significant change can only come from collective action. Consider for example a 'Manifesto for Liberation of Women' which was presented for discussion at the 6th National Women's Liberation Movement conference in Edinburgh:

> Women cannot be individually liberated within a society that oppresses women. When you convince your husband that he should help with the washing-up, you have not made employers pay you an equal wage. When you have learnt to express your disgust at sexist advertisements to your sisters, you have not found the means to ensure that the educational hierarchy provides girls with a common curriculum (Dundee Women's Liberation Group 1974: 1).

Consciousness-raising remains one of the key successes of the Women's Liberation Movement, witnessed by the numerous references to it in the diverse papers of differing groupings. It was certainly a draw for women new to feminism, who saw CR as part of the educational process to becoming a feminist. As I shall argue later, the other CR mechanism at work during this period is the clutch of bestselling women's novels which also invite the sharing of experiences specific to women. Given that it is my contention that such novels acted as unofficial consciousness-raisers for the Movement, I shall also assert that this was a missed opportunity to get on board women who would never actively join a feminist group, but were in every other way entirely sympathetic to feminism's demands.

Unfortunately, feminism's internal wranglings were to become the most newsworthy element about the Movement – a clear way to contain the threat of feminism as a serious challenge to the *status quo*. It was always the extremes and the extremists which came under scrutiny and gradually these wings of the Women's Movement would be the source of much lampooning by the media. For instance, Boston's Cell 16 had a policy of celibacy, intended not only to keep women free from other distractions and focused on the revolution, but also to help women deprogramme themselves from feeling that they needed to court male attention. The ultimatums from such a group were clear and incontrovertible, as Dana Densmore demonstrates in her essay 'On Celibacy': 'until we say "I control my own body and I don't need any insolent male with an overbearing presumptuous prick to come and clean out my pipes" they will always have over us the devastating threat of withdrawing their sexual attentions and worse, the threat of our ceasing even to be sexually attractive' (Densmore 1968). For the members of Cell 16 these delusions were ones to be actively worked through in the process of demystifying romantic love and the rules of heterosexual attraction; this group seemed to have a brisk no-nonsense approach to the pulls of romance as set against the responsibilities and necessities of revolution –

> Erotic energy is just life energy and is quickly worked off if you are doing interesting, absorbing things. Love and affection and recognition can easily be found in comrades, a more open and honest love that love you for yourself and not for how docile and cute and sexy and ego-building you are . . . And if despite all this genital tensions persist you can still masturbate. Isn't that a lot easier anyway? (Densmore 1968)

The New York group The Feminists, which included the notorious Ti-Grace Atkinson and briefly counted as one of its members Valerie Solanas (author of the famous *SCUM Manifesto*, but actually more infamous for having shot Andy Warhol), also had a manifesto that might be off-putting to many, since they adopted a quota system for membership so that no more than one third of their members could either be married or cohabiting with a man (Koedt et al. 1973: 374). They also mooted (but did not adopt) the proposal that they all wear a uniform to forge greater equality within the ranks (Echols 1989: 179). Both Cell 16 and The Feminists' views on sexuality were hardly going to be popular since they suggested that 'sex was something that women needed to be liberated from' (Echols 1989: 174), a rather retrograde suggestion when the majority of young women, duped or not, were feeling very much a part of the much-hyped 'Sexual Revolution' of the 1960s and 1970s.

While these views are not representative of the majority of radical feminists, they hint at the infinite variety of such groupings and indeed the lengths that some were prepared to go to in the name of revolution, requiring total dedication from their membership. Obviously such dedication was something not possible or desirable for those with other primary emotional commitments, and such demands threatened to alienate and baffle many women otherwise instinctively drawn to becoming involved with radical feminist politics. Sex remained a thorny issue at the heart of radical feminist politics; first, heterosexual sex was put under scrutiny and attempts were made to demystify the female orgasm and educate women about their anatomy with the clear view that heterosexual sex was ripe for feminist intervention. However, somewhere along the line the more negative take on sex – that penetration was inevitably a hostile patriarchal act – took over. Gradually it became almost impossible to speak positively about straight sex and lesbianism, subject early on to discussions and even implicit strictures about what was and what wasn't acceptable sexual practice (role play was out, for instance), became a more vital topic of debate. Despite the popular view that all feminists were lesbians, homophobia in the Movement was a real problem, demonstrated by the oft-expressed fears that advertising the extent of the lesbian membership would put off 'ordinary' women. Betty Friedan, for example, was well known for her remarks about the 'Lavender Menace'. Lesbian feminists such as Rita Mae Brown and the group Radicalesbians asserted that homophobia in the Movement compromised its inclusivity and from these skirmishes emerged the concept of political lesbianism – the principle that women should give over all their energies to other women as an act of solidarity (Koedt et al. 1973: 240–5). As Freeman notes of the drive towards political lesbianism, the 'high personal cost of engaging in such acts often serves both to symbolize and to deepen one's commitment to the movement. Thus, those women who chose lesbian/feminism, often at great personal cost, as a means of demonstrating their commitment could easily perceive those who didn't as possessing less conviction, and thus not to be trusted' (Freeman 1975: 140). Feminism's relation to sexuality became so contorted that heterosexuality became more of a taboo subject, since it proved impossible to move beyond its being termed 'male identified' to a place where women's heterosexual desire could be reviewed in a more positive fashion. Consequently, lesbian sexuality was to some extent desexed and became, uncomfortably, the moral core of the Movement.

Despite these issues about structure, national identity, sexuality, and small group dynamics, the boundless enthusiasm of these early groups is infectious, even when some of their rallying cries can be viewed in retrospect as hopelessly optimistic: '[A]s soon as the Leader groups have established themselves in each town and city and defined their aims, they must then strive to gain the support of all women in those towns and cities [. . .] The majority of women are still asleep. They must be awakened from their nightmare and educated by other women' (Skinner 1970: 33). Refreshingly, this call to the barricades takes the radical stance of suggesting that all women go on strike at home until the men of the world submit, but:

> if after a certain time has elapsed, the government still shows no signs of building good nurseries, or of reconverting some of all those empty houses dotted over the country, then we must be prepared to take our under-fives (unless a better course of action can be found) with the exception of babies, into the Houses of Parliament and male dominated concerns all over the country for one day of every week until we get what we and our children need (Skinner 1970: 34).

There is here, as elsewhere, an awareness of how extreme such proposals seem, but the captured rage felt at the dawning realization of the impact of 'hundreds of years of men's dictatorships' (Skinner 1970: 35) was potent enough to encourage groups to think up more unusual strategies to achieve their ends. While in the US it was only really NOW that attempted some kind of national consensus about the central issues for women, there was a semblance of some early agreement between British feminists, forged at the Ruskin conference. Four key demands were agreed to be at the heart of the modern British Women's Movement: first, Equal pay; second, Equal opportunities and education; third, Free contraception and abortion on demand; and fourth, Free 24-hour nurseries. These were later revised to seven demands at the Women's Liberation conference in Birmingham in 1978:

1  Equal pay for equal work
2  Equal education and equal opportunities
3  Free contraception and abortion on demand
4  Free 24 hour nurseries
5  Legal and financial independence for women
6  An end to discrimination against lesbians
7  Freedom for all women from intimidation by the threat or use of male violence. An end to the laws, assumptions and institutions which perpetuate male dominance and men's aggression towards women (Fairbairns 2003: 94).

In both Britain and the US there seemed to be a consensus that childcare difficulties prevent women entering the professions and that without control of their own bodies women remain at the mercy of their biology and the roles they are seen traditionally to perform. Debates about domestic roles, whether there should be wages for housework, fierce battles over abortion rights, and the more educational dimensions of the Movement, with bestselling publications such as *Our Bodies Ourselves* coming from the Boston Women's Health Collective, all fused together in a heady mixture of both exciting and ultimately life-changing discussions.

The strengths of this new Women's Movement continued to lie in its diversity and inventiveness and the fact that the energy was supplied by small semi-autonomous groupings.

Its weaknesses were in the sharp divisions this created and the confusion among potential members with regard to what Women's Liberation was really all about. While sisterhood was a powerful image and said a great deal about how the Movement wanted to see itself and how it wanted to be seen by women at large, there were numerous incidents, since retold in accounts and memoirs, which demonstrated some deep-seated tensions at its heart, even before the really important debates about the place of identity in feminism began to take hold. Greater than early ideological splits were the interpersonal disagreements that culminated in some fairly bloody culls. Although it has served the mainstream media well to characterize the movement as riven by splits and to suggest that this is indicative that it is bent on self-destruction, it doesn't do justice to its surprising moments of cohesion or to the changes it managed to champion. Another way to look at feminism of this period is as an anxious movement; anxious not to repeat the petty corruptions and power-play of the New Left or Civil Rights and anxious to engage with all women by making political statements and organizing demonstrations that could be embraced by all. This is the ambition, but on a day-to-day basis petty rivalries could escalate into full-scale rifts and within a small group of women in any cell this could rapidly become fairly serious.

This process, dubbed 'trashing' by 'Joreen' (Jo Freeman) and other important US Movement figures, is the practice of isolating and punishing a member of a group who is seen to stand out in certain ways and therefore becomes an object of suspicion. Joreen later found out that her only 'crime' was to be quoted in a news article without the permission of the group. From her point of view, '[t]rashing is a particularly vicious form of character assassination which amounts to psychological rape' (Freeman 1976: 49). She notes that trashing is 'much more prevalent among those who call themselves radical than among those who don't; among those who stress personal changes than among those who stress institutional ones; among those who can be satisfied with smaller successes; and among those in groups with vague goals than those in groups with concrete ones' (Freeman 1976: 97). Radical feminism had after all demanded a movement based on structurelessness, where everyone is working to the one motive with one voice; needless to say this works against those with unusual skills of public speaking or writing or creativity, since they are likely to stand out as more proficient, as natural 'leaders' and even as self-appointed spokespeople, which is likely to provoke the ire of their sisters. This is reinforced by a resolution reached at the Class Workshop of the Second Congress to Unite Women in the US in 1970, which included the proposals that:

> 1. Anyone who appears in the media is to be drawn by lot from her group [. . .] The lot is to be rotating. No one is to participate in the media alone. 2. Women's liberation is getting popular enough that the media needs us as much as we need them. We can and must dictate our terms to them: present prepared statements and refuse to give personal information. From now on anyone who refuses to follow this policy must be assumed to be doing so for her own personal aggrandizement. 3. No member of a group can appear as an independent feminist – whether for fame or money. 4. No individual or group can earn a living by writing or speaking about women's liberation. 5. Anyone who wants to write should write for the movement, not for the publishing industry. 6. Any individual who refuses collective discipline will be ostracized from the movement. (quoted in Echols 1989: 208)

As Freeman has said elsewhere, 'feminists often failed to make a distinction between those who were "using" the movement and those who were "strong" women or had valuable talents [. . .] as a result, some of the most talented women in the movement withdrew from it entirely, bitterly alienated' (Freeman 1975: 121). Judith Hole and Ellen Levine's book on these early years also conjures up scenes of bitter struggles and misunderstandings, noting, '[a]s a result of the charges of elitism, so frequent during this period, some individual women felt forced to leave groups and withdraw from all activity in the movement [. . .] With mixed degrees of bitterness and humour they called themselves "feminist refugees"' (Hole and Levine 1971: 161). Feminist groupings conceived in a utopian fashion as without hierarchy of systems of privilege were imbued with hierarchies to their very fabric; they were susceptible to infiltration by other politicos as well as being vulnerable to the perceived tyrannies of the more charismatic members, not to mention the casual assumption of the central ground by white, middle-class, heterosexual women.

It wasn't just 'trashing' that sent shockwaves through the Movement and drove many an energetic woman from its groupings, but the fact that modern feminism on the face of it brought to women a clean sheet rather than a pre-set agenda; the cost of this being radical disagreements about what feminism was for:

> The rage, the sensitivity, and the overwhelming, omnipresent nature of 'the enemy' drove parts of the Women's Movement into ideological rigidities, and the movement splintered as it grew. Who could say what was *the* central issue: equal pay? abortion? the nuclear family? lesbianism? welfare policies? capitalism? Groups formed around particular issues, constituencies and political styles, many sure that they had found the key to women's liberation. After 1970, women's liberation groups in all parts of the country suffered painful splits variously defined as politico/feminist, gay/straight, anti-imperialist/radical feminist (Evans 1979: 225)

For good or ill these painful splits and differences of opinion were well documented and yet of less importance to the majority of women, who identified themselves as feminists because they were more interested in 'the kinds of responses it made possible' (Evans 1979: 226). After all, the radical wing of feminist activity probably only accounted for the minority of women who chose to call themselves 'feminist', not the many women who read all the literature they could lay their hands on and attempted to change their own lives. For them, the Movement facilitated and energized individual actions and decisions. It may not have been the preferred response of those feminist activists, but it did amount to a massive groundswell of support for feminist issues and a broadening interest in women's concerns.

Looking at numerous Women's Liberation pamphlets and magazines, it is clear that many are aware of the problems of communicating feminism to a broader constituency and of the tension arising between putting forward an accurate view of the Movement yet not allowing 'stars' to emerge. As the UK magazine *Shrew* noted, '[t]he whole question of leadership, responsibility, elitism, ego-trips, communication, media figures is becoming crucial to our growth as a healthy movement and our communication with other women' (*Shrew* 1971:11). But without the funds to produce glossy eye-catching material these publications were never going to reach a mass market used to the more sophisticated techniques of magazine empires and advertising moguls. There were of course attempts at more glossy magazine publishing, the most well known being *Ms* magazine and in the UK the slightly less glossy but relatively popular *Spare Rib*, but these just did not have the circulation and therefore the visibility to compete with mainstream magazines.

*Ms* magazine emerged in 1971 and 'became on the spot the name of the only feminist mass magazine in history. It would become, like the acronym NOW, a verbal symbol of the women's movement' (Cohen 1988: 325). The format offered a link between classic women's glossy magazines and a weekly political periodical. It aimed to counteract the more pernicious effects of the mass media in the US by offering a more reliable account of Movement activities and of issues of importance to women. It also opened up the Women's Movement to a mass 'membership', bearing in mind Robin Morgan's assertion that 'this is not a movement one "joins". There are no rigid structures or membership cards' (Morgan 1970: xii). This allowed women, even those most isolated, to feel they belonged to a community of radical women with whom they could at least vicariously share a sense of political direction through an organ that addressed their concerns solely and recognized the ways in which women were not represented in mainstream social policy.

This serves to reinforce the point I made in the Introduction to this book, that there was no accepted 'language' of feminism that people could resort to. Rather, every new concept was an alien one and a suitable word or phrase had to be wrought out of the language that was available – some of the topics that feminists wished to cover were, from a broader perspective, still seen as mundane and trivial. Authors who chose to pick up on the writings of the Movement reflect this grasping for conceptualization and in fiction perhaps this dictated the choice of gritty realism at a time when more avant-garde forms were favoured. Sue Kaufman's *Diary of a Mad Housewife*, produced at the time when left-wing women were setting up their caucuses and challenging male power, was lauded by radical feminist Susan Brownmiller as producing the 'first feminist novel of the new generation' (Brownmiller 2000: 40). It portrays Bettina Balser, whose diary gives an account of the minutiae of her privileged yet mundane existence; she uses the diary as a means of confession in order to prove to herself that she is not going insane and in doing so it dramatizes the deteriorating relationship between her husband, Jonathan, and herself. This and other novels coming out a few years later, which I shall go on to discuss in the next three chapters, were crucial in hammering home the feminist message in a more palatable fashion. What fictional heroines such as Bettina and her ilk demonstrated was that feminist principles might be a utopia that you held up for scrutiny as a measure with which to compare your own life. These women sometimes failed to gain the freedom they so urgently desired; their affairs were just proof that men wanted ownership of their women; their children were a source of guilt and the deepest love of their lives. Their weaknesses and fallibility spoke to a generation of readers, who perhaps felt that they lacked the resolve to join a group as demanding as Cell 16 but wanted to effect some changes in their relationships in order to combat their sense of utter domestic suffocation.

These novels are exciting because they purvey feminist ideas in a more popular parlance, sometimes without purporting to be 'feminist' at all. They consciously or unconsciously reinforced the key political principles of feminism while showing an understanding that the sacrifices feminism required were not always easy. This, in particular, demonstrated how rapidly some of the central principles of feminism were filtering through to become household words. In addition to this, key phrases and words devised by the Women's Movement were co-opted to quite different and interesting ends. For instance, in 1972 in the UK one popular advertisement in women's magazines was for Libresse sanitary towels, which were sold with the shout line, 'Women's Liberation. Throw away your belt and special panties and switch to new Libresse' (see, for example, *Honey* May 1972). The picture of a women's torso and the top of her legs, cut off below the breasts and showing her wearing a simple pair of white panties with her hands on her hips avoids a sexualized image of a woman – so much a topic of feminist critique at the time – and nothing about the pose is suggestive. In the same issue of *Honey* there is a playful article on male chauvinism which offers some uncompromising advice to its young women readers:

> 1. Remember to remember what male chauvinism adds up to: thousands of years of slavery. Be sensitive, be prickly. If you're assaulted by hints of male arrogance, smash back. 2. If you want to take control of a situation, to ask somebody out or tell someone not to pester you, do it. It may be taken amiss, but if it is you shouldn't want to have too much to do with that person anyway. 3. Bear in mind that Lysistrata stopped the Athenian men from going to war by leading the women on a sex strike (Anon. 1972: 55).

In 1968 in the US the cigarette brand Virginia Slims first produced the strapline, 'you've come a long way' (later adding the word 'baby'), suggesting either that women were still different enough to require their own cigarette or that separatism could be extended to every aspect of a woman's life, even her commercial tastes. This advertising campaign continued in the 1970s and 1980s and slogans were accompanied by humorous and stylish images, some of supermodels and other famous faces, to draw women into the myth that somehow this cigarette brand contributed to women's wider social freedoms as well as the visible successes of individuals such as the supermodels included in the campaigns.

Such advertisements, exploitative of feminism though they were, in common with popular magazine articles and the novels of the period, all contribute to the ways people learned about feminism and to some extent shaped their ideas about it. While the risks were that some of these messages served to undermine, exploit, or trivialize feminist slogans (as does the Virginia Slims ad), the positive by-products were those articles and novels which allowed women to feel that feminism included them, whatever their 'political' qualifications. By the mid to late 1970s there was an anxiety and degree of disillusionment about the success and reach of the Women's Liberation Movement both in the US and the UK. An article in the British feminist journal *Catcall* asks,

> [w]hat will happen to our movement? Will this second feminism survive, or will it go under, like the first? In the year two thousand, will some pioneer activist again have to expose the horror of women's lives? [. . .] Will this generation's children, like the children of our great-grandmothers, be forced back into the shadows of husband and home, despised for their labours, doomed to endless service and suffering? (Weisstein and Booth 1978: 17)

The authors warn of a cultural recidivism and remind us that by the later 1970s the US and the UK were hitting recession and job shortages were beginning, and that such forces might ineluctably drag us into backlash.

While there were numerous reasons to be increasingly gloomy about the fate of feminist activism by the mid-1970s, it was at this time that feminist fictional writings were reaching their height, with novels which are fast-paced, thrilling, and reassuringly ambiguous. While the politics of some of these authors might have failed the close scrutiny of WLM, their message was hitting the mark for the millions of readers who had their consciousnesses raised through their responses to the novels. I shall spend the next three chapters evaluating the contributions of these key novels and shall note in particular how they do – or don't – relate to live, ongoing debates in the Women's Movement.

# 3

# Mad Housewives

The novels that began to appear around the time the Women's Liberation Movement emerged are testament to the attractions of feminist thought for a wide range of women. Fiction allows for the luxury of experimentation and can give voice to taboos and contradictions, and these writers, some card-carrying feminists (in the sense that they concerned themselves with the political agenda of Women's Liberation), were able to depict scenarios familiar to their readers, but which perhaps had never been articulated in words before. The life stories which are the staple of these feminist bestsellers tantalized the readers with the promise of the kind of deep dark revelations of autobiography. In these popular novels we find evidence of the twin pulls of Friedan's call for a new individual self-determination and a utopian wish for collective action resulting in massive social change. Whether or not the writers were feminists, the themes chimed with the feminist debates being held on both sides of the Atlantic. Quite often these novels included an account of each stage of a woman's life, from adolescence through to motherhood, and these shared thematic concerns revealed a recognition that the indoctrination of women into the ways of femininity runs deep. From pre-pubescent girlhood, females are aware of the intense pressure to perform their femininity in the most appropriate way. The glossy magazines and the billboards, the beauty pageants and the approbation of their peers will all begin to embed themselves into the female consciousness, even for those women who feel able to challenge such unrealistic standards. In these novels we find the anguished sense of entrapment of the suburban wife, echoed in books from *Diary of a Mad Housewife* right through to *The Women's Room*. For the group of young married women described in *The Women's Room*, the unspoken, unthought-about conditions that made it [housewifery] oppressive had long since been accepted by all of them: that they had not chosen but had been automatically slotted into their lives, and that they were never free to move (the children were much more effective as clogs than confinement on a prison farm would be). Having accepted the shit and string beans, they were content (French 1986: 75).

The image of the shit and stringbeans underlines the mundanity of these women's daily lives and the focus on servicing others; they are portrayed as recluctantly accepting a state of affairs they had never chosen nor could have predicted, underlining the way women's expected social role is a million miles away from the freedoms of teenage courtship and the promises of romantic love. Similarly in *Up the Sandbox!* (1970), Anne Richardson Roiphe describes the tedious cycle of Margaret Reynolds's housework duties and their anachronistic primitiveness in a modern world:

Eat, eliminate, prepare food, clean up, shop, throw out the garbage, a routine clear as a geometric form, a linear pattern that seems almost graceful in its simplicity. Despite computers and digit telephone numbers, nuclear fission, my life hardly differs from that of an Indian Squaw settled in a tepee on the same Manhattan land centuries ago. Pick, clean, prepare, throw out, dig a hole, bury the waste – she was my sister (Roiphe 1970: 18)

Charlotte Perkins Gilman, writing about housework at the turn of the twentieth century, also comments on its enduring primitiveness in an age of rapid technological developments – '[b]ack of history, at the bottom of civilisation, untouched by a thousand whirling centuries, the primitive woman, in the primitive home, still toils at her primitive tasks [. . .] by what art, what charm, what miracle has the twentieth century preserved *alive* the prehistoric squaw!' (Gilman 1904: 84)

The feminist novel itself has a long pedigree and critics such as Norma Clarke remind us that, in addition to writers and critics such as Gilman, writers of the 1890s such as Sarah Grand and Elizabeth Robbins used feminist thinking of their time in their writing, observing, '[t]hroughout the nineteenth century, novelists had explored the contradictions in women's lives, the lack of fit between ideal and reality, the stranglehold of myth and ideology' (Clarke 1985: 93). She notes that Sarah Grand's *The Heavenly Twins* (1893) sold 20,000 copies in its first year and was reprinted six times, to become a bestseller in the US. In a real sense the novels of the late 1960s and 1970s are carrying on the tradition of exploring the contradictions that women have to live with, but on the whole they are less didactic in their methods, less closely associated to the feminism of their time. The preferred mode of representation for all of these writers is a stark form of realism, strikingly at odds with an era where literature is becoming more generally self-conscious, and for some this might seem a reactionary or naïve retreat. Equally, though, it could be interpreted as a deliberate strategy to expose those unwritten truths of women's contemporary lives rather than an inability to cope with more 'sophisticated' and fashionable literary styles. Nicci Gerrard's explanation of this is, '[w]e needed novels to "tell it like it is" ' (Gerrard 1989: 111), which certainly echoes feminist consciousness raising imperatives.

There was a significant band of women writers who favoured a novel which took the form of a *Bildungsroman,* recounting life stories which invited women readers to recognize their own lives therein – not least because these were stories of contemporary living and part of their essential material was showing how our personal relations shape social relations and how the whole forms a backdrop to the choices and decisions we feel able to make. This kind of writing can still contain within it a utopian dimension which imagines future possibilities, and this is achieved through the positioning of the reader. This is most evident at the end of the novels where the chief character may be on the threshold of a life-changing decision or simply may be unable to make the move that would change her life but could still inspire others to do it instead. Perhaps a twenty-first-century reader would have less stomach for some of these tales and Maroula Joannou, for one, suggests that the reception of these confessional novels has by necessity changed with time – 'the very novels which empowered and helped to politicise a generation of women may appear lacking in subtlety, formally conservative, and sometimes even hectoring in tone' (Joannou 2000: 106). The way they dutifully record and describe menstruation, abortion, childcare, and sexual desire seems unnecessarily grim and heavy-handed, even formulaic. But for readers of the time these stories of urban isolation and self-doubt allowed them to feel less cut off from the world and, in the spirit of the consciousness raising group, allowed for the experience of a shared reality which suggested that these feelings weren't just a response to personal inadequacy or maladjustment but were actually a justified reaction to being positioned as unequal to men.

Gerrard's defence of this novelistic form is about celebrating their quotidian dreariness and understanding its purpose: '[F]ictional women sitting at kitchen tables drinking peppermint tea and discussing their problems is not a mundane literary event if real women see through the conversation a commentary of their own lives' (Gerrard 1989: 112). Needless to say, not all of these confessional novels possess any enduring literary or other worth and in any case a form too often exploited rapidly becomes tired and loses its novelty value. Some of these novels do endure and strike a chord, but these seem to be the ones that dwell very little on domestic detail, such as *Fear of Flying*, which makes no great attempt to anchor itself in a particular period and features a childless woman. The emphasis here, rather, is on the attempt to 'fly', to create the self beyond the prisonhouse of femininity. Those which feature a campus setting, such as *Braided Lives* (1982) or *The Women's Room*, present a politics that is simply alien to the post-Thatcher and Reagan generations. Some of the novels fall short of the mark, perhaps, because their intention to be 'feminist' in some straightforward way means that they can fall peril to the straitjacket of correctness, like any politically intentioned novel. The successful confessional novels are those that not only possess the qualities of good writing and a slightly different take on the unofficial narrative formula, but also escape the impression that they are simply 'brave and slightly worthy' (Gerrard 1989: 114), and should be admired because of this.

This chapter will go on to focus on some early examples of the feminist confessional novel, which I shall dub the 'mad housewife' novels because the central characters seem at times in danger of losing their hold on rationality in face of the ways domestic duties threaten to rob them of all sense of self. As we shall see, these novels anatomize domestic labour and its impact on the married woman and in doing so bring together both First and Second Wave accounts of the housewifely role. Before looking at the novels in further detail, it is important and useful to chart feminist responses to these texts from the late 1960s to the contemporary period. I hope that this will help the reader understand why it is interesting to review these novels now; as well as serve to contextualize my own critical responses to the texts. Early accounts of the 'feminist novel', as they were called by some contemporary critics such as Jane Larkin Crain, note what she regards as the tedious attention to detail (as opposed to Gerrard's view of its political possibilities). Crain notes, '[the] sorts of things that ladies' magazines have been handling in little articles and short stories for years – the housewife's sundry duties and chores, her sexual and other marital difficulties, her endless labours as a mother, and so forth – have been transferred en masse, and in the same exhaustive, obsessive detail, into the pages of the feminist novel' (Crain 1974: 58). Dismissed by Crain as 'all too steeped in ideology to pay the elementary respect to human complexity that good fiction demands' (Crain 1974: 59), such novels are characterized as whining and self-indulgent, lacking both the culture and complexity of their literary forebears. Even though she acknowledges that 'they constitute a phenomenon', she finds 'something repugnant in all this celebration of cowards, cripples, and losers' (Crain 1974: 59; 62). Of course it has not been uncommon for novels with a radical political perspective to be seen as overly ideological, and these novels simply aren't striving for the 'literary' cachet that Crain wishes to judge them by. It has become much more common since the 1990s to regard Second Wave feminism as promoting a victim mentality among women and Crain seems to suggest that this view existed as an undercurrent a lot earlier; it smacks of the assumption that feminists exaggerated the ways in which women's oppression was manifested in material ways and implies that women who bemoan their lot should simply strive for self-improvement. Those Crain describes as losers are the central characters who are depicted as failing to live up to their own aspirations, the point being that circumstances militate against them. If you don't believe that women were actively presented with obstacles that denied them certain opportunities, then you are going to blame the women who don't manage to succeed in a culture that favours exceptionalism; the high profile of the few successful women in any given field which supports the idea that it is as open to female as male advancement. This mentality became powerfully enacted by Margaret Thatcher, to name just one example, in the 1980s.

It has become something of a tradition in books about consciousness raising novels to give central space to a discussion of Rosalind Coward's short article, ' "This Novel Changes Lives": Are Women's Novels Feminist Novels?', which appeared in the British journal *Feminist Review* in 1980 and which is itself a response to Rebecca O'Rourke's 'Summer Reading', published in the same journal during the previous year. As the first substantial article to devote itself to the genre of what Coward also calls 'the feminist novel', it is an important piece of writing and anticipates further commentary on this theme in her book *Female Desire* (1984). A key theme of the article is the questioning of what a 'feminist reading' might be and the interrogation of the real relation of fiction to politics: 'No one is quite sure about the political validity of the admixture of conventional entertainment with a serious political message' (Coward 1980: 53). The issue of how one determines whether a woman's writing is feminist needed to be addressed and has been raised, in various guises, over and over in the reflective practices of feminists as critics and readers. After all, can the reading of any book by a woman result in a feminist event? Or by producing a feminist reading of some conservative texts are we papering over their flaws? Might there be so much energy invested in producing feminist readings which give legitimacy to the constituency of women as critical readers emerging since the late 1960s that issues such as literary value, formal skills, and political content become redundant? For Coward, implicit in her argument is the suggestion that only appropriate feminist/political credentials on the part of the author could legitimize the writing and that any nod to the popular in style or tone is to sacrifice the author's credibility. Feminist criticism was developing at a time when the literary critical establishment was being challenged by radical voices which demanded more reflexivity about what we do and who we do it for. In relation to theoretical developments, early feminist literary criticism was going to seem naïve and impressionistic in its focus on images of women and the histories of female authors. Feminist literary criticism began in the spirit of exploration and perceives its duties not only as hermeneutic, but also as archaeological in many cases – trying to excavate those women who were important and successful in their time, but have since been erased from the hall of 'greats'.

If the novel in question is also a runaway commercial success, this can make a book even more problematic from a feminist critical perspective because marketability and political credibility are conventionally seen as incompatible. Coward directs us to take into consideration the wider conditions of the text's production – marketing, construction of the author, and even the institution of literary criticism itself – and in this approach one can identify in the young Coward the heavy influence of French literary theory, that of Roland Barthes and Michel Foucault in particular. In retrospect the article appears a little fragmentary and the theory rather heavy-handed, creating difficulty in following the central argument about what makes a feminist text. She is tough on O'Rourke for what she sees as her lack of theoretical awareness and for the fact that she doesn't distinguish between genres and form when she talks about women's writing:

> Rebecca admits to the pleasure experienced in reading what are in many ways politically reactionary books, only to justify that pleasure by the fact that these books were written by women. It would be far more important to understand what these pleasures are, how they can be used and transformed (Coward 1980: 56).

Coward seems disturbed that O'Rourke can cheerfully celebrate women's writing as a category worthy of critical appraisal without distinguishing whether or not a feminist political commitment is in evidence. In order to enforce the point that women-centred novels do not necessarily have anything to do with feminism, she cites the example of Mills & Boon as a retrogressive genre. When it comes to the feminist bestsellers she makes distinctions between *The Women's Room,* which she claims does make clear its allegiance to Women's Liberation, and *Fear of Flying* and *Kinflicks,* which she feels do not, and she makes some fairly sweeping value judgements on this basis. The novels' status as works of popular fiction cause her some methodological difficulties, and it does seem to be that the fact of their popularity and their explicit references to sexuality prevent her from assessing their feminism in a broader perspective, because their popularity, the pandering to the mass reader, rather than their feminism, might be the source of their success. When it comes to their confessional qualities and concomitant preoccupation with sexuality, she questions O'Rourke's reading of the novels as representative of experience that can be translated into feminist politics, suggesting that such a reflectionist model of reading is naïve - 'feminism can never be the product of the identity of women's experiences and interests – there is no such unity' (Coward 1980: 63).

At the end of this challenge to O'Rourke it's still pretty difficult to gauge Coward's own response to these novels. Concealed beneath the protective layer of Barthesian analysis, it is difficult to know whether she is condemning popular fiction or just grasping for a more worked through form of analysis. What is unmistakable, whether intended or not, is the excessive hostility of the response – this is not just a correction of O'Rourke's piece but a wholesale attack on her methodology, which Coward reads in ways it was clearly not intended to be read. Of course, during the growing academicization of feminism from the late 1970s onwards, political divisions were still rife and arguments common. O'Rourke's aims are simple: she wants to draw some classics to the attention of a wider readership and does argue for the importance of a community of women's writing that I'd want to endorse, whereas Coward is clearly tired of the impressionistic criticism that she associates with early Second Wave feminism.

In 'Summer Reading', O'Rourke identifies a change in women's writing from the early 1960s and says, 'this women's writing of the last fifteen years or so raises and explores the problems of women's existence but it offers only resistances, never change', continuing, 'no fictional heroine joins the women's movement, there is no overt politics of these precisely worked-over personal lives' (O'Rourke 1979: 1; 1–2). One of the intentions of her essay is to encourage feminists to read contemporary women's writing and consider its relation to feminist politics. Talking about *The Women's Room* as one of the examples of these contemporary texts, she makes the crucial point, '[f]ar from being the mouthpiece of feminist propaganda, Mira is on occasion the devil's advocate, asking questions of feminism which are sometimes naïve, sometimes obvious, but which come from within a culture which oppresses women most effectively through their own internalization of patriarchal values' (O'Rourke 1979: 5). She admits that in making her selection as an active feminist, she has high expectations of these texts and their feminist context – 'as if I still have some notion of The Feminist Text, a rarefied, perfect work which would balance and represent all the conflicts and contradictions of contemporary feminism' (O'Rourke 1979: 8). In saying this, O'Rourke articulates not only her own desires, but also those of numerous feminists who look to contemporary fiction expecting it to offer them this impossible balance, and when they find it wanting they are much harsher in their critical reception than they are with regard to books from an earlier period. Here, O'Rourke picks up on something that subsequently gets lost again until some time later: that feminist fiction of this kind does not and never intended to have a phatic relationship to feminism; it was sometimes acting as devil's advocate and addressing some of the gaps and unanswered questions that feminist politics was constantly batting back to the individual.

One of the reasons I have chosen to discuss Coward's article before looking at some of the features of O'Rourke's is to demonstrate the degree to which they were doing two different things. O'Rourke is captivated by the possibilities of identifying powerful books by women from different periods and genres which provide interesting counterpoints to feminism and politics; Coward is more interested in offering a disciplined and rigorous model of feminist criticism. In her book *Female Desire*, Coward again touches on the properties of the confessional novel and is struck most of all by each heroine's garrulity – their need to tell all and their closeness to the ideals of the so-called Sexual Revolution. She acknowledges that in such novels 'consciousness raising is used as a narrative device' (Coward 1984: 179), also noting that the confessional becomes a popular mode in men's writing too - if one thinks of texts such as Philip Roth's *Portnoy's Complaint* - and also in popular autobiography of the day. Coward remains sceptical about the power of such narratives to change women's lives because she questions the extent to which many of them are able to explore the constructedness of female identity. As I hope to show later on, many of these books seem painfully aware of this constructedness and it is a key legacy they left to popular forms which emerges again in urban fiction of the 1990s.

One of the objectives of this book will be to find uniting threads among these CR books, whether by self-declared feminists or otherwise. One way of reading these novels is to forge a link with readings of some of the key feminist non-fiction texts of the period. As Katherine Payant observed in her book on contemporary women's fiction and feminism, and as I asserted earlier, non-fiction was consumed as avidly as fiction, and Payant's memoir of this period reinforces this sense of a dialectical link between the two forms:

> *Sexual Politics* is, no doubt, one of the few works of criticism read by large numbers of nonacademics. In my own small northern Michigan town, in my consciousness-raising group composed of teachers, artists, other professionals, and housewives, we avidly discussed it and other works at the same time that we explored our experiences as women. The tie-ins were excitingly obvious to us. Equally exciting were the new novels by women writers that spoke to the experiences of being a contemporary woman, and we began to read and discuss these, too (Payant 1993: 16).

She notes how some reviewers were disappointed by these novels because they wanted stronger central characters, but this, of course, is to miss the point. Fallible heroines allowed these writers to explore the gap between politicizing one's life and changing it for good.

I am particularly interested in the consciousness-raising dimensions of these texts and the way the reader is positioned to respond to these women's stories and agree with Gayle Greene that 'whatever a writer's relations to the women's movement, we may term a novel "feminist" for its analysis of gender as socially constructed and its sense that what has been constructed may be reconstructed – for its understanding that change is possible and that narrative can play a part in it' (Greene 1991: 2). Lisa Hogeland was to note, years later, '[p]opular texts, both fiction and film, have been and continue to be used to draw lines and set limits about what feminism is and what it means' (Hogeland 1998: 156). Whether we like it or not, feminism is characterized and defined by the fiction and films that attempt to represent it, echo its ideas, or even discredit it. It is better, surely, to acknowledge 'feminist' interventions wherever they appear rather than try to section them off into two wings of writing – one from the party faithful and the other of the writers who may also have enjoyed commercial success from their works.

While Coward tires of the repetition of similar events and daily happenings in the feminist bestseller, one could equally interpret this constant revisiting of the same ground as a will to dramatize the boredom, to make an event out of tedium. Gayle Greene sees the repetitions and returns to the same territory as the act of naming the unnameable or the unmentionable –'central events in these novels derive from the fact that women live in women's bodies – this becomes the focus of fiction for the first time' (Greene 1991: 60). That they touched a nerve with thousands and thousands of readers is proven by the books' sales figures, but as regards critical success they were viewed with suspicion by feminist critics, whose poor opinion of these texts would only be confirmed if they were praised by the mainstream literary establishment, because that reinforced their concern that the author has sold out for the glittering prizes. Looking back, they were bound to act as an incendiary in feminist political circles where individual voices were always regarded with scepticism. Unfortunately, this meant that any feminist writings which became popular were going to be viewed with enormous scepticism by those who thought that the gaining of a revolutionary consciousness should be done at vanguard of the Movement rather than in the safety of one's own home. Lauret suggests that though many feminists found sustenance from such novels (and some had come to feminism via the fiction), they also felt that they captured a particular moment which could not comfortably be revisited: 'Perhaps some feminist critics, for who the reading of these novels was a formative experience but who have since "moved on", are reluctant to return to them for fear of being disappointed. Like meeting an ex-lover: the reality matches neither the fantasy nor the memory' (Lauret 1989: 98). I have already noted that some of these writings have not aged well and may prove incomprehensible or dull to the new reader. But Lauret's comments are themselves now over fifteen years old, and it is quite feasible that as the distance between the novels and their new readers grows so our perspective on them may change further, in the light of new concerns with the domestic in terms of the 'mumlit' that grew from the success-ful chick lit genre and a renewed focus on the sexual division of labour in current social debates.

John Sutherland suspects the uneasy relationship of femi-nism to fiction had much to do with unresolved problems of how to treat a popular text:

> 'Authenticity' required either poetry (with its minimal read-ership and consequent freedom from commercialism) or the straight talk of non-fiction. In terms of sexual politics *The Female Eunuch* was generically sounder than *Fear of Flying*. The superselling novel with emancipated themes [. . .] was inevitably suspect as being indirectly exploitative of women (making money for male publishers, fuelling male mastur-bation fantasies) or indicative of a repressive tolerance which insidiously sapped revolutionary energy and confused protest with entertainment (Sutherland 1981: 83-4).

Sutherland (controversially for some feminists) notes the correlative rise of Mills & Boon mass market romance fiction at the same time as the rise of feminism and in some ways the two genres continued to comment on each other, with feminist bestsellers such as *Fear of Flying* conducting romance through the lens of feminist anti-romance and Mills & Boon incorpo-rating 'feminist' elements in their books in order to attract the more liberated reader.

In 1964 the US television series *Bewitched* was launched and became so popular that it has seen endless reruns up to the present day. I remember not being allowed to stay up and watch it when I was about seven, but, when I was allowed to watch it finding it absolutely riveting, in ways quite similar to my enjoyment of the cartoon show *The Flintstones*. Samantha (or Sam) the housewife/witch, whose family, magic, and commitment to good causes was a source of exasperation to her husband Darrin, reminded me of Wilma in *The Flintstones*, who was always trying to conceal her worst consumerist excesses from the perennially bad-tempered Fred. Both shows offer an image of what a good housewife might look like and both showed the ways in which the housewife was always seeking to undermine the structures which defined her. This is particularly true of Sam, whose magical powers tie in to a fantasy of being able to eradicate the drudgery of housework in an instant. Sam is a perfect housewife and hostess because she is a witch and this perhaps links in to a more compelling fantasy – to be able to accomplish everything that a good woman should while actually having a rewarding life outside the home. Inevitably Samantha exposes the contradictions of mass media of the period, 'trying to acknowledge the impending release of female sexual and political energy, while keeping it all safely in a straitjacket' (Douglas 1995: 126). Both shows were underlaid by an impossible dream, that housework could be effortless and fun and that the rewards lay in the pleasures of a spotless, well-appointed home. Wilma's wonderful labour-saving devices spoke to the dream of the 1960s housewife in a time of economic boom: to buy their way out of drudgery. But the reality was that labour-saving devices often created an increased burden of labour, with correspondingly higher standards of cleanliness and efficiency expected. The cat was already out of the bag, and by the late 1960s women's fiction was also echoing a clear frustration with a role that cast otherwise talented, intelligent, and single-minded young women as passive and eagerly selfless unpaid servants.

The central protagonists of these 'mad housewife' novels are well educated, intellectually questing and often artistically inclined women. Their marriages are based on the solid foundation of compatibility and companionship. They freely enter into these partnerships, secure in the knowledge that this is a new era of equality and self-definition and that their marriage will be different to that of their parents. These are not novels of breadth and incident; much of the drama takes place in the women's heads or arises in the narrating of the most mundane of incidents. The form is confessional or confiding and almost all novels are written completely in the first person. In cases where the novel is presented as a diary or journal, the act of writing is seen as therapy. Cosseted in their youth, these women are baffled by the intricacies of domestic life and the fact that their husbands, so self-sufficient when single, become entirely dependent on them after marriage. The eponymous mad housewife novel, *Diary of a Mad Housewife*, offers us a first-person account of the life of Bettina Munvies Balser. It could not really be described as a 'liberation novel' in Hogeland's sense of the term, because there is no concerted coming to consciousness through an awareness of feminist political positions; yet Sue Kaufman's novel shares several of the structural features of later feminist fiction as well as reflecting back on novels such as *The Bell Jar*. In face of Bettina's increasing solipsism and anxiety about her role as wife and mother it is as if she has indeed entered the private totalitarian state that Esther in *The Bell Jar* so feared. The means by which male power is sustained is less consistently addressed, but the focus on married relationships is an emotive and effective representation of how feminists were to articulate the effects and frustrations of patriarchy. Bettina's diary, which spans about six months, becomes for her an 'account book', the purpose she claims the book she buys will be put to when quizzed by one of her two daughters. She feels the term is more appropriate than 'diary' or 'journal', and the reader quickly feels that it is the means by which Bettina can both give an account of the minutiae of her privileged yet mundane existence in order to prove she is not going insane and dramatize the deteriorating relationship between her and her husband, Jonathan, so that he is, in a sense, called to account at the same time.

In common with other fictional diarists, the entries provide the possibility of self-help where psychoanalysis and talking to others has failed. Bettina uses her creative imagination to think of possible alternative spaces beyond the four walls of her spacious but imprisoning apartment. Domestic life is presented here as an exhausting cycle of guilt and boredom where Bettina, freed from absolute drudgery and physical exhaustion by her maid Lottie, spends her time organizing all the accoutrements which will allow Jonathan to feel that his apartment truly reflects his professional and social status – decorating, buying objects and furniture, organizing parties. Her children disappear and reappear around school and social schedules which she juggles with shopping expeditions, while her husband frequently works late or makes business trips. It is clear from the first entry that Bettina is being called to account by her husband, who has noticed a change in her behaviour – particularly since he observes that she no longer takes an interest in the clothes that she wears and she is behind with the chores she used to do so well as to render them invisible. Bettina has her own concerns about descending into insanity and as the diary develops many of her fears seem to stem from her inability to fit into the role of housewife, which seems to require no description. The diary, like the writings of the anonymous heroine of Charlotte Perkins Gilman's *The Yellow Wallpaper*, is hidden from the view of her family – first in her underwear drawer and latterly in a purpose-bought locked security box. The extreme measures employed to keep a mere diary from prying eyes suggest the extent to which Bettina is concerned about her own sanity and paranoid about the possible scrutiny of her husband. Clearly she is not literally imprisoned by her husband, but she senses the same disapproval and connection of creativity with unfemininity which we witness in the anonymous narrator's account of her attempt to stop writing to please her husband in *The Yellow Wallpaper*. While her own efforts at writing must be suppressed, Bettina's bedtime reading is weighty indeed – including Thomas Mann and Proust. Unlike Esther in *The Bell Jar*, who in the process of analysis is praised for hating her mother, Bettina's hatred (caused by years of neglect as a child) is turned into an uncomfortable 'understanding' through psychoanalysis.

As a young unmarried woman, she studies art history and paints and sculpts and has a relatively sexually liberated set of experiences culminating in a liaison with a married sculptor, who ends their affair and leaves her with anorexia, migraines, and eczema. Therapy follows this plunge into mental and physical disorder and her 'cure' is to find an undemanding clerical job and rent a small apartment. Her analyst,

Dr Popkin, requests to see her pictures and dismisses them as 'Foetal shapes! Fecal smears!', exhorting her to 'be what you are', but, for Bettina, 'that took a lot of doing and in terms of time took another year and a half, but I finally learned to accept the fact that I was a bright but quite ordinary young woman, somewhat passive and shy, who was equipped with powerful Feminine Drives – which simply means I badly wanted a husband and children and a Happy Home' (Kaufman 1968: 28; 28; 28–9). The tone of this last quotation suggests that what Bettina learns is to ventriloquize the views of her analyst rather than accept his view of reality. We are reminded of Isadora Wing's own tussles with the psychoanalytical establishment when one of her analysts declares that she must 'ackzept being a vohman' (Jong 1974: 12) but, unlike Bettina, Isadora laughs in the face of the more reductive analyses she receives and retains her aspirations to write, her understanding of being a woman remaining far more complex than his. Bettina remains a frustrated artist and her frustrations find creative outlet in her diary. After marriage and the rapid production of two children Bettina has learned to perform her feminine role with éclat. But as Jonathan becomes more powerful and wealthy he becomes more the 'Forceful Dominant Male' (Kaufman 1968: 188), as Bettina puts it. Not only is he made a partner in the law firm, but he also plays the stock market and becomes a patron of the arts, particularly enjoying funding new plays. Bettina's 'madness' seems to stem from Jonathan's sudden successes and his need to be with the 'new people' - the artists and patrons who accept him because of his money. Not only does the novel set the inner life of Bettina against her daily life as a conduit for her husband's comfort and status and the care of her children, but it also shows powerfully the ways in which women can become depersonalized in both these roles where how they are seen to act on behalf of husband and children is more important than their own motivations. This novel, anticipating the frank language of the later consciousness-raising novels, is open about Bettina's sexual feelings and motivations in her fling with playwright George Prager and, surprisingly, foregrounds the male body as object of desire:

After so many years of Jonathan's long loose body covered

with its furze of pinky-blond hairs, looking at this one was like seeing a man's naked body for the first time. Compact, powerful, flatly muscled, almost hairless and startlingly white, it made me shudder – and not from pure pleasure either, or the memory of what it could do (Kaufman 1968: 162).

George, like other romantic heroes in CR novels, is a bad man and his badness accounts for much of his attractiveness. Bettina seems to be aware of her own delusions as she falls for him, but convinces herself that her insanity has made her the type of woman who would fall for a heel: 'And it would follow that the sex would be fantastic; the violent pleasures to be derived from the sado-masochistic relationship have been adequately documented by experts' (Kaufman 1968: 188). The lure of the bastard and the conflict which arises when the more exciting sex is to be had from the bad man recurs in later CR novels too and is part of the way in which these novels attempt to return a more honest expression to the contradictions of heterosexual love and desire.

Bettina's madness has real physical manifestations – recurring bouts of sweats, vertigo, frustration when she's out being a housewife (for example, doing Jonathan's Christmas shopping, attending boring arty parties) – and only her affair releases her from these, as it allows her to shed this adopted identity. In common with later novels there is a pregnancy scare. Her final scene with George ends in violence as he questions her motives for telling him she may be pregnant and the affair is ended by this brush with reality. The denouement of the novel has Jonathan confessing he's lost practically all his money on the stock market, he's been in analysis, and he's had an affair. She decides not to confess in return, and they reverse roles – he stops accusing her of being insane and looks to his own precarious psyche while she is released by being able to be generous in her understanding and make no fuss about the money or the affair. The ending, characteristically, is open and enigmatic enough to defy some of the questions that the reader naturally wants answered – the finer points are left for the reader to imagine. At the close of the novel, we are simply left with the bizarre imagery of a cockroach stuck in the face of the kitchen clock. Smashing the clock face, Bettina releases the cockroach – 'From there it ran down the clock's side and across the counter to the wall, where it vanished down a hole in the plaster between the tiles – damaged but undaunted – home to wifey and kids' (Kaufman 1968: 286). The domestic imagery used to anthropomorphize this rather unpleasant insect also conditionally returns us to some kind of domestic quietude, but certainly one wherein Bettina has a great deal more agency (since it is she who smashes the clock to release the insect). This circling of the narrative is important, in that it emphasizes that for Bettina at this time there is no point of exit. The emphasis on the mundane is deliberate, reasoned, and essential to our understanding of Bettina's life, where she suffers no material hardship, because the depiction of these women's lives where 'nothing' seems to happen offers the perfect insight into examples of the seemingly invisible and constant re-enactment of male power.

Femininity, it seems, takes some balancing and it is all too easy to lurch into the hectoring shrew; motherhood similarly brings out the schizophrenic in some of our mad housewives. Lois Gould in *Such Good Friends* (1970) describes her own conflicted identity as a mother, as she has her central character Julie say of her son, 'he was the kind of second baby that made you wonder what you'd done right the first time, because it didn't work any more [. . .] When he screamed in his crib at two a.m. I used to go in and pummel him in the dark. Then I'd come back a second time to pick him up, cuddle and rock him with the light on, so he'd only see the good Mommy and never be able to pick me out of the line-up as the other one' (Gould 1972: 71). This description of wilful violence ruptures the passage in which it lies, beginning as an innocent enough description of her children's anxiety at her having to leave them when she goes to her husband's hospital bed. Margaret Reynolds in *Up the Sandbox!* echoes some of these feelings when she describes her daily trip to the park with her children. While studying the baby perched on her lap, she evenly observes, 'I could starve him – or leave him behind me, dropping him on the cement, crying in the park till the police come and assign him some nameless future', adding, 'but he has nothing to fear because despite an angry thought or two, we are connected deeply and permanently' (Roiphe 1970: 12). While feminists in political writings dispassionately delineate the nature of the power relationships at the heart of the family, these fictional characters focus on the emotional and affective ties which have them celebrating the lives of their children while wishing that their routines could be arranged some other way.

The daily chores are tyrannical and mind-numbing in their repetitiveness and yet the mothers' love for their children is both unconditional and nourishing, inspiring strong waves of guilt at feeling hostile or trapped in the first place. Anne Roiphe dramatizes the active life of the mind rebelling against the predictable spaces the housewife occupies, so that in one chapter she will delineate her day down to the most uneventful detail while in every alternate chapter she fantasizes an alternative life for herself. In the first of these she is the only white member of a radical black cell called PROWL who successfully blow up the George Washington Bridge. While her husband Paul writes his doctoral thesis, she imagines herself a politico in Cuba, the lover of Fidel Castro, who turns out to be a woman and tells here, 'At the end of my next five-year plan, I will reveal the secret to the country, and then women will go dancing in the streets, and they will rush to their desks, capable at last of higher mathematics and musical composition, revolutionary leadership and all the things that make manifest true equality between the sexes, and then and only then will the total revolution have been achieved, the revolution of women against their oppressors – men' (Roiphe 1970: 71–2). Other fantasies place her as a doctor in an emergency room; in Vietnam, and finally on an expedition up the Amazon. The last chapter brings us crashing back to reality when she announces that she is pregnant and closes the book wishing for a healthy child.

In Sheila Ballantyne's *Norma Jean the Termite Queen* (1975), Norma lives in the aptly named Pleasant Valley and imagines a life for herself which like a man's remains unfettered by the fact of her fertility, yet her novel ends with the celebration of women's unique powers of reproduction. The novel details the many arguments she has with her husband when he demands that she act more like a wife (she keeps going to the garage and making pots), her analysis of her own discontents, and her hunger for an identity outside the home, which she shares with her friends. Norma has access to feminist texts, which she uses to try to find answers which aren't always welcome: 'I sometimes get to reading things like *Patriarchal Attitudes*, and instead of saying, well, that's interesting but it has nothing to do with me, I discover lots of things that confirm exactly how I feel. It's always disturbing' (Ballantyne 1983: 260).

Alix Kates Shulman's *Memoirs of an Ex-prom Queen*, published two years after *Diary of a Mad Housewife* in 1969, shows how quickly consciousness of feminism was spreading in the US, as the writer's own involvement in radical feminist politics testifies. The novel itself does not focus on organized feminism, but its dedication to the New York radical feminist chapter the Redstockings makes clear Shulman's overt political association of the fiction with the Movement, as well as suggesting that she makes a principled attempt to play down her own individual contribution as an author. As is so often the case with these texts told in the confessional mode, the novel will look backwards as well as forwards, as Sasha Davis the narrator announces, 'I shall begin my story neither at the beginning, moving forward as a reader expects, nor at the end, moving backward as a writer recalls, but rather somewhere in between, where the truth is said to lie' (Shulman 1985: 3). Chapter 1 sees Sasha on the Orient Express from Madrid to Munich about to split up with her first husband Frank, a history academic. She is 'twenty-four and married and old; a has-been like last year's Miss America. Please God, I prayed, let me be beautiful at least until after my money runs out' (Shulman 1985: 6). She has married Frank almost by accident and describes how she drifts easily into the routine of marriage while studying for her PhD: 'I hadn't really wanted to marry at all. I wanted to make something of myself, not just give it away. But I knew if I didn't marry quickly I would be sorry. Only freaks didn't' (Shulman 1985: 163). Again and again it is made clear that, in spite of Helen Gurley Brown's revamping of spinsterhood in the early 1960s, these fictional heroines view the prospect with utter drad.

Something which becomes a feature in later texts is the explicit reflections on sex; but being from a female point of view and more candid than those descriptions found previously in fiction by women, they act themselves as educative components of the texts. They are rarely erotic and are in fact more often about sex which is abortive or unfulfilling. After her defloration by her high school sweetheart Joey, Sasha reflects:

> Watching him move up and down on me in the darkness, I wondered: *is this all there is to it?* I had loved Joey to the melting point, but now I resented him. I received each thrust of his body like a doubt. Really all? When it was over a few moments later and Joey came groaning into his handkerchief as always, it struck me as hardly different from our usual sex. The only thing to recommend it was that it was ultimate. But, really, kissing felt much nicer (Shulman 1985: 67)

She spends much of her adulthood trying to resolve the 'growing gap between mind and matter' (Shulman 1985: 138) that she identifies at college and seeks constant affirmation of her attractiveness, but this doesn't lead to self-confidence and impels her to visit a shrink, diagnosing herself as 'frigid'. Sasha meets her future second husband William Burke on the ship home from Europe to the US and later, pregnant by Will, she leaves Frank. The abortion scene, which becomes almost stereotypically a part of such novels, is harrowing even by the standards of later texts such as Marge Piercy's *Braided Lives*: 'I sat on the toilet and pushed and pushed. Then out it popped, my first baby [. . .] A nightmare. I looked again. It hung there like a corpse [. . .] It was too awful: the first baby I produced in this world I deposited like a piece of shit straight into the toilet' (Shulman 1985: 230). Once married, Sasha goes on to have two children, reflecting, 'Willy expected it, poets encouraged it, it was part of the package' (Shulman 1985: 232). Marriage for Sasha is the death knell on her youth and attractiveness and she beautifully conjures up how femininity and motherhood are fundamentally incompatible: 'In time comes the ugly crease in the brow between the eyes hewn by incessant anxiety and sporadic rage, the rasp in the voice, the knot in the gut, the regret. Fear alters the features, and in time the sweetest child will make a shrew of her' (Shulman 1985: 359–60). The tricks of beauty so reliable in early adulthood would come back to haunt her in her later years as she struggles to recapture youth – and Willy's attentions – by a visit to the beauty parlour. In a passage that anticipates *Bridget Jones's Diary*, Sasha notes:

Suddenly under the dryer I saw that those very remedies
I had come to count on – haircuts, diets, sun, lovers – would
produce in time such terrible symptoms of their own that
more cures, more tricks, more devices would be necessary
to control them. Bleach your hair and it will turn out
coarser; shave your legs and it will grow in thicker; have a
mole removed and two more will pop out. My own once-
radiant skin had begun to show imperfections which to
camouflage would be to aggravate. It would dry out in the
sun, hang loose if I dieted, puff up if I slept; and even if I did
nothing at all, the pores would enlarge, hairs sprout,
dimples crease, pimples scar. The whole process was out of
control. Once the grey got a start in my hair, it could only
spread. And a lover – the ultimate cure – a lover was
absolutely out of the question for the simple reason that
I could not bear for him to see my thirty-year-old thighs
quiver! (Shulman 1985: 265–6)

Having had her hair cut, which symbolically announces the
emergence of a new Sasha, she returns home to find that Willy
doesn't like it and in fact tearfully overreacts; but the change
is prophetic and she leaves the room to ring her friend
Roxanne (the poet who represents her unawakened creative
impulses), signifying the end of this relationship. Willy cannot
bear to spend time with her and their two daughters – 'A high-
chair did not go with candlelight, nor mashed bananas with
white wine [. . .] We bugged him, we bored him to tears, we
were united against him' (Shulman 1985: 273). For Maria
Lauret, *Memoirs* 'is a good example of a novel poised between
sexual revolution and women's liberation, one foot in each
camp – a spreadeagled text' (Lauret 1994: 36); and in a sense
the text importantly foreshadows the most significant of the
consciousness-raising novels I shall discuss in the following
chapter. Feminism could politically and philosophically fence
itself off from what was regarded as the soft sell of the Sexual
Revolution, but day to day many women felt that society had
shifted towards a more permissive attitude to sex, and for the
better, and Sasha attempts to explore such new freedoms after
her first failed marriage. That she fails to enjoy the fruits of this
sexual freedom (and indeed that she is punished by contract-
ing a nasty venereal disease in Europe) suggests that readers

are encouraged to view announcements of a new permissive society as somewhat premature.

Marge Piercy's review of *Memoirs of an Ex-Prom Queen* in the US journal *The Second Wave* in 1972 accords with later views that a key role of these books was in their consciousness-raising potential: 'The book is extremely funny with the same kind of laughter often heard in a C-R session when someone sets out plainly and honestly the horrible thing she has just done to herself: everybody identifies with her sudden aware-ness, and laughs' (Piercy 1972: 46). This is not of course comfortable laughter, but the consolation of recognition that so many of the CR novels provoked, and Piercy particularly admires the use of narrative voice, which encourages the reader to treat Sasha sympathetically and actively prevents the distance that would allow readers to dismiss her as unremittingly foolish. We will return to this question of degrees of distance between reader and narrator when we look at the relationship of the reader to contemporary chick lit and the question of whether we are in a position to view the character as foolish and hapless or whether we approach her choices from the point of view of our own understanding of the obstacles she will have to encounter.

I have already mentioned Shulman's solid feminist creden-tials, which might have given added credibility to this work and encouraged a wider readership. At the time of writing the book she was as a member of Redstockings and WITCH (Women's International Terrorist Conspiracy from Hell) and was involved in the 1968 Miss America protest. As well as for her fiction she became well known within feminist circles for writing 'A Marriage Agreement', which set out a proposal to divide all household tasks between husband and wife, something she tried to do in her own relationship. But her activist pedigree would not prevent her being seen by some of the Movement members as either self-indulgent or openly betraying the collective will of the group. As has already been discussed, the act of writing either feminist analysis or creatively was treated ambiguously by the Women's Liberation Movement. While the Movement had its unofficial stars, it emphasized its leaderlessness and was clearly fearful that a charismatic figure might hijack its public face and offer singu-lar answers where a multiplicity of reponses was encouraged and preferred. In taking at times a tough stand against writing and creativity, feminists missed more opportunities to support those in the Movement with a talent for self-expression and for crystallizing the ideas of their group. This policy of leaderlessness and rotas for media appearances as well as everything else had its cost because:

> the one thing that feminists could peddle were their ideas, and as a consequence, women writers were especially mistrusted. Even dedicated movement veterans like Shulamith Firestone whose book, *The Dialectic of Sex*, was a tremendous contribution to radical feminist theory, were reportedly criticized for trying to 'cash in' on the sudden trendiness of the women's movement. The distrust of writers was so great that Alix Kates Shulman recalls being 'terrified' that she might have to choose between being a writer and being an activist in the movement (Echols 1989: 206).

To write one's own account, whether creative or theoretical, was to risk being seen as trying to assert a leadership role and to court visibility and individual kudos, which might be viewed with hostility and suspicion by the Movement. This is more lamentable because writing and self-expression are so much a part of the strengths of feminism's Second Wave and are themselves part of the educative process. This is reflected in the fiction of this period, where time and again the central character either is or aspires to be a writer or artist. Additionally, the creative expressions of women from previous generations became a very positive part of early feminist scholarship in literary studies. In these novels of the 1960s and 1970s acquisition of education, formally through college and university but often less formally where characters encounter radical ideas which challenge their views of their own lives, is an important recurring trope. Women's looking to literature to find models of behaviour to express their own desires allows an intertextual connectedness with their readers which posits literature as a form of exchange between writer and reader.

The year 1972, when the US feminist magazine *Ms* was first published, also saw the publication of *Ella Price's Journal* by Dorothy Bryant. Barbara Horn in her afterword to the

Feminist Press edition explains why this novel was so important, being,

> One of the earliest, most moving novels about conscious-
> ness-raising, the novel slowly, irrefutably establishes how
> one woman can transform her existence. That Ella (an
> everywoman) is approaching mid-life, comes from the
> working class, is only beginning to develop her skills and
> confidence, and still moves forward, relatively unscathed
> by an unwise affair and an unsympathetic family, makes
> her story truly groundbreaking. And that our heroine's
> survival depends upon something as seemingly mundane
> and universally available as a few courses at the local two-
> year college makes her example as provocative, under-
> stated, and inspiring today as it was in 1972 (Horn in Bryant
> 1997: 234).

This novel takes the form of five notebooks (the same number
as in Lessing's *Golden Notebook*), the reason for their inception
being part of a coursework requirement for Ella's English
courses at college. Ella is a mature married student whose
view of education is a far cry from her teacher's, and she can't
initially see the relevance of writing a journal to improving her
English. She is conscious of her oddity as a mature student
and is uneasy with any aspect of the work which she sees as
morally questionable or as a diversion from the 'real' business
of learning grammar: 'Half the students here are just playing,
and the other half are always marching and carrying signs and
trying to stop the rest of us from learning anything' (Bryant
1997: 22). At the start of the journal, she is constantly asserting
how normal she is and that she has no real problems, but as
she gains the language to understand and articulate the problems that are niggling at her she reinterprets the relationship
she has with her husband Joe. Strikingly, it is clear that Ella is
from a working-class background: talking to a friend who
doesn't go to cultural events because she believes that such
events are directed only at whites, Ella responds, 'It's not race.
I feel the same way. It's as if you have to be born in it, like
being part of a different world, where people talk about books
and go to the ballet when they're young. That's what the division was to me when I was a child: the big line between the

kids who went to the ballet and the ones who didn't' (Bryant 1997: 61–2). Ella's access to ideas at college is seen to directly facilitate the gradual questioning of her own life, her marriage and most particularly her sense of self.

At college, her teacher Dan Harkan gets Ella reading novels by male authors with female heroes, such as *Madame Bovary*, *Anna Karenina*, and *Washington Square*, but when her readings of these novels take on a decidedly feminist turn she has her first disagreement with him:

> These men, the authors, didn't really want the women to succeed. They liked their heroines, but being men they were prejudiced about what a woman ought to be. Soft and weak and all. So they couldn't make their women strong enough to make a go of the rebellion. They couldn't imagine a woman like that. They couldn't go on liking them as women, feminine, you know. So they had to destroy them (Bryant 1997: 79).

Harkan does not share Ella's more radical re-readings of these texts and it is Laura Wilkens, another ex-student of Harkan's, who lends her *The Golden Notebook* and gives her a wider political education. As her journal progresses, it becomes clear that she too has to conceal her writing from her husband. Her short affair with her teacher ends in disillusionment when she realizes that he regularly takes up with his bright students (Laura, her friend, had also been his lover) as one of the perks of his position of power over his female students. He is sexually inexpert and unconcerned about Ella's pleasure and angry at her own naïvety she gives up college, but, like Bettina, determines never to tell her husband of her affair. At the end of notebook four she is pregnant and decides to burn her journals to 'remove the last obstacle between Joe and me' (Bryant 1997: 184), but by the fifth and final notebook she realizes she doesn't want the baby; with one teenage daughter, she is on the verge of liberation from the labours of motherhood and she is torn between seeing the pregnancy as a symbol of her reconciliation with Joe and her acceptance of her feminine destiny and Joe's desire for the return of a proper wife or as a trap in her marriage which denies the workings of the mind and privileges the functions of the female body, both of which seem

irreconcilable to Ella. As she awaits the abortion, she decides
to start classes again, realizing that it is her domestic role, not
the demands of her classes, which is making her depressed.
Her analyst has encouraged her to seek her repressed feminine
self, recalling earlier 'mad women' in fiction who are urged to
give up all forms of creativity to vouchsafe their sanity; but
Ella actually discovers that she is trying to find a self that
authenticates her will to know things, to live in the realm of
ideas. As she confides to her husband earlier on in the novel,
'[j]ust writing in the journal has almost changed my life'
(Bryant 1997: 55), and in giving verbal expression to her own
experiences she gets more adept at sorting the authentic from
the inauthentic: 'I must have fallen into the oldest, stupidest
woman's attitude – seeing myself and my problems and my
needs in terms of men' (Bryant 1997: 208). This develops her
awareness that male authors have written their female characters inaccurately; and her journal might also be interpreted as
a contribution to a tradition of women's writing of self-discov-
ery. There are echoes, for example, of Kate Chopin's *The
Awakening* (1899) when Ella reflects, 'I'd take off my shoes and
stockings and just walk along the water, letting it lap up over
my feet as the waves came in. A lot of people did that; nobody
thought anything of it. I'd walk further and further out, until
the waves splashed my skirt. Then I'd stop. But I wondered
what it would be like just to walk out and keep walking'
(Bryant 1997: 40). So ends Chopin's novel, with Edna walking
further and further out into the water; however, this novel
ends with less finality in that Ella renews her life through
severing the links with her husband and with the termination
of her pregnancy on Christmas Day. The symbolism of having
this event fall on Christmas Day is stark and chilling and the
conclusion does nothing to alleviate this starkness. The last
journal ends on an unfinished sentence, 'I feel' (Bryant 1997:
227), and this novel, like those which succeeded it, presents life
choices as messy, upsetting, and contingent. None of these
kinds of novels will end with a satisfactory resolution and
many will conclude reflectively with an awareness that women
are repeating the mistakes of their mothers and that marriage
becomes a site of conflict the moment the woman attempts
to forge an identity beyond motherhood and domestic servicing.

In *The War Between the Tates* (1974) by Alison Lurie, we have an early campus novel not written in the first person confessional mode which at best exists on the borders of the 'mad housewife' genre. Erica and Brian Tate are the classic academic couple who met at college. Brian is a political scientist and Erica has written and illustrated three children's books about an ostrich called Sanford who, it turns out, is modelled on her ex-college beau Sandy Finkelstein, now called Zed and the hippie owner of a radical bookshop. Focalization shifts across the main characters but is mainly fixed on Erica, who has reached some kind of mid-life crisis, recognizing that her kids are growing into teenagers who bear little relation to the children she bore and who seem to point accusingly at her own childrearing skills. Her relationship with Brian has become rather cold and distant and their best friends, Danielle and Leonard Zimmern, have split up. She discovers a letter from a graduate student which makes it clear that Brian has been having an affair with Wendy, an amoral figure whose alternative hippy lifestyle politics don't allow for guilt or remorse. She becomes pregnant and Erica forces Brian to marry her. The novel is very much an intellectual comedy about ageing and that one's problems are the mundane ones shared by others. Erica wants not to be like Danielle, but in fact her plight becomes the same and she accepts Brian's return for the most pragmatic reasons. Her growing friendship with Wendy is striking in all of this, suggesting that women always have more in common with each other than with husbands and lovers, being 'all in the same field, yet not in competition. Brian must hoard his ideas for publication; but if she passes on a new recipe she earns her friends' gratitude and loses nothing' (Lurie 1994: 211). Her affair with Sandy confirms for her the need for physical as well as emotional involvement – she's not remotely attracted to him and their 'affair' is really her gift of gratitude – which he's unable to live up to. Subsequently Erica flirts with feminism in the form of the local women's group, but she isn't sure, for instance, that she believes in day-care centres and finds the other women loud and aggressive. In common with Bettina and Sasha, Erica has to confront the passage of time and the invisibility of the ageing female form, a form that is displayed nowhere but in the mirrors of these sad and lonely women:

Now, on this cold March night, Erica sits before the mirror she knows best, and the first time in weeks looks close into it, smiling gently, anticipatively. A woman whom she scarcely recognizes looks back at her, first with a blank, then with an injured and startled expression. This person is whey-faced, middle-aged and skinny, with a hollow goose-flesh chest above her ill-fitting, inappropriately girlish dress. Her dark hair has been chopped off too short above a too-long neck, and what remains shows crinkled threads of grey. The stranger's nose is pinched, her mouth tight. Only the eyes – large, grey, thick-lashed – are familiar to Erica, and now they blink and turn in nets of tiny wrinkles, like caught fish (Lurie 1994: 211).

In common with *Diary of a Mad Housewife*, this is a novel of reconciliation which shows an awareness of the perils of patriarchy but doesn't attempt to move beyond it, for the chief characters at least. Wendy, the most rounded feminist character, is not ultimately drawn that sympathetically and the only feminist demonstration is a bogus one orchestrated by Brian in a prank which backfires horribly. The final scene is that of a peace march that Brian has been instrumental in organizing and offers vignettes from both Brian's and Erica's viewpoint about their probable reconciliation: 'They will put their arms about each other and forget for a few moments that they were once exceptionally handsome, intelligent, righteous, and successful young people; they will forget that they are ugly, foolish, guilty, and dying' (Lurie 1994: 314). The peace march represents their reconciliation, the withdrawal of troops from Vietnam and perhaps a wish for the end of the fighting within feminism as it draws to a close with a child's voice asking, 'Mommy, will the war end now?' (Lurie 1994: 314)

The next chapter will look at how the consciousness-raising novel emerged from mad housewife fiction, producing three of the most enduring novels at this time of heady feminist activism, each in its own way becoming a byword for feminism. As I write about these quite disparate novels I'm reminded of Maria Lauret's proposition that 'feminist politics created a new gendered discursive space in which all women's writing would henceforth be written and read, whether it had allegiances to feminism or not' (Lauret 1994: 74), and this is the spirit in which I shall revisit these novels and provide the framework with which I shall scrutinize so-called chick lit. I have discussed books here that, bar one, have no strategic relation to feminism, but all characterize the oppressiveness of the domestic sphere and feature the recognition that femininity is a construct frozen in aspic for the under-twenties and after this stage something to be lamented forever. Husbands are seen as unthinkingly arrogant, draining their wives of all their emotional reserves and expecting this performance of femininity to be re-enacted *ad nauseam*. What the writers discussed in this chapter share is a quest to re-evaluate women's lives and to search for a language to express the differences of women's experiences of marriage, sex, and parenthood specifically. The novels discussed in the following chapter are all concerned more acutely with space – both geographical and physical - and the fact of women's liminality in the spaces – both creative and professional – traditionally regarded as a masculine domain.

# 4

# Women's Spaces: Marilyn French, Erica Jong and Marge Piercy

The developing Women's Movement confirmed that housework was drudgery and politicized the perceived relationship of women with the home. The 'mad housewife' novels also contributed to this changing and radical response to housework and were better suited to chart the ways in which the housewife felt oppressed – especially since the source of their oppression had up to this point seemed invisible, because there was no language in which to describe it. The consciousness-raising novels of the mid-1970s were to show further how women's domestic identity allowed for no creativity or sense of self. Ann Oakley's analysis of domestic labour in *Housewife* (1974) crystallizes these views and demonstrates, ' "Housewife" is a political label after all, a shorthand symbol for the convenience to a male-oriented society of women's continued captivity in a world of domestic affairs – a one-word reference to those myths of woman's place which chart their presence in the home as a natural and universal necessity' (Oakley 1974: 240). Having rejected the naturalness of the association between women and housework once and for all, women writers were concerned with the means by which the authentic female self could be constructed beyond this sphere.

Marilyn French's *The Women's Room* and Erica Jong's *Fear of Flying* are two of the most memorable feminist novels from the 1970s and in many ways define the feminist fiction of the period. It was as if there was a sudden thirst for stories of 'real' women's lives and novels often teased the reader with a closeness between author and narrator, between fiction and historical event. Some writers, struck by the powerful changes wrought on women's lives by the political radicalism of the 1960s and the rebirth of feminism, approached their writings as means to document this memorable period. For example, Sara Davidson's *Loose Change* (1977) combines history, memoir, and the plot construction of fiction to preserve something precious and ephemeral. By the time most of these novels were published, the real crest of feminist activism had passed and local groups were starting to fall apart. Popular as the mad housewife novelists were, *Fear of Flying* and *Women's Room* were the defining bestsellers which women found life-changing. An anonymous reviewer writing in the UK Newsletter *Women's Report* is effusive in praise of the impact and scope of *The Women's Room*:

> It says so much, so very much more readably than any other writing, fiction or non-fiction, which has come from the women's movement. It can be tiring to be asked to explain one's 'consciousness'. Ms French has relieved me of the necessity, and given me a basis from which to start discussion (*Women's Report* 1979: 11).

The novel was successful because, as this reviewer implies, it seemed to contain every possible dimension of a woman's existence from courtship to young married life and children, through college, politicization, and the inevitable confrontation with the dynamics of male power. The novel shows Mira's gradual coming to feminist consciousness, largely through her contact with other women and her entry into higher education. The process is shown as long and torturous and at one point the narrator herself apologizes for the mundanity of her narrative, but claims, 'it's all true, it happened and it was boring and painful and full of despair' (French 1986: 147). It is, looking back, an unremittingly gloomy book, as if French is determined to emphasize that women still have a long way to go and that the way is treacherous. French articulates her own view of patriarchy in her later critique *The War Against Women* (1992), asking, 'what other system can depend on almost half the population to enforce a policy daily, publicly and privately, with utter reliability?' (French 1992: 184) *The Women's Room* details numerous acts of literal violence and oppression by men and anatomizes the ways men unquestioningly assume dominance in family life. Mira's husband Norm – aptly named as the unprepossessing everyman of patriarchy – understands marriage as the means to facilitate his professional life and personal comfort, yet his relationship to the house is as that of a visitor, distant from its mysterious workings. In suburbia, Mira is part of an accidental community of other women, equally isolated in their homes, whose lives become so inter-connected as to force a close intimacy – 'they spent most of their free time in each other's kitchens and yards. They sat over coffee, hot or iced, and a home-baked, packaged coffee cake, watching the children' (French 1986: 74). This sharing of their lives and intimate experiences, however, remains benign and 'no one ever suggested that the situation could be changed; no one ever challenged the men's right to demand and control' (French 1986: 77). Once Norm leaves Mira the changes are swift: in common with Ella Price, along with her college education comes politicization.

Structurally the whole novel is framed by Mira's story, even though it is narrated in the third person. At the beginning she is to be found hiding in the ladies' lavatory – symbolically suggesting that women have yet to find their own space in the world and that the spaces they currently occupy are resolutely gendered – and by the end it is revealed that this disembodied narrator who seems to be able to shift focus in the minds of other characters is in fact Mira herself. The ending fails to promise a changed self or the onset of an exciting new set of life choices despite all the lessons Mira has learned. It is clear that Mira regards her life, despite the important odyssey of education and feminist politicization, as a series of failures and tragedies, the most notable of the latter being the death of her friend and role model Val, who is shot at the hands of the FBI. The issue of women's relationship to men, and how it might be improved to accommodate changes in the life of women, is unresolved, and Mira's lover Ben is eventually rejected because he expects her to take on his life plans and start another family. The sex and companionship have been almost perfect, but motherhood signals inevitable subordina-tion for Mira. But does Mira hate men? The Mira-narrator is chillingly frank – '[m]y feelings about men are the result of my experience. Like a Jew just released from Dachau, I watch the handsome young Nazi solider fall writhing to the ground with a bullet in his stomach and I look briefly and walk on' (French 1986: 209). At the point of these narratorial interventions, when the action proper stops, the narrating voice comes across as preachy and uncompromising, conforming to every stereotype of the angry radical feminist. Yet the tone is at other times one of unremitting sadness, as if Mira truly laments her inability to forge change in the relationships between men and women and believes that changes will not be witnessed by her generation. The passage quoted above is controversial of course, because of its association of gender conflict with the Nazi's treatment of the Jews, but maybe the sentiment is also incomprehensible to a subsequent generation of readers, because the moment when anger was directed at individual men as direct representatives of patriarchy has passed. In many ways there is now a movement to a more inclusive view of gender construction which sees men as potential victims too.

Many critics have noted *The Women's Room*'s total lack of irony as well as the impression that 'the atmosphere of the novel is unrelievedly gloomy, a catalog of oppression of women by men' (Payant 1993: 37). It is certainly the case that all the women are presented as victims at one time or another, and the men as primarily brutal and self-seeking. For some the book does not make a clear distinction between polemical tract and literary work and this makes it less rewarding, especially if the reader feels that their own behaviour is implicitly under scrutiny. As Nicci Gerrard points out, '[t]here is a missionary zeal to *The Women's Room*, a kind of nannyish hectoring [. . .] The "truth" of *The Women's Room* was its recognition that something was very wrong with the majority of women's lives; its success lay in its potboiler form' (Gerrard 1989: 138). This tension between a book's politics and the attempt by its author to write as accessibly and engagingly as possible is one shared by Jong, Alther, Piercy, and many others, but French is markedly less successful in achieving the right mix of entertainment and education, perhaps because of the uncompromising message she felt she had to convey. The problem with many early responses to these texts was the generally casual dismissal of the 'popular' as not being worthy of closer scrutiny. Therefore the possibility that there might be any radical potential in writing genre to communicate politics is never really considered, so strong is the assumption that commercially viable fiction is incapable of carrying within it weightier themes. This is disappointing, given the commitment to make feminism as accessible as possible in the political domain.

While *The Women's Room* may arguably be 'the first and last international bestseller of the women's movement' ((O'Faolain 2003) if Jong is disqualified because of her more distant relation to feminism), it is not the novel new readers today would either find most pleasurable or most instructive. As Nuala O'Faolain remarks, '*The Women's Room* was conceived of as food for the starving, even if the cooking was crude and the food was bitter herbs. Its first readers [. . .] might as well face it; they just aren't hungry that way anymore' (O'Faolain 2003). Continuing Rosalind Coward's argument, discussed in the previous chapter, the question is not only whether a 'feminist text' has the correct political credentials, but whether a text which fits the criteria actually can work to influence the reader at the same time as maintaining the momentum of plot and incident. We can usefully set this book against the more commercially savvy *Fear of Flying*, published three years earlier, as a point of comparison. Most people would agree that *The Women's Room* is not itself an accomplished work of fiction, even though it is fondly treasured by its original readers and those who remember its significance in the wider communication of the feminist message. It bears too much the imprint of its age and does not seem to have endured, so that it can even seem anachronistic whereas Jong's first novel still has a vivacity and passion understood by contemporary readers. Jong is really primarily concerned with how women can write their lives and elevate quite individual concerns and themes to the stuff of literature; her argument is as much with the literary canon as it is with the broader social effects of patriarchy.

Erica Jong has been regarded as a celebrity author, with all the negative connotations that the term still has, with at best a tenuous relation to feminist politics. What she had over French, perhaps, was that her engagement with feminism was at a level consonant with many of her readers – intellectually engaged, but politically distant. She is a witty and self-consciously literary writer who focuses more single-mindedly on the experiences of her central character Isadora Wing, while offering intertextual links to other fictional characters and writers. This upbeat confessional narrative, which has at its heart a scathing account of the ideology of femininity and the imprint it leaves on her heroine as she grows up, is often seen primarily as a celebration of heterosexual freedom at the beginning of the Sexual Revolution. Jong's work was reviewed both favourably (by John Updike and Henry Miller) and unfavourably (by Paul Theroux) by men, but whether the response was positive or negative, the fact that the book was reviewed by men at all led feminists to view it with instant suspicion. John Updike was highly complimentary about this first novel, characterizing it as, 'a notably luxuriant and glowing bloom in the sometimes thistly garden of "raised" feminine consciousness' (Updike 1976: 411), going on to place Jong's work in the tradition of confessional writing best represented by J. D. Salinger and Philip Roth. He notes with approval the ways in which she appraises the male body as a thing of desire, indicating his hope that such a reversal of representation would 'hold out some hope of renewed negotiations' (Updike 1976: 412) between the sexes. Maria Lauret concurs that one of the key impressions when reading Jong and others like her was that they 'were among the first to "write back", to represent men in their fiction the same way that women were being treated in American literature: on their backs, with their sexual equipment exposed for the world to see, all hairless balls and missionary delusions, not to mention the shit marks on the sheets' (Lauret 1994: 29). Rather than inviting comparisons with the mad housewife novels, Jong was more regularly compared with her male contemporaries and especially with other Jewish writers. Particular links have been made between *Fear of Flying* and Philip Roth's *Portnoy's Complaint* (1969), not least because they both 'feel powerfully autobiographical and sincere, and if sincere, therefore authentic'[1] and possess powerfully frank sexual content. Among the numerous intertextual references, it is not really surprising that Jong has Isadora cite Portnoy, when she cries, ironically, 'if only I had a *real* Jewish mother' (Jong 1974: 138).

By far the most controversial aspect of this novel was its

alleged sexual explicitness. It doesn't actually dwell on sex scenes or draw them out in great detail, but it is uncompromisingly frank about female sexual feelings and masturbation, and consciously posits its heroine as sexually aggressive. Jong's own view was that while the novel is about sex, a lot of the sex is failed sex. This is particularly true of Isadora's affair with the Laingian psychoanalyst ironically named Adrian Goodlove, who is rendered impotent by her active desire, the clear inference being that he is emasculated by strong autonomous women. The controversy about the sexual nature of the novel and Jong's own view that it's about failed sex means it is worth pausing to reflect on this most remembered (and misremembered) aspect of the novel. It is Jong herself who confirms in her essay 'Writing a First Novel' that 'the sexual *acts* in the book are nearly all abortive or unfulfilling, and that was what I intended. It was *meant* to be a saga of unfulfilment, and it was *meant* to challenge the notion that intellectual women must be heads without bodies' (Jong 1974: 267). Helena Eriksson observes that in women's novels of the 1970s, 'representations of marriage often involve an explicit positing of sexuality as central to the marriage relation; dissatisfaction with marital sex becomes a staple element in women's novels' (Eriksson 1997: 47), and this is certainly a thread which runs through Jong's work. This is not surprising, given the sheer bulk of discourse about sex circulating during the 1970s, including manuals such as Alex Comfort's *The Joy of Sex* (1972) which asserted that sex should be mutually satisfying, to the point where women began to feel the pressure to perform orgasmically and couples strove for the holy grail of the simultaneous orgasm. Jong's work certainly engaged with this discourse and we're never completely sure whether Isadora is as aggressively sexual as she presents herself or whether she is a child of her time, obeying the call to express the self through sex. Her dissatisfaction with marital sex is misplaced, since Bennet can at least satisfy her; what is actually missing is the trappings of romance and the lack of fit between her soupy longings and the actuality of her marriage. Jong, more than any of her fellow writers of the time, recognizes the importance of romance as a genre through which female sexual desire has been mediated; her novel is in some senses an anti-romance, a feminist literary intervention into the genre which anticipates later critical re-evaluations of the link between romance and women's social experience of relationships.

There has been more nonsense talked about the zipless fuck in particular than anything else in the novel. Ever since Jong coined the phrase, this episode has been distorted beyond recognition to suggest that Jong was putting forward some kind of feminist utopian sexual moment. Yet this fantasy of uncomplicated coupling on a train where no names are exchanged becomes a nightmare tinged with sexual threat when Isadora finds herself alone in a railway carriage with a man who takes the fact of her being unaccompanied as a sexual invitation – ' "You are *seule*?" he asked again, flattening his palm on my belly and pushing me down toward the seat. Suddenly his hand was between my legs and he was trying to hold me down forcibly' (Jong 1974: 272). This scenario of the zipless fuck, the perfect anonymous sexual congress with no follow-up or complications, remains a fantasy in the novel – even though some read Isadora's relationship with Adrian, rather contradictorily, as conforming to this fantasy. The zipless fuck is more accurately a means by which the fundamental differences between the genders can be underlined and it can be established that it is their material experiences of the social world which determine their appropriate access to sexual pleasure. A woman alone on a train is unlikely to experience the pleasures of such a covert encounter; rather, as Isadora discovers, she is likely to be bothered by unwanted male attention and possibly abused or attacked. Throughout the novel, Jong is trying to work through ideas about the compatibility of feminism with heterosexual desire – 'the big problem was how to make your feminism jibe with your unappeasable hunger for male bodies' (Jong 1974: 88) – and she problematizes this by deliberately having Isadora fall in love with a bastard, just as other key fictional characters in women's literature had done before her. There is no resolution offered, where feminism might find new strategies to focus on heterosexual desire, setting aside questions of abuse, reproduction, and power. As I have said elsewhere, although Jong announces the impossibility of getting one's heterosexual desire to gel with one's politics, the issue 'is never critically addressed, and Isadora's failure to achieve this speaks volumes' (Whelehan 2004: 28). Feminist politics became increasingly silent on the topic, leaving women to negotiate privately the best solutions they could.

In other ways, Jong goes beyond the brief of many of her contemporary writers, who, while writing acutely about marriage and its accompanying problems, say little about what it means to be single. Jong confronts this problem and offers a clear explanation about why so many women of that generation rushed into marriage:

> It is heresy in America to embrace any way of life except as half of a couple. Solitude is un-American. It may be condoned in a man – especially if he is a 'glamorous bachelor' who dates starlets during a brief interval between marriages. But a woman is always presumed to be alone as a result of abandonment, not choice. And she is treated that way: as a pariah. There is simply no dignified way for a woman to live alone (Jong 1974: 18).

Here she notes that it is social censure and the fear of scrutiny by one's family, rather than just the prospect of material hardships, which prevent a heterosexual woman carving out a life alone. This principle underpins the rest of the novel, so that we better understand the obstacles confronting Isadora in her attempt to realize her independent self as well as recognizing and sympathizing with her failures. This includes the rather warped messages she gets from her mother, who regards herself as a failed artist because she could not combine motherhood and a career and although part of her wants Isadora to succeed as a writer, she also encourages her to become a mother. Here Jong shows us how ambivalent parental socialization can be, especially on the part of the mother who may want her daughter to leap out of the mould the mother has become trapped in, but also understands the pressures and the temptations to fall in with universal expectations about feminine destiny, because '[y]ou could never escape your femaleness. You had conflict written in your very blood' (Jong 1974: 148).

Here we have the portrait of the artist as a young woman, and as a young woman Isadora assumes she has to write as a man because 'nobody would be interested in a woman's point of view' (Jong 1974: 113). Yet in describing her own rite of passage she gains maturity enough to accept that she is a 'woman writer' and that in her own time this is a political challenge to the literary mainstream. As I wrote elsewhere, the 'confessional voice which predominates threatens to confirm some long-held assumptions that women can only write their lives; yet this voice is also the perfect consciousness raiser which unseats the very critical assumptions it invites' (Whelehan 2004: 26); additionally, the voice demonstrates that the women's lives are an essential part of the feminist political process. The material of her own adventures provides Isadora with the material for her first bestselling novel, which is an unashamed celebration of the woman's point of view.

In 1977 Jong was interviewed by Rozsika Parker and Eleanor Stephens for *Spare Rib*, who attempted to tease out what they saw as tensions in *Fear of Flying* and its sequel by suggesting that while Jong rails against marital fidelity she also seems to celebrate the return to monogamy in the choice of Josh at the close of *How to Save your Own Life* (1977). She retorts by saying, 'You know it's so dangerous when we read novels as polemics' (Parker and Stephens 1977: 17), and one is left wondering whether Jong is being disingenuous here or actually denying the presence of a critique underpinning the themes of the novel. She rejects the idea that such novels, because they are feminist, can simply be read as literal political tracts, reminding us that Isadora is portrayed quite deliberately as conflicted and constantly failing to live up to her own feminist ideals while at the same time holding feminist precepts up for the scrutiny of the reader. It is possible that Jong is overwhelmed by the critical response to her first novel and simply refuses to be embraced by the Women's Movement, because, as the tenor of the first questions of this interview suggests, she will be tried and found wanting. Of the hotly criticized lesbian scene in her sequel she says, 'I was really doing a send up of that whole period in the Women's Movement in the United States when everyone said, "If you don't try it once whether you like it or not, you're not a good feminist." I think that's absurd and an insult to people who are inclined to be gay, or seriously gay' (Parker and Stephens 1977: 17). She seeks to explain her own fragmentation from the Movement by asserting,

I never got a lot of nourishment from the movement. I've always been a person who loved other women and had women as friends, but the first time I ever came intellectually to blows with another woman was after the movement began. There was such incredible pressure. And there was this awful feeling that if you wanted to do your own work, if you said, "I'm sorry, I can't come to the benefit/poetry reading, because I'm writing a novel," you were selfish, not contributing enough, too interested in your own career. You had to be out there stuffing envelopes, you had to be doing this and doing that, and what you were best at – writing was the thing that got lost, there was no time for that. I made a very conscious decision that I had more to give by writing novels (Parker and Stephens 1977: 17).

It appears as if Jong, in common with Jo Freeman and Susan Brownmiller, regards herself as a casualty of the Movement's striving for purity of principles, where creative writing is framed as potentially divisive and self-indulgent. Interestingly, later in the issue of *Spare Rib* which includes this interview is a clear acknowledgement that feminists are not good at keeping track of their recent history and an acceptance that 'one of our main weaknesses as an organised Movement is that we do not record our activities as they are happening or the effects we experience/observe later' (*Spare Rib* 1977: 33). Feminists were also slow to recognize or perhaps acknowledge the wider impact of their activities on women's social experiences or to record these as part of the Movement's recent history. The success of these bestselling novels with such close ties to the Women's Movement was something of a cultural event, which could effectively have been utilized to celebrate feminism's continuing dynamism and its widening appeal to huge numbers of women.

The feminist critical responses at the time of publication of *Fear of Flying* seemed promising, however. Elaine Showalter speaks more presciently about the potential impact of such novels when she comments, '[b]est sellers are a very potent political force in any era. A novel like Erica Jong's *Fear of Flying* is tremendously important to contemporary feminism because it reaches an enormous audience that *Spare Rib* and *Ms* and *Daughters Inc.* are never going to reach', adding later, 'feminists have a responsibility to writers more than writers do to feminists' (Parker and Sebestyen 1979: 29). This interestingly suggests that feminist critics have neglected a duty to support such writers and instead hold them up to trial in order to examine the purity of their intentions; of course, most critics would not acknowledge the importance of such a 'duty' and the examination for authenticity of feminist motive underpins much subsequent criticism. Negative responses predominate later, such as that of Lorna Sage who sees nothing of value in such works, claiming that they 'tried for a special kind of transgression, and became instead (or as well) a voyeuristic spectacle, a liberation striptease' (Sage 1992: 114). For Gayle Greene, *Fear of Flying* is particularly significant as 'a vehicle for the dissemination of feminist ideas and for the controversy it sparked, and it deserves attention as a cultural document' (Greene 1991: 87); but this rather arid statement again leaves a question mark over the precise nature of the attention they deserve. There seems to be a marked reluctance to engage with the novel as a work of fiction, registering that its success lay in the pleasure of recognition it gave to readers about their own complex relation to feminism and to their sense of their selves, rather than as some kind of dispassionate historical document, important for capturing the spirit of its age.

For many of these writers communicating feminist views to the popular audience, the power of their work lay in their emphasis on women at the same time as problematizing how (and if) women writers communicate to men. As Jong remarks, 'if we women approach women as our subject, we are not only shocking male (and many female) reviewers, but we are also stealing the favourite subject of male writers – which is: *woman*. No wonder they hate us' (Jong 1974: 267). The humour of Jong's book has perhaps been most widely misunderstood, rejected, or ignored as a fruitful or serious narrative strategy and, as I shall show in chapter 5, this recourse to humour can be seen to inhibit the scope of the work, especially if it is seen to be incompatible with gritty realism. For Charlotte Templin, who evaluates the negative reception Jong received, '[m]ost dismissals of Jong have rested on her thoroughgoing and assertive heterosexuality. Jong has been charged with repeating the same "old story" of female fulfilment through relations (sexual and otherwise, but especially sexual) with men' (Templin 1995: 179). There was very little acknowledgement of the way Jong rewrites the romance or how she has Isadora accept that fulfilment, sexual or otherwise, is not going to be obtained simply through men. Although Lisa Hogeland notes that Jong offers a 'revisioning of the romance plot that marks the failure of everything romance is supposed to provide for women' (Hogeland 1998: 71), as Maroula Joannou observed, 'much of the feminist distrust of *Fear of Flying* can be attributed to the fact that the novel appears too male-identified, too "pro-sex", and too heterosexual even for white, middle-class heterosexual feminists' (Joannou 2000: 113). It offers, as Joannou suggests here, a pro-sex antidote to the classic romance narrative, but at a time when positive feminist representations of heterosexual sex were thin on the ground.

The novel is punctuated with images of freedom and autonomy throughout, not least the metaphor of flight (from America and from her marriage) and Isadora's ongoing battle with analysis. Her quest for her true self is rendered absurd by Adrian's pretence at therapy, when he takes her on a seemingly existential tour of Europe but in actual fact has a planned rendezvous with his lover and children for a rather bourgeois family vacation in Brittany, leaving Isadora '[u]tterly free. It was the most terrifying sensation I'd ever known in my life' (Jong 1974: 245). The novel exploits its own fictional status and invites the reader to make connections between narrator and author as Isadora observes, 'I had written myself into this hackneyed plot' (Jong 1974: 161). The links between the names Isadora Wing and Erica Jong alert the reader to the possibilities of playful autobiography, but the voice of Isadora becomes simultaneously the voice of 'everywoman'; and the psychoanalytical sub-plot facilitates commentary on the means by which we re-evaluate childhood and determine the route to becoming a woman as mediated by powerfully gendered assumptions. Isadora's identity in all its complexity – Jewish, white, married, heterosexual, writer, feminist – is exploited in order to make feminism work at the level of the quotidian. There is a recognition that male power functions by stealth and won't be overturned overnight, and that meanwhile one continues to live the daily mundanities of contemporary existence. For Rita Felski there is nothing revolutionary about this

text and therefore it does not fit her category of feminist literature because Erica Jong's novels 'do not seem to me to reveal
any serious questioning of the existing basis of male–female
relations or any sustained refusal of the values of a male-
dominated society' (Felski 1989: 14–15), suggesting that Felski
also requires a much 'purer' offering to satisfy her own definition of what constitutes a feminist text. Feminists have histor-
ically asked a great deal of fictional female characters,
demanding that they be role models rather than accepting that
texts can question male–female relationships while failing to
find answers.

What surprises many about this novel are the number and
variety of literary references – to the eighteenth-century
picaresque tradition (with Isadora herself as something of a
picaresque heroine) as well as to writers such as Tolstoy, Joyce,
Lawrence, Roth, Woolf, Plath, Lessing. These references
become organic to the novel because they represent the way
Isadora situates her own identity as a writer, charting her
influences and the process by which she shifts to embracing
the title of *woman* writer. It is not just a novel that very much
exploits the political and social context in which it was written; it is also centrally about writing and finding a voice. There
is a coherent plot concealed beneath a meandering trail of
events, reminding us of the arbitrariness of memory and the
significance of context to allow us to make sense of the world.
The relationship between fiction and fact is continually played
with, coming to a head in the sequel *How to Save Your Own Life*,
which portrays Isadora's coming to terms with the runaway
success of her first novel. All is ordered chaos in *Fear of Flying*
as Isadora searches for a convincing plot to write amid the
debris of her own past and present; when she reads her notebook in the hotel in Paris she says, 'I began to be drawn into it
as into a novel' (Jong 1974: 260). What she learns in the course
of the novel is how women are brought up to believe in very
crucial fictions about femininity and the costs of refusing to
accept to be a 'woman' as defined by analysts, literary greats,
and husbands.

The ending frustrates many as Jong leaves us in a freeze
frame with Isadora taking a bath as Bennet returns to his
London hotel room. Most readers assume that Isadora will try
again with Bennet, but we are left to imagine the terms on

which this might be negotiated. This denies any romantic ending, but also forestalls any fuller explanation of what independence would mean for a woman. Isadora's return to Bennet suggests a need for her to evaluate what marriage can now mean, quite separated from romance. The interpretation of Isadora's decision as a retrograde step depends on what the reader regards as the way forward for relations between men and women. One thing this ending powerfully signals is that the emotional baggage Isadora carries and the meanings she attaches to this relationship cannot easily be dispensed with, in spite of her recognition that women's autonomy is inevitably compromised in marriage. In a way (despite the fact that there is a sequel) the novel has several points of resolution which deny the primacy of the ending, from the episode where Adrian taunts Isadora as he leaves her for his partner by saying, 'I wanted to give you something to write about' (Jong 1974: 244), to where Isadora, journeying alone, sees her zipless fantasy dwindle into something rather more distasteful.

If this is seen in part as a book about the woman artist, we see that Isadora comes away triumphant, having found a voice and accepting that writing about everyday life and the self is a viable form of expression. Crucially, from a consciousness-raising perspective, Isadora asserts, 'I stopped blaming myself' (Jong 1974: 260), an almost identical declaration to that made by the unnamed narrator of Margaret Atwood's *Surfacing* (1972). The heroine's refusal to accept victimhood at the hands of dominant men is seen to be a powerful step forward for many readers, despite the ambiguities of the ending. Erica Jong isn't in the business of writing utopian fiction – it's enough that Isadora had grasped her life afresh from another angle. Her consciousness has been raised and her life story is that of Everywoman and, worse, the source of her empowerment is at the hands of the man who duped her into the romantic soft sell. As Adrian leaves her, he says, 'doesn't this make the perfect ending to your story?' (Jong 1974: 244), but Isadora does not allow him to figure the ending; neither does feminism come to be seen as providing all the answers. Jong's exploration of the position of a woman who wants both a relationship and the space to pursue her own aspirations possesses the fullest political resonance. Certainly millions of readers (over 12 and a half million copies have been sold worldwide[2]) found this novel enriching. It might be argued that the open ending is the only recourse for the woman writer committed to realism, in that resolution would only be perceived in the healing of a relationship between a man and a woman or the movement to a utopian space of female self-realization – something much in evidence in early feminist science fiction, naturally enough.

Many detractors felt that the book was exploitative in a number of ways. For example, Elizabeth Cowie et al. assert,

> Jong's *Fear of Flying* illustrates all that is worst in the 'new' literature, where the woman speaker, deliberately collapsed into the 'real' writer, is represented as an author with writer's block, seeking both sexual gratification and release into prose [...] Neither writing nor sexual pleasure as valorised activities are queried in relation to social and political meanings. Both are complacently offered as individual satisfactions, and silently substituted for a feminist politics (Cowie et al. 1981: 242–3).

Time and again feminists drew a clear line between individual experience and politics, without seeming to realize how confusing this was for those on the periphery of feminism who were attracted by the idea that 'the personal is political' and who assumed that maybe their politicization began at home. Even though these critics go on to assert that the politics of a piece of art can only be worked through in the reading and interpretation of it, they seem curiously quick to damn writings such as these, seemingly for all the qualities regarded as their strengths by readers – the teasing connectedness of writer and reader, the explicit descriptions of sexual anxiety – and they overlook Isadora's own questioning of the relation of sex to politics. Popular fiction consistently baffles 'serious' critics and, unlike their approach to more literary fictions, there is a tendency to produce depressingly literal readings of the novels, which don't allow for nuances and the playful ambiguities of metaphorical language. Feminists were especially hard on contemporary texts that boasted their feminist credentials and expected them to live up to much higher ideals than those by women from earlier periods. In addition, the motives of such writers were constantly under scrutiny for political bad faith and clearly all too often a bestselling text could be adroitly dismissed as evidence of the author's materialistic and exploitative relationship to feminist politics. Gayle Greene offers a much more nuanced reading of *Fear of Flying* but laments, echoing the sentiments of many readers, that the old patriarchal realities are ultimately reinstated in the novel's closure. While Isadora admits to thinking in romantic clichés when she falls for Adrian Goodlove, Greene feels that rather than offering a knowing critique of the power of gender socialisation, Jong rather happily resorts to this cliché as an avoidance of real critical intervention. I think that actually Jong is reinforcing how deeply embedded such longings are: as she says, 'even if you were *clever*, even if you spent your adolescence reading John Donne and Shaw [. . .] you *still* had a mind full of all the soupy longings that every high-school girl was awash in' (Jong 1974: 17), and many readers agreed with her.

For Lauret, such fiction is 'marred by an undertow of defeat belying [its] surface exuberance' (Lauret 1994: 29), and it is true that the humour of the narrative can obscure the more bleak messages within, just as is the case with contemporary chick lit today in 2005. Of course, these novels were never self-consciously produced by a group of writers with common interests or any contact or reference to each other's work, just as feminism of the Second Wave can never be neatly summed up as one dynamic movement. The writers mentioned in this and the previous chapter are also gripped by the possibilities of the so-called Sexual Revolution – the perception that social mores were rapidly changing and increasing openness about human sexuality might itself (along with the availability of the Pill) change women's lives. Feminists generally saw this vision of a Sexual Revolution as a chimera where women were being sold the idea of sex as liberation but often it cast them in just as strong a thrall to men, with new pressures to perform sexually at every occasion.

*Fear of Flying* dramatizes in part the conflation between the Sexual Revolution and women's liberation, where the Sexual Revolution announced a sea change in social attitudes but beckoned in a new libertarianism which didn't necessarily change women's sexual identity or their power relationships with men. On the one hand, Jong's sexual frankness, her creation of a heroine who is always hungry for sex and fuelled by fantasies of freedom in the 'zipless fuck', fits in with the ideal type woman of the Sexual Revolution who loses her inhibitions the better to service men; but you only have to scratch at the surface of this image to see how Jong makes Isadora constantly frustrated and disempowers her in the sexual encounters she has. Her quest for sex is more often a quest for affirmation of her self, something she has only been socialized to seek through other people's responses to her. She discovers that her own feminism and self-belief render Adrian Goodlove impotent – something she takes to be an almost militant refusal to accept a changing set of sexual relations on his part. His inability to achieve erection becomes itself a slap in the face of female autonomy: women have for years faked sexual ecstasy only now to be spurned by the reality of male mechanical failure. The burden of the argument is that men are turned off by female autonomy, that women's liberation is an anaphrodisiac. Here we see the germs of Jong's feminist critique of the Sexual Revolution and her acknowledgement that sexual freedom does not necessarily free women from other forms of oppression; moreover, Isadora is a complex feminist, aware of the rhetoric of feminism, but determined to seek her own individual solutions as well as finding real difficulties incorporating feminist solutions to daily problems to do with family, relationships, and romantic love. Adrian's existential advocacy of free love only works if the women he courts occupy a more traditional feminine role.

As Rosalind Coward avers, in the 1950s and 1960s men as well as women were writing more frankly about sex, and in confessional mode, with notable male writers including Philip Roth, Kingsley Amis, and Henry Miller. For Coward, 'women-centred novels represent a fictionalized version of our culture's contemporary obsession with autobiography and with intimate relations' (Coward 1984: 182). It is as if, for her, these novels represent nothing but a pandering to the nation's voyeurism and follow a fairly predictable formula, where certain stock female experiences are described and it is suggested that the woman comes to feel through evaluating these experiences that she 'has become her own person', with this impression reinforced through the form of fictional autobiography used. I would argue that while it is true that whole personhood is very much what these central characters are seeking, and while it is also the case that many of them are creative as writers or artists themselves and seem directly to be writing their own stories, it is important to note how far from being their own person these women still feel. Often they feel fragmented, trapped, or simply liberated from past torments and are reluctantly ready to live in the present (as in *Kinflicks*, discussed in chapter 5). We may feel that Jong has cheated us and has not allowed Isadora to fulfil her quest for sexual autonomy, but what has in fact occurred is that Isadora discovers that her search for sexual adventure is a displacement of a search for self: sex becomes a way of affirming a man's affections, yet losing one's quest for identity in the love of another. The sexual behaviour of the men in this novel shows just how tight a grip men still have on definitions of sexual expression and women still remain, critically, objects of exchange. This theme continues through to the third Isadora novel, *Parachutes and Kisses* (1984), where an increasingly lonely and isolated Isadora seeks affirmation through a mixed batch of sexual encounters. Now she has a young daughter, sex takes on more profound emotional resonances. Sure enough the element of sexual confession recedes, and Isadora has yet to reconcile all the fragments of her self, as writer, lover, wife, mother, daughter, sister, and Jew, suggesting that women experience their selves through fragments and in relation to powerful social institutions represented by partners and parents.

Coward acknowledges, 'the autobiographical voice of these contemporary women-centred novels often appeals to a collectivity. I am, but I am a representative of all women. The history of my oppression is the history of all women's oppression' (Coward 1984: 185). What she dislikes about such novels is the way she feels they define women through sexual identity, which, while a means to explore the construction of female identity, is also a way to repetitiously depict the heroine as victimized and grimly enduring patriarchy. Perhaps Coward's view itself is overly pessimistic or perhaps these grim portrayals suited the sentiments of the times – and maybe they can more usefully be read against formulaic romance-writing such as Mills & Boon or Harlequin, which suggested that relationships were the site of women's power.

Moreover, writers such as Jong refuse the ending which needs a man to wrap it up: Bennet's entry on this last line suggests that women's destinies are all too clearly governed by the shade of their men, but here Jong fuses acknowledgement of the too clear realities of women's lives, set against the utopian space being opened by mainstream feminism where women could think beyond the box within which patriarchy had confined them. For Jong, 'I write about women who are torn, as most of us are torn, between the past and the future, between our mother's frustrations and the extravagant hopes we have for our daughters. I do not *know* what a writer would write about if all her characters were superwomen, cleansed of conflict' (Jong 1999: 43).

Just after publication, when *Fear of Flying* had sold in excess of 3 million copies in its first year, Jong was positively fêted by feminist academics, interviewed by Elaine Showalter in 1974 and asked about the future of feminist writing, and lecturing to women at colleges all over the US, yet latterly 'Jong's work is now largely ignored by the feminist establishment' (Templin 1995: 64). It seems, according to Templin's research, that there was a backlash against her writing soon after she published her sequel and that much of the spleen vented against her was precisely because of her feminist political viewpoint, which makes feminist rejections of her work all the more ironic. She concludes that Erica Jong's reputation has been marred in the media, by academics and particularly by feminist academics because of her media celebrity and the fact that her books are considered popular more than literary – also because she herself embraced attention: 'An author can be forgiven, even admired, for having the media swoop down on her and thrust her into the spotlight, but can she be forgiven for staying there?' (Templin 1995: 180) The fact that the media, literary men, and feminists all picked her up at the same time only to drop her soon after meant that a fair evaluation of her work was long in coming.

Marge Piercy's connection to the Women's Liberation Movement was more straightforward since her essay 'The Grand Coolie Damn', setting out the ways Movement men excluded women from political activism, was collected in one of the earlier Second Wave anthologies (Morgan 1970: 473–492). Several of her novels feature feminist political activism as a central feature of the work and *Braided Lives* (1982) is representative in this respect. The novel features Jill Stuart at its centre – another artist, but this time a poet trying to explore the specificity of a woman's voice in poetry, yet frequently accused of naïvely spewing her emotions on paper. Jill is dismissed by both her teacher and her boyfriend as using naked emotions on the page as an excuse for poetry and her boyfriend Mike, a poet himself, remarks, 'you're a woman first. And most of what you write is just *merde*' (Piercy 1982: 169). Her own challenge to over-intellectualizing tendencies in male poetry criticism was one shared by the Women's Movement's approach to theories of women's oppression, which initially were kept accessible and polemical and inevitably mistaken for naïve and simplistic rants. Jill is another narrator–artist, facing deep prejudice about what it is legitimate to write about, let alone whether women are intrinsically incapable of writing great literature; yet although her boyfriend perceives her poems to be 'formless', she finds she can use experience effectually to create her own artistic expressions:

> I was taught to see poems as complicated intellectual constructions full of carefully layered ambiguities, ironies and ironically treated myths, alluding in a complex web to other similar works. But you can write about fucking, you can write about supermarkets, you can write about your mother, you can write about the Bomb. You can write your politics. You can actually write poems that say what you feel and think (Piercy 1982: 403).

Jill's triumph lies in having the commitment to follow her own voice and find her politics through it; what she cannot control, like Jong in the real world of literary reviews, is the way in which critical reviews are written on the actual body of the author that produces them as much as they are about the work itself. Piercy sends this up wonderfully in *Braided Lives*, offering a parody of biologistic assertions of women's writing with her description of a male reviewer's response to Jill's poetry: Piercy's mock review by 'Sydney Craw' in the '*Bloodstone Review*' asserts, 'Her poetry is uterine and devoid of thrust. Her volume is wet, menstruates and carries a purse in which it can't find anything' (Piercy 1982: 404). This clearly reminds us of Paul Theroux's likening of Isadora to a giant pudenda in an early review of *Fear of Flying* (Theroux 1974: 554).

The book opens in a nominal present of the late 1970s/early 1980s, but we never return to this point in narrative terms – instead, there are italicized passages that interrupt the narrative occasionally to give a sense of the self Jill will become and offer an understanding of how events shape her life. Josh, her current partner and the question of her happiness or otherwise, remains a hazy image. The narrative 'proper' begins when she is sixteen in March 1953 and, as with Plath's *The Bell Jar*, the Rosenbergs are mentioned to set the political temperature of America at the time. Her best friend is Howie, whom she much later becomes involved with; because of the use of flashbacks and foreshadowings, we also learn pretty early that he is going to die young, and later we find out that this is tied into his Civil Rights activities in the South. Jill is characterized early on as sexually unformed and has a number of casual 'seductions' with girls of the same age. When she goes to university and shares a room with her cousin Donna (another girl she seduced when younger), Donna infers that she may be a lesbian and Jill, defending herself, asserts, 'The truth is I don't feel particularly feminine as defined by Mother and the girls in the dorm. I don't feel male either. I must be something else altogether, like a giraffe maybe' (Piercy 1982: 48). Her first boyfriend, the poet so critical of her 'formless' poetry, is depicted as increasingly controlling and almost violent. She loses her virginity to him, and is shocked to find out that the details of their sex life are shared out among his friends, just as his friend Lennie brags about her cousin Donna to Mike.

Jill's relationship to her mother is striking not least because at first her mother seems simply cruel, aggressive, and manipulative of her, especially when she pretends to have had a private detective follow her and Mike to get her to admit they've been sleeping together, information she uses in order to attempt to force them to marry. Like Isadora, Jill has the worst confrontations with her mother but also the fiercest love, observing, 'I do not know a girl who does not say, I don't want to live like my mother, I don't want to be like my mother. Is it our mothers, ourselves or our men who mold us?' (Piercy

1982: 163) When she becomes pregnant it is her mother who helps her perform an abortion. While this episode had by the time of this book's publication become almost a prerequisite of such writing, another narrative intervention in the form of an italicized interlude suggests that already the complexion of feminism in the 1980s has changed again and the debates about abortion are becoming a taboo subject:

> *If it were a couple of years ago I would tell you more, but if I do so now, desperate young girls, desperate middle aged women, the victims of rape, incest, battering, far more numerous than we like to believe, all the women who simply do not believe in catching a baby as you might the flu of pneumonia, would be tempted to do as I did, just because I survived it but barely. There have to be better ways, I cannot include a recipe for action that is likely to kill you* (Piercy 1982: 179).

After this and the end of her relationship, Jill gets her diaphragm, so often the badge of liberation for the women in novels since *The Group*, and also witnesses the beginnings of her involvement in campus politics. Donna, now working successfully in television, will come to Jill after a botched abortion and bleed to death in her apartment. This crystallizes Jill's politics and she will use Donna's name as a code for women ringing up and wanting to get access to a safe abortion (this is taken from an actual feminist strategy outlined by Brownmiller in her memoir *In Our Time*). The ending, with its discussion of the cat and its nine lives, is as jarring as that of *Diary of a Mad Housewife*: 'Freedom is a daily necessity like water, and we love most loyally and longest those who allow us at least occasionally to vanish and wander the curious night. To them we always return from the eight deaths before the last' (Piercy 1982: 445). The emphasis is that Jill is luckier than some of her compatriots, having survived abortion, rape and exploitative relationships; but more than this it underlines that the majority of women are directly affected by these major issues as they are the penalty for entering into heterosexual relationships.

For Lauret, Piercy's work 'read[s] like the proceedings of a feminist debating club: people "talk politics" a lot of the time, a narrative technique which is reminiscent of the old-fashioned novel of ideas' (Lauret 1989: 99). Piercy's novel is established with the backdrop of active feminism and it is clear that for Piercy both the political and the literary are essential to social change. The melancholy aspects of the work encourage the reader to think of the consequences if feminism once again disappears. Fiction and memoir remain close at this time (Sara Davidson's *Loose Change* and Kate Millett's *Flying* of 1974 are cases in point) and Piercy's work on one level seems to be part of the effort to keep the memory of feminism's recent history alive. A reviewer appraising another of Piercy's novels, *Small Changes* (1973), raises what for many is so distinctive about this kind of literature – 'Piercy's basic assumption – and it is a revolutionary one in literature – is that the every-day lives of women – our problems, our work, our sexuality, our growth – are of central importance not only to us but to the world' (Palmer 1973: 45). This review reminds us again that these books instantly throw us back on our experiences and emphasize shared values, and that this very simple strategy of making fiction appear to evoke the harshest realities is what causes such mixed reactions from critics.

Whereas some of the rhetoric of radical feminism is hard to swallow, if women felt they were being exhorted to accept one constricting view of patriarchy and if they denied it or questioned it they might be seen to be collaborators, fiction seductively presents fallibility and women exposed to the contradictory pulls of everyday life. While feminist discourse had trouble giving positive expression to love, sexual attraction, and maternal feelings, because these emotions were regarded as tied up in the mystifications of patriarchal ideology, the CR novels portrayed them in all their ambiguity. There may be no space for the classic romance ending, but love is portrayed multifariously, as attached to contingency, need for security, money, eagerness to please parents, and sometimes as wrenchingly irrational and ephemeral. The point is that these characters' feelings dominate their lives and they are constantly battling against life choices based on custom or others' expectations or their own cowardice, most often resisting marriage, as does Jill Stuart in *Braided Lives*, or retreating from it, as do Sasha and Isadora.

British writer Sara Maitland comments, 'one of the things a feminist could do in fiction which is difficult in other forms of writing is introduce some of the real contradictions without being heretical. Somehow you can say that women are not always very sisterly, that women – including feminists – are often confused about what they want and how they want to do things. I felt a kind of freedom in writing fiction, a freedom to say it's not that simple' (Radford 1978: 16). Michèle Roberts pursues this theme and adds, 'I think the practice of writing is in one way like consciousness-raising, the practice of women talking together in groups. Because in writing you claim for yourself what many women still can't do – take time for yourself, experience pleasure and strength in thinking about yourself. I feel that's something we're still struggling to do as women' (Radford 1978: 16). These views crystallize my own thinking about the strength of the CR novels, which is that they offered freedoms to the feminist writer beyond the necessary compromises of shared feminist politics and that they spoke to an unexpressed need among readers to understand feminism as a process in which their own lives were tied up and, as such, was the sum of thousands of life stories offering women the opportunity to put their own concerns first.

In this chapter I've looked in detail at some more of the critical responses to the CR novels – specifically to those, such as Jong, who proved to be huge commercial successes. They're frustrating to feminist critics because they aren't afraid to vaunt independence and quirkiness and their heroines take Second Wave feminism on their own terms. Readers do not have to be feminist or have any specialized understanding of feminist politics to be drawn into these novels. It is impossible, however, not to come away with a clear sense of critique of the patriarchal order and the limits romance, courtship, and sex place on young women's lives. So even though these novels don't in general politically propagandize, they ultimately demonstrate a long-running tension between feminism's history as a movement and feminism's pull as a politicizing of individual self-realization and change. What is powerful is that not only do they focus on the trials of becoming a woman but they also examine the ways in which that becoming is achieved in the style of the *Bildungsroman*. These reflections on teenage life are often the crux of the novel where the heroine, looking back, identifies the extent of the social pressures applied to her to force her to conform to constricting ideas of femininity. Novels such as Lessing's *The Golden Notebook* 'opens and closes with the now-familiar scene of two women in a kitchen talking about their particularly female concerns' (Gerrard 1989: 146), and women talking to each other is very much a feature of a number of the novels, showing how important women are to each other as support but also looking at the ways in which patriarchy makes them hostile. What should be emphasized is the sheer 'mainstreamness' of these novels and their appeal to a wide range of readers. Zoë Fairbairns, whose dystopic novel *Benefits* (1979) was written on the back of the fierce wages for housework debate, remarks, '[a] novel that set out to "prove" the rightness or wrongness of a general principle would be pretty boring' (Fairbairns 1981: 256–7), and the success of these novels lay in the ways in which they maintain interest through a strong plot and the possibility for readers to choose their own pathway through the feminist dilemmas presented without losing the integrity of these issues. Apart from the (often acrimonious) conferences and networks, the literature of feminism – both fiction and non-fiction – was the glue that held the movement together: 'It would not be an exaggeration to say that Women's Liberation as a leaderless amalgam of dispersed groups and practices was held together not by organisation, but by an infrastructure of magazines, touring speakers, broadsheets, films and exhibitions and – last but not least – creative writing' (Lauret 1994: 72). When we look back at these books we are often disappointed by the homogeneity of their heroines (pretty much all of them middle-class and white and heterosexual), but these books did hold on to the belief that there was a power in portraying the everywoman who had to be imagined to be at the centre of feminism. These themes were not going to survive the ruptures of identity politics on both sides of the Atlantic and of course their vision of everywoman was always to be compromised by their own narrowness of view, but to regard them as interconnected with the business of the Women's Movement is to remember their shared history and to give space for further examination into how these books led women to organized feminism, or at least to a broader feminist consciousness.

# 5

# Forbidden Fruit: Sexuality

I have already noted that the consciousness-raising novels were often seen derogatively as owing more to ideas generated by the Sexual Revolution than the feminist movement, and when it came to the massive success of writers like Erica Jong it was assumed that the titillating content of her work drew in the mass readership, rather than any new insights she may have had on feminism and contemporary relationships. Novels such as *Fear of Flying* were launched more noisily than the mad housewife novels at the turn of the decade; whatever Jong's feminist or writerly credentials, *Fear of Flying* was also being aggressively marketed for its 'sex appeal'. Lisa Alther's *Kinflicks* was similarly marketed as a sexually explicit exploration of female desire and, given the huge success of *Fear of Flying*, it was inevitable that Alther's novel would be branded similarly and that the publishers would be attempting the twin aim of marketing the novel both as a 'woman's book' (a category feminism had made most lucrative for mainstream publishing) and one which could be read by both sexes as a thrilling take on the new sexual freedoms available to young people.

Just as chick lit today has its trademark covers, so then these feminist novels were marketed in bold colours with eye-catching typography. *Fear of Flying* had a photograph of the author inside the cover and this served to enforce the link between author and character, showing a very attractive and confident young Erica Jong in an open and even seductive pose. In the case of the UK edition of Lisa Alther's *Kinflicks*, the front cover has a painted illustration of a voluptuously contoured cheerleader leaping in the air, her face open-mouthed, directed at the viewer. Although the author photos were presumably done with Jong's blessing, it is claimed that Alther very much disapproved of the Penguin cover of her novel.[1] Either way, these novelists would find themselves at the mercy of the marketing strategies of their publishers and the reception of their work would be profoundly influenced by its packaging. Having verified that 'feminist' subjects could sell, publishers presumably expected authors to acquiesce to strategies which further 'sexed up' their work.

I am going to spend time looking at the way sex and desire are depicted in CR novels, making specific reference to Alther's *Kinflicks* and *Original Sins* (1981) and Rita Mae Brown's *Rubyfruit Jungle* (1973). These novels problematize sex in some ways, but they also both question the origins of desire and sexual motivation further, as their central characters go against the grain even of the sexually liberated 1970s America, and seek other kinds of experiences which expose the nature of power relations in sex, ultimately implying that the idea of sex as central to the self is painfully misguided. This seeking authenticity through the abandonment of sexual desire is exposed as all part of the psychoanalytical sell, which Jong had already dissected in *Fear of Flying*. None of these characters experience their sex as in itself liberating or insightful; and despite Isadora's most heartfelt fantasies, sex is never decoupled from the messiness of life. What these novels tell us most of all is that individual integrity comes from acceptance of change and awareness of how others' perceptions govern the dominant perspective of the self as vulnerable and fragile. All the novels speak to the tendency to look for signs in our past to understand our present; but in all cases this proves to be an inexact science. Both Alther and Brown reflect on where the authentic self emerges from: Molly Bolt, the heroine of *Rubyfruit Jungle*, doesn't know her real mother and relies on her stepmother Carrie's account of her, only having the vaguest notion of her father; Ginny Babcock has a landed pedigree as daughter of Major Babcock, but her post-adolescent years are characterized by rebellion and political motivation. While her mother lies dying, Ginny has time to reflect on her family background, whereas Molly realizes that nature has little to do with the way she turns out, since while she is told she physically resembles her natural father she also emulates the desires of her stepfather Carl.

Molly Bolt learns that she is a bastard near the beginning of *Rubyfruit Jungle*, after being punished for making money by showing a friend's penis to other schoolchildren. Her stepmother Carrie uses this shock tactic spitefully to disassociate Molly's immoral behaviour from her own mothering skills, but Molly replies, 'I don't care. It makes no difference where I come from. I'm here, ain't I?' (Brown 1977: 7) This comment sums up Molly's philosophy, which focuses on the fact of her *being*, rather than an ability to be defined by labels or categories which attempt to explain her existence or anatomize her behaviour. Molly's friendship with her cousin Leroy allows Brown to examine the arbitrariness of gender construction, and it is the teenaged Leroy who first observes to Molly that he thinks she is 'queer', while at the same time speaking of his own gender confusion: 'I dunno. I like you the way you are, but then I get confused. If you're doing what you please, out there riding around on motorcycles, then what am I supposed to do? I mean how do I know how to act if you act the same way?' (Brown 1977: 63) The novel demonstrates that new sexual and other freedoms don't help people come to terms with gender confusion where ascriptions of femininity or masculinity lag behind the liberatory potential of sexual expression, and Brown presents heterosexuality as an institution in much the same way as Adrienne Rich does in her essay 'Compulsory Heterosexuality and Lesbian Existence' (Rich 1986). Leroy's first passion is for another man, something he confides to Molly who urges him to pursue what gives him pleasure on the grounds that, 'why would people get so upset about something that feels so good?' (Brown 1977: 70), rather than be concerned about what such desires make him. Later Leroy retreats to solid married heterosexuality, presented as a domestic trap from which he dreams of being released. Molly, like several of her school friends, lurches through teenage identity crises and has intimate passionate liaisons with a couple of them; but the first lesson she has to learn is that people will betray her for the sake of holding on to their fragile grasp of normality. It's not so much heterosexuality that Molly resents, although she claims to find men dull, and her intimate liaisons with them are always described as absurd and laughable, but rather it's the pressure to be monogamous and deny the fecklessness of her own passions which she rebels against.

Molly's take on lesbianism is unusual for the period in which the book was written and would gel just as easily with the development of queer theory and politics in the 1990s. She says to one of her teenage school friends early on, 'why does everyone have to put you in a box and nail the lid on it? I don't know what I am – polymorphous and perverse' (Brown 1977: 107), at the same time casually referring to Freud's ostensibly liberal assertion that everyone is born bisexual. She continues seeing both women and men when she starts at college – though the boyfriends she has seem strictly for form's sake – and having seduced her room-mate, Molly is expelled from college for moral turpitude. Faye her lover is rich and protected from the consequences of her dalliance by parents who cart her off to be 'rehabilitated'; while for Molly, estranged from her stepmother with no income, this expulsion means the end of her scholarship and is the last straw from Carrie's point of view. Molly decides to go to New York, because 'there are so many queers in New York that one more wouldn't rock the boat' (Brown 1977: 136), and there she is helped off the streets by a young gay man who earns his living precariously as a rent boy. She works to earn enough money to study film at university and encounters a number of people with multifarious sexual peccadilloes: the man who pays $100 to have grapefruits thrown at him; her lover who is a 'kept woman' to a famous actress; an archaeologist whom she meets at the publisher where she works and eventually seduces, only to find that she can only make love to her favourite fantasy of being a man in a urinal being seduced by another man. Molly, who feels no need to assume a gendered identity in her love-making, swiftly moves on to the archaeologist's sixteen-year-old daughter. Despite Joannou's view that '[w]hat lesbianism predominantly signifies for Molly in *Rubyfruit Jungle* is good sex' (Joannou 2000: 114), the message also seems to be that sexually everyone is unique and carries their own baggage around with them, giving the lie to the idea of 'normal' sex, whether straight or gay.

In her final reunion with Carrie, Molly learns the identity of her natural father and Carrie uses his difference – he was French and bookish – to explain Molly's character, not just in terms of her sexuality, but also her beauty and her precocious cleverness. In a perfect framing of the narrative which starts out with Carrie's using biology to condemn Molly, the fact that Carrie can find a positive aspect to Molly's birthright underlines their reconciliation and the fact that each of the character's lives are more sharply affected by nurture than biological inheritance. Thus Molly's escape from poverty is all the more surprising, not least because of her lesbianism. Molly's final year project will be her filming of Carrie delivering a long unstructured monologue while sitting in her rocking chair. It is a clear signal that Molly can move on, her understanding of Carrie's motivations being much clearer once she has heard her life story. In common with the other CR novels, there is no happy ending and Molly will continue to be up against the social inequalities brought about by poverty, gender, and sexual orientation. Despite coming out top in her year she is the only graduate who can't find work in the industry; yet she remains determined to pursue her dream to make films, just as earlier she pursued her bookish wisecracking even when it alienated her peers. What Molly never suffers from is self-doubt, and where other confessional novels aim to some extent for recognition through empathy Molly declares her difference and seems to be proud of her uniqueness, which is positioned as something to do with her lesbianism, but her sexuality is in fact only part of it. Molly, more than everything else, is an advocate for people doing what feels good for them, despite what others think, a philosophy she shares with her adoptive father Carl, who advises her to 'do it all you want but be quiet about it' (Brown 1977: 92). For Patricia Duncker, 'Carrie's story of unhappiness and betrayal has its counterpart in Molly's history. Women have more in common with each other than they do with any man' (Duncker 1992: 182), yet Molly is aggressively following the lead set by Carl, even though she later comes to understand that Carrie's marriage to Carl is another kind of trap, since she finds he is sterile, due to syphilis, after their marriage. There's almost a kind of arrogance about Molly's self-belief which is reminiscent of the character Jeanette in Jeanette Winterson's *Oranges are not the Only Fruit* (1985), a narrative device which has us aligning our personal beliefs with the narrator's and seeing casual homophobic prejudice thrown into sharp relief. Rather than offering us the voice of everywoman and allowing us to forgive ourselves a little for our flaws, *Rubyfruit Jungle* offers belief in self-certainty and the rightness of taking risks. Molly is moral too in her own way, refusing to sell herself to gain advancement and insisting on love, though never finding it in any pure form.

This novel gained its bestselling status through word of mouth and for readers its impact was powerful because of its refreshing and shocking approach to sexual self-determination. Dorothy Allison says 'I picked up *Rubyfruit Jungle* from a friend in 1973 and felt the world shift around me. Rita Mae Brown wasn't just a lesbian novelist, and her book wasn't just a reassuring romance. Molly Bolt was a completely new way to imagine myself' (Allison 1995: 199). As a coming-out novel this is a far cry from Jane Rule's *Desert of the Heart* (1964), the previous most significant lesbian novel, which is very evocative but fundamentally sexually coy when compared to Brown's work. Evelyn, a middle-aged academic, meets Ann in Reno, while she is staying at Ann's stepmother's house waiting for her divorce to come through. Their passion is described by innuendo and in the strange backdrop of the Nevada desert where people come to gamble, marry, and divorce. The motif which accompanies the couple throughout the novel is the fact of their close physical resemblance which has people mistaking them for mother and daughter, also reflecting the difference in age between the two. The powerful backdrop of the desert underscores the fact that their love can only thrive in a vacuum, since the people who pass through Reno are mainly in transition, moving from married to divorced and then destined to return to their 'real' lives. The developing relationship is described with strong maternal imagery and suggests, consciously or not, that their love is more nourishing than either Evelyn's failed relationship with her husband or Ann's long-standing liaison with her close friend Silver, who is shortly to be married. The name, Evelyn Hall, has striking echoes of another lesbian foresister, Radclyffe Hall, with the first name being equally androgynous. Brown's work, in contrast, signals a period of more confident lesbian writing and the assertion of identity and sexual autonomy which chimes with the work of straight women writers who are also negotiating a path for women's freedom via sexual expression.

Lisa Alther's *Kinflicks* divides into first- and third-person narrative to correspond with the story of how Ginny Babcock came to be by her mother's deathbed, separated from the flash-backs on her own past narrated in the first person. The third-person narrative sections also allow for the mother's perspective on her own life and that of her daughter's – both a far cry from the bright and lively 'kinflicks', the home movies her mother made of her children when they were young and which echo the way Ginny rewinds the stories of her adolescence and adulthood up to the point that she arrives at the hospital to visit her dying mother. The third-person narratives are dated entries and cover just under a month; they anchor the thrust of the narrative in a condensed time frame from which we understand the first-person sections to be the act of remembering while Ginny waits for her mother to die. The book caused consternation for some feminists because it was seen as sending up aspects of the Women's Liberation Movement, especially in the nature of the way one of the female characters meets their death and another is horribly disfigured. As is characteristic of these novels in general, the humour can often clash with the very real tragedies which are narrated and Maria Lauret, for one, feels that novels such as *Kinflicks* and *Rubyfruit Jungle* try to present a kind of self-mocking humour that is often at odds with the narratives of pain recounted within the main body of the texts. The humour, for Lauret, represents, 'the wisecracking wit of the insecure loudmouth who talks too much for fear of exposing herself' (Lauret 1994: 34). She is right to note the disturbing violence within these books and the inability of the heroines to take it seriously, yet the humour in many ways helps to underline the absurdity of the choices the women have to make in a male-dominated world. Rosalind Coward confirms Lauret's view and observes. '*Kinflicks* embodies a real tension in trying to make serious points about women's experience in a form which is basically "playing for laughs" [. . .] The central protagonist is shown making sense of the world as a child makes sense of the world' (Coward 1984: 181). This strategy of having the central protagonist look at the world askance does of course allow the reader to review their own complacent assumptions with a colder eye, although writers such as Coward would still contend, with reason, that the narrative of books like *Kinflicks* is structured by sexual confession and the risk is that women are then perceived as confined and defined by their sexual history.

In common with *Rubyfruit Jungle*, preconceived notions of sexual identity are challenged through Ginny's relationships over the course of the novel – firstly her teenage liaisons with Joe Bob and Clem Cloyd and then her lesbian relationship with Eddie at college and their subsequent life together with a small group of other women on Stark's Bog Farm. Of this latter relationship, Ginny remarks, 'I had to keep reminding myself that I was now officially a "lesbian". I felt that, although I now wore wheat jeans and turtlenecks and sandals and a braid like Eddie's basically *I* hadn't changed' (Alther 1977: 302). From the outset Ginny rails against the supposed fixity of lesbian or straight identity, leading to one conclusion that Ginny's lesbianism is never authentic or fully embraced; but this dismissal of Eddie's part in the novel would be to underestimate the importance of their love affair to Ginny's life. This relationship marks a number of shifts for Ginny, not simply her sexual orientation, but also her growing politicization and her realization of her previous privileges as a little rich girl, daughter of Major Babcock, owner of an armaments factory. She shares Eddie's involvement with anti-Vietnam and Civil Rights protests and they move to Stark's Bog Farm, which turns into a woman-only commune when some of the women become tired of men expecting domestic as well as sexual servicing. Nonetheless, roles still seem to remain divided among the women and Ginny takes on a traditionally feminine one, where she 'stayed in the cabin and cleaned. I also spun and dyed wool, and used it to crochet rainbow curtains for our bare windows. I felt like Snow White, the others of course being the dwarfs' (Alther 1977: 331). The division of labour between Ginny and Eddie takes on increasingly traditionally gendered connotations as Ginny stays at home and Eddie works in the field, becoming more and more suspicious of Ginny's sexual motivations and suspecting her of wanting to sleep with the local men. Eddie previously has taken the 'male' role in acting as Ginny's political educator, instructing her on what to do with her income derived from the Major's armaments business and, like a domineering husband, taking away from her any ability to make decisions on her own. Alternatively, Eddie's assertiveness in both their personal and political lives could also be seen to mimic the early power struggles within Women's Liberation, with the more vocal politicos taking over and suppressing the more conflicted viewpoints of their less assertive sisters.

The commune decides to hold a women's festival and the chaos that ensues surely is intended to resemble the chaotic and multitudinous beginnings of the Women's Movement. The tone is at its most humorous here and for many there is the sense that feminist activism of the time is merely being sent up:

> Laverne's group, 'Women and Their Bodies,' in Eddie's and my first-floor bedroom, was in a fascinated cluster around Laverne herself. She sat in a chair, her knees drawn up to her shoulders like chicken wings. With the aid of a complex arrangement of an inserted plastic speculum, mirrors, and a flashlight, Laverne was demonstrating to the intrigued gathering how it was possible, if one possessed the flexibility of an Olympic gymnast, to view the inside of one's vagina and the mouth of one's cervix. I stood transfixed, gazing at the moist red hole. But for the life of me, I couldn't grasp why anyone would *want* to view the mouth of her cervix as reflected in a mirror (Alther 1977: 354).

There is a suggestion throughout this section of the book that Women's Liberation became diverted into practices only distantly related to the aim of freeing women from male oppression, and that it lost its way. This can clearly be interpreted as demonstrating Alther's own conservative responses to Second Wave feminism; but it seems more likely (as we shall see in the later discussion of *Original Sins*) that she is sceptical of dogma and the means by which even the most radical organizations can be taken over by those who seek to dominate for their own purposes. The peace of the commune ends horrifically after the women are troubled by the male locals riding their snowmobiles on a pond nearby. Eddie becomes consumed with jealousy, convinced that Ginny really wants to be with one of the local landowners, Ira Bliss, and stretches a length of wire between two trees in order to ruin the young men's games on the lake. Instead she is decapitated as she drives off on Ira's snowmobile in a rage after finding him and Ginny in what she thinks is a compromising position – 'just before Eddie reached the pond, Ira's Sno Cat appeared to hesitate slightly. The next instant, Eddie's head flew off her shoulders and bounced and spun across the ice like a crazed basketball' (Alther 1977: 380). Just before this episode, the perpetually horny Laverne is electrocuted by her mains-connected vibrator and has to go home to have skin grafts on her thighs, only later to admit herself to a convent. The house itself blows up in a freak gas-leak left unattended as the women misinterpret the warning smell as the mystical odour of death, and this catalogue of absurd calamities sees the utopian intentions of the commune literally go up in smoke.

Unlike the heroines of other CR novels, having been politicized, Ginny then falls into a traditional marriage in a reversal of the normal narrative trajectory. For a while it appears as if she openly embraces her domestic slavery – '[i]n short, my married life was harsh and tediously predictable. I loved it. I adored knowing exactly what I would be doing for the entire upcoming month' (Alther 1977: 420). Her sex life with Ira reads like something from a 1970s sex manual as they try all sorts of positions and tricks to bring Ginny to orgasm, culminating in another absurd scene where they are literally left dangling, handcuffed to a wooden roof beam until they are rescued by Ginny's hippie friends still living at the farm – 'Mona came over and gazed up through her purple-tinted goggle lenses and said blowsily, "Like far out, Gin"' (Alther 1977: 435), as Ginny makes formal introductions to her new husband. It is clear that Ginny will tire of domestic incarceration and that it has just been a reaction to the 'tyranny of structurelessness' she experienced at the commune, yet it is also the case that Ginny is portrayed as acted upon rather than an actor. Even when she returns to stay at her childhood home while her mother is in hospital and tends to the nest of upturned young swifts she finds abandoned, they die one by one, the final swift's death heralding that of her mother. The death of the mother is characterized as a weaning process and Ginny, cast adrift, finds that she doesn't want to return to Ira, not even for the sake of her daughter. Her attempts to kill herself, first by drowning and then by shooting, end in anti-climactic absurdity:

> Her leg hung out of the boat and was being wrenched out of its pelvic socket by the heavy stone. The entire right side

of her body was badly bruised by the fall. As she lay there becoming slightly seasick, she considered the unappetizing nature of what she was about to do. Either the rope would rot and she'd float to the surface for some poor trespassing fisherman to find, or she'd decay among the seaweed and be nibbled to bits by scavenging bluegills. She'd befoul the water, which supplied the cabin sinks (Alther 1977: 566).

So Ginny, a failed suicide, yet ever-practical, embarks on one of those now familiar journeys that mark the end of such novels, having 'wrapped her mother's clock in her faded Sisterhood is Powerful T-shirt' (Alther 1977: 569), suggesting perhaps that, though faded, her feminism prevails.

Alther's *Original Sins* (1981), published five years after *Kinflicks*, is a multi-narrational novel charting the lives of five youngsters – two white brothers, two white sisters, and one black boy (the grandson of the girls' domestic help). Alther focuses on class, as well as looking at racial divisions in the US, Civil Rights politics, and the differing perceptions on racial segregation in North and South. The novel begins with the five as children and their blissful lack of awareness of class and racial divides or how these divides come to frame their life choices and politics. In the case of the two pairs of siblings, Alther depicts their personalities as totally polarized and in doing so seems to create a natural pairing off between them, so Jed and Sally effortlessly achieve popularity and sporting/cheerleading excellence while Raymond and Emily are on the social margins, the gawky teenagers lacking finesse and resenting the 'in-crowd' as a result. Donny, the young black boy, must attend an all-black secondary school and can't understand why his mother leaves him with his grandmother and moves up to New York (he is kept ignorant of the fact that she is raped and harassed by her employer, attacks him in self-defence, and leaves town for her own safety and livelihood). The North/South divide is explored by showing how Emily and Raymond are both ridiculed on their arrival at college in New York because of their accents, small-town mentality, and their attitude to blacks. Both become involved in student politics and the Civil Rights movements, but are made uncomfortable by the heavy-handed and patronizing treatment by rich northern students to southern blacks when they go down south. The situation as they see it is more complex than allowed for by the militants, who don't understand the black families' fear of the nature of the support they are being offered.

Meanwhile, Jed gets Sally pregnant and they forego college ambitions to stay put and start a family. Both are frustrated by this and Sally feels (but cannot articulate) a sense of entrapment in the happy housewife ideal, which makes her seem more like a character from an earlier 'mad housewife' novel. When she finds a way to escape the mundanity of her housework through her handicrafts, meeting with other housewives to discover new techniques and eventually through producing a book and presenting a television series, her success predictably threatens Jed. His politics have turned in the opposite direction to those of Raymond and Emily and he has become part of a group of white vigilantes who are policing the movements and activities of blacks seen to 'invade' white domains – so that at one point he confronts Donny himself.

Emily's college friend Lou further confuses her notions of the meanings of racial identity and politics because she doesn't conform to the idea of black militancy subscribed to by the Civil Rights movement. Lou refuses to play to the role of the downtrodden poor black waiting to be politicized by student radicals and they get their revenge by dubbing her an 'Oreo', ('black outside but white inside' (Alther 1981: 256)). She tells Emily about her middle-class girlhood in a poor white neighbourhood:

> I always thought I was just about the hottest thing on two legs. We were rich, and all my playmates were poor. They were dirty. I was sparkling clean. I could do an arabesque, and they couldn't. Huh. It was the shock of my life one day when I was playing house with these trashy white kids and they made me be the maid. *The maid?* Hell, my mama had a maid, and none of theirs did. I wasn't about to be no maid (Alther 1981: 240).

Meanwhile, switching back to Sally's narrative, the book begins to read more like a Mad Housewife novel – 'As she picked up Jed's dirty clothes, she wondered if she could ask him to put them in the bathroom hamper himself. Or should a

wife be in charge of her husband's dirty clothes?' (Alther 1981:
379) This is followed closely by quite a typical 'mirror' scene,
reminiscent of that found in *Memoirs of an Ex-Prom Queen*,
where the heroine evaluates her own body for signs of ageing:

> After she dried and oiled herself, she plucked her eyebrows,
> then examined the roots of her hair. She used cleansing
> cream on her face, reapplied her makeup, and rolled her
> hair. She sprayed herself with cologne and deodorant. She
> douched. She took her eyebrow pencil and put it against her
> ribs, underneath her right breast. When she removed
> her hand, the pencil stayed in place, instead of falling to the
> floor as it always had. She felt the pencil with horror. She
> had failed the *Glamour* magazine two-piece bathing suit
> test' (Alther 1981: 380).

At the same time that Sally is having her own identity crisis at
home, Emily is coming out of Civil Rights to set up a group
with other women – 'For the next several months they
discussed what the format should be, given that they all
loathed the hierarchical pattern bequeathed them by the patriarchy' (Alther 1981: 401). This is set against the increasing jealousy of her husband Justin, who characterizes their gatherings
as counter-revolutionary, 'a bunch of spoiled middle-class
women coffee-klatching' (Alther 1981: 401). Emily's lesbian
affair with Maria helps her to contextualize her own frustrations with Justin and they become estranged.

Jed dies ignobly after having an affair with his best friend's
wife (the woman who, at high school, he used to have sex with
when Sally wouldn't 'put out'), and the others meet, literally,
over his dead body. They watch their children as they play on
the Castle Tree where they shared their innocence and Donny
announces, 'Gon be different for them' (Alther 1981: 585), even
though we see that Donny in particular has had his life
dictated by the social realities which govern and restrain his
ambitions. We're left with this image of the tree and its gnarled
branches waving in the wind – a positive note of change or the
depressing cycle of old? This lacks the anxious humour of
*Kinflicks* and instead seems committed to producing a kind
of social history of the 1970s which expresses doubt about
whether feminism or anti-racism or radical politics alone is the

answer. In a sense Alther is agreeing with Kate Millett's model of sexual politics which firmly places individual desires in a wider political context, since 'coitus can scarcely be said to take place in a vacuum [. . .] it is set so deeply within the larger context of human affairs that it serves as a charged microcosm of the variety of attitudes and values to which culture subscribes' (Millett 1977: 23).

Heterosexuality dominated the debates in the Women's Movement – both in its association with male power and institutional practices of oppression, such as marriage, and in debates about how women might seek liberation through sex. Anne Koedt's 'Myth of the Vaginal Orgasm' (Koedt et al. 1973: 198–207) challenged the dominance and the purposes of penetrative sex as the best way for women to achieve orgasm, although her disavowal of the vaginal orgasm stops short of endorsing lesbian relationships. Penetrative sex became associated with the tropes of pornography and violence against women so that 'sweet sex, the great unmasker, is dragged in the gutter again' (Jong 1984: 75). The Movement became torn between the need to offer a model of patriarchy that explained the way women were entrapped in their most intimate relationships and the pursuit of a new mode of sexual engagement that might offer an approach to female sexuality powerful enough to unseat normative heterosexual relations. Were women to assert their freedom by reclaiming their sexual potential or by rejecting heterosexuality in favour of celibacy or political lesbianism? The theories and processes of political lesbianism became a central topic of discussion and gradually the choices seemed to be presented as more a decision about whether to choose lesbianism and invest in the love of one's sisters, despite one's sexual orientation, opt for celibacy, or simply keep silent about one's relationships with men. Jill Johnston's perspective on political lesbianism helps to demonstrate its essential contradictions:

> The word lesbian has expanded so much through political definition that it should no longer refer exclusively to a woman simply in a sexual relation to another woman. The word has in fact had pornographic implications as though lesbian was a woman who did nothing but enjoy sex, an implication employed as a tool of discrimination. The word

is now a generic term signifying activism and resistance and the envisioned goal of a woman committed state' (Johnston 1973: 278).

There might have been much mileage in feminism's embracing the concept of political lesbianism but, as the above statement demonstrates, there is mass confusion over what this label might mean for individual women and their sexual choices, and these discussions succeeded in the main in alienating straight and lesbian feminists and making them evasive. As the group Radicalesbians observed, 'They would rather not talk about it. If they have to, they try to dismiss is as a "lavender herring." But it is no side issue [. . .] As long as the label "dyke" can be used to frighten a women into a less militant stand, keep her separate from her sisters, keep her from giving primacy to anything other than men and family – then to that extent she is controlled by the male culture' (Koedt et al. 1973: 243). This call to political lesbianism, and the confusions around what this could mean, summed up how sexuality became shrouded under discussions about political practice and the problems of how to channel women's vital energies to collective enterprises.

New York's Cell 16 maintained a programme of celibacy and separatism and seemed to regard *any* sexuality as a diversion from the political aims of the group. Other groups would come to political lesbianism as a strategy, but not always to the delight of their lesbian sisters. There remained no agreement on how to approach these issues, but a gay–straight split that became more apparent in the Women's Movement and meant that feminists became more circumspect about how women were expected to express themselves sexually and to what extent one's politics could inform one's sexual choices. To some extent the CR novels were able to address this gap without falling into the trap of political debate, yet the majority of the novels were going to portray resolutely heterosexual women at their heart, with lesbianism either portrayed as an adolescent episode (*Braided Lives*), a possible experiment in political lesbianism (*Kinflicks*),or as all part of the rich tapestry of 'swinging' (*How to Save Your Own Life*). Exceptions of course include the complex Molly Bolt in *Rubyfruit Jungle*, the character of Emily in Alther's *Original Sins* and Zane in Alix Kates

Shulman's *Burning Questions* (1978), none of whom present lesbian relationships as any freer from power struggles and strife than straight ones, but show how social institutions impact upon them much more keenly.

Where lesbianism is a key issue – and even a space for celebration, as in *Rubyfruit Jungle* – there lies the possibility to consider these portrayals of young lesbian women in comparison to coming-out novels of the past, such as Jane Rule's *Desert of the Heart* (1964). Here there is an emphasis on clandestineness and the impossibility of being a 'practising' lesbian, just as in the consciousness-raising novels that deal with lesbianism it is recognized as a lifestyle tolerated in the radical settings of the Women's Movement but punishable by exclusion elsewhere, so that Molly is ejected from her college for her liaison with her room-mate. In *Desert of the Heart*, Ann has casual sex with women who go on to marry – for example, her flamboyant friend Silver. She has also been engaged for a long time, but this relationship clearly acts as a smokescreen for her own desires. The desire between her and Silver is made overt and yet it is equally clear that Silver will never acknowledge her own lesbianism and will instead end up marrying, potentially acting in bad faith. Evelyn, conversely, is seen as both mother and lover, as if Rule is playing with Freud's notion of male inversion as narcissism.[2] Rita Mae Brown was active in the Women's Movement, joining various groups such as the Redstockings and the Furies, and she spent much of her time trying to get visibility for lesbian issues as well as introducing class dynamics to debates: these aspects of her politics clearly inform her writing, since it is clear that Molly's life chances are compromised as much by her poverty and class background as by her lesbianism.

Obviously another issue which dogged debates on sexuality was the inevitable link for all heterosexual women between sex and reproduction. Of course, the right to control reproduction and the right to women's bodily autonomy was one of the unique features of radical feminism, also more mutely echoed by NOW. The New York Redstockings group, set up by Ellen Willis and Shulamith Firestone in 1969, organized 'speakouts', where members would confess to having had illegal abortions in order to pressure for a change in the law (later, de Beauvoir was to testify that she, too, had had an illegal abortion). As Susan Brownmiller remembers, 'back then, personal testimony was a political act of great courage' (Brownmiller 2000: 109). Sue Kaufman's Bettina Balser, Erica Jong's Isadora Wing, Marge Piercy's Jill Stuart, and Alix Kates Shulman's Sasha Davis all wait for their period: for Bettina and Isadora its arrival is a chance to make a new start on their own terms; Jill and Sasha have to deal with the choice of barbarous self-induced abortions or illegal expensive ones. After her best friend's death from such a botched abortion, Jill's life's work becomes making safe abortions available to other women; for Sasha, the abortion is a gesture of resistance to domestic submission, an assertion of continued independence. More startlingly of all, perhaps, Ella Price's abortion on Christmas Day marks her resistance to matrophilia as a means of covering up the cracks in a disintegrating marriage. Mothers themselves are treated ambiguously, their love for their children either destroyed by their sense of loss of both identity and femininity through children (Bettina's mother), or Jill's mother's brand of tough love which only comes through for her when she needs to give herself an abortion. Bettina has to be analysed out of her hatred for her mother; Isadora faces the burden of living up to the failed aspirations of hers to live the impossible binaries of motherhood versus artistic freedom and the tensions in the feelings of such mothers who give up their ambitions to have children. Isadora, in the third novel of Jong's series, is a single mother discovering why her mother gave up her own artistic aspirations after childbirth – 'raising a child and making a living were no easy feats. One always felt divided. One always felt that one's vital organs were being torn apart' (Jong 1984: 415).

The ways in which men are portrayed in these novels is worthy of note here because although in many ways these novels broke new ground in attempting to posit men as objects of desire, strengthening the feminist view that the creation of a new woman warrants the creation of a new man, the moody Byronic hero of the classic romance was a tenacious figure in these novels too. These novels remain dominated by arrogant and insensitive men who only have a notion of their own worth and are clearly comfortable with the privileges that patriarchy has granted them; these are the men that women often go on to fall in love with, whereas the sensitive and supportive men get short shrift. Isadora's choice of Adrian over her husband Bennet becomes increasingly perverse when it becomes clear that sexually he is unable to satisfy her; yet he seems to provide all the dangerous attractions of the romance hero, with the enigmas around his own personal life and the fact the he offers her the appearance of completely free choices as they make their oddly aimless tour of Europe. Isadora confesses that she wants love 'to feel whole' (Jong 1974: 226), and at times she fantasizes about giving up her ambitions and becoming a housewife; in this we see echoes of Ginny's embracing of domesticity with Ira after her chaotic life at the commune. Isadora is cured of her romantic longings and when, alone, she finds herself being appraised by a man with a look similar to Adrian's, 'all I saw in it at this point was bullying and sadism' (Jong 1974: 247). Ella Price's romantic ideals about her teacher Dan Harkan are crushed at the moment of the consummation of their affair, when 'suddenly he blinked, moaned hoarsely, then lay still' (Bryant 1977: 167) and it becomes clear that all Harkan seeks is physical relief from his lovesick students. She overhears some other tutors talking about Dan's reputation and understands that she is part of a cycle of affairs he has with mature students, wives like her. Ben seems to offer Mira an antidote to the crushing conformity of Norm, but when he is invited to go and work in Africa he assumes she will join him and, more than that, wish to have another child with him. From being the sensitive, almost perfect, male lover, Ben is seen to suffer from some of the same traits as Norm, seeing his partner as someone who can fit around his needs and ambitions. Mira refuses, discovering that still '[s]he felt smaller than he, she flattered him sincerely, because she found him more important, larger, better than herself' (French 1986: 494). Even Sasha's romance with Willy, which is set in contrast to her first marriage to Frank, is destined to change once she has their children and recognizes that their development and the world of childcare in which she is now immersed is of no interest to him. Eriksson makes the point that often the lover who is sensitive and non-aggressive is seen as questionable or less desirable, and certainly this association is confirmed by the nature of the male characters presented in these novels:

> It would seem, then, that, when a sensitive man is intro-
> duced and compared to more aggressive and sometimes
> even violent lovers, he is often given characteristics of being
> either physically disabled or at least physically inadequate
> [. . .] or dysfunctional in a social context [. . .] and he is
> sometimes perceived as an unreliable provider by the
> protagonist (Eriksson 1997: 81).

These writers still found it hard to write desire without
recourse to fairly stable notions of masculinity. In common
with feminist politics, these novels failed to give us the model
of the new man who would be able to negotiate the changing
social relationships so much desired by the new woman. The
sensitive man, when he is depicted, is seen as tragically
flawed, as Eriksson has observed, and this legacy can still be
felt in women's popular fiction today.

All the novels discussed in these last three chapters offer the
opportunity to concentrate on the fate of the individual within
the Women's Liberation Movement, since their focus is almost
single-mindedly on personal life, loves, family ties, and the
difficulties involved in maintaining any kind of relationship –
more so if you are trying to disinvest in the notion of romantic
love. This has to be set against the activities within the
Women's Liberation Movement during the late 1960s and
early 1970s, which desperately sought to pool a collectivity of
experience and offer some kind of structure of political
activism while at the same time denying any framework
which might limit the individual will. Out of these contradictions feminism wrestled with the ways to mount a significant
challenge against patriarchal authority from a consolidated
front. Ultimately, this meant some suppression of individual
expression in the name of the group, but this succeeded in
driving out some of the most charismatic figures in WLM and
allowing the media to select the spokespeople they preferred –
Gloria Steinem and Germaine Greer, for example – who,
because they had no group allegiance, were not largely seen as
authentic spokespeople for feminists. Nonetheless, these were
the kind of people, along with Kate Millett, Shulamith
Firestone, and Betty Friedan, that the majority of women had
heard of through their writings and whose media appearances
caused such controversy from within feminism.

From a retrospective vantage point it is clear that feminism might have done well to play the spin game to a greater extent: it was mistaken in its belief in its own power, in that it did not harness that power to its own best advantage. However, to do so would have lost feminist politics those characteristics that were unique to it, not least its refusal to play the power games that characterized mainstream politics. At least at the heart of feminism there remained the hope that change could be effected without the motivations of greed and corruption. Nonetheless the media proved a sophisticated antagonist, treating feminism as harshly as it would any political grouping. The media is always hungry for personal details and was clearly thrilled when it was able to 'out' Kate Millett as a bisexual or catalogue the numerous factions and splits within the Movement: in the face of such revelations, the Movement went into defensive retreat, rather than attempt to play the media game. Even though Robin Morgan declared that feminism was not a movement one joins, feminists weren't beyond expelling people summarily if they were felt to have betrayed the central principles of feminism. In fact, feminism of the modern age depended on personal testimony and the charisma of key individuals strong enough to appear and voice their beliefs in public, so that by these culls they risked losing their most effective communicators. For many of the protagonists of the CR novels, the act of writing becomes the path to self-knowledge, yet within the Movement these novels were not counted as part of its vast array of documents and many would persist in believing, as Rosalind Miles did, that 'there are always the commercially-minded who are quite ready to climb up on their sisters' backs to make their impact (and their fortunes)' (Miles 1974: 183).

# PART 2
# 'Post-feminism' and Third Wave Feminism

# 6
# Crashing of the Superwoman: The 1980s

Feminism didn't invent the career woman, yet moving into the 1980s it is surprising that the term didn't become enriched with more positive indications that the status of women in the workplace was changing or that women's rights were increasingly protected by feminist-informed social policies. Sadly, the clear tension between the two words – after all, one doesn't talk about career *men* – said it all. Women with careers would continue to be seen as oddities, and by the late 1980s they were often portrayed as selfishly putting their own needs before that of their family. There would be no straightforward way for women to gain access to the top of their professions without the perception that their success had cost them dear in personal terms. Thinking back to Helen Gurley Brown and her manifesto for the working woman in *Sex and the Single Girl* in addition to the emergence of career-oriented women in more significant numbers after the Second World War, it is clear that the career woman is a product of women's increased access to education, a buoyant post-war economy, and a changing ideology of femininity, not to mention less consensus about what is or isn't expected of women.

At the level of introducing new ideas and emboldening women to challenge inequities, feminism can surely take a great deal of credit for changing the dynamics of the workplace, as this is something for which the mainstream liberal wing (exemplified in the US by NOW, for example) worked tirelessly. Feminists hadn't necessarily come up with clear-cut solutions to the problems women would have juggling family commitments, except to assert that this was not solely a women's problem. They certainly didn't anticipate women's mass entry into the professions and full-time careers as being in addition to everything else they were traditionally expected to do at home. Feminists from the liberal to the more radical recognized that housework was boring and thankless and often a complete waste of an individual's effort – '[t]he appropriate symbol for housework [...] is not the interminable conveyor-belt but a compulsive circle like a pet mouse in its cage spinning round on its exercise wheel, unable to get off' (Williams et al. in Malos 1980: 114); and worse, it was something being repeated by millions of women in their separate homes. Key to the demands that feminists made was that the private sphere should be socialized to the extent that the roles associated with it would no longer be assumed to be women's work, but as activist feminism waned and common-sense, individualist feminism came to the fore, there was no substantial shift in the association of women with domestic work.

When one looks at the fairly static figures for who does what in the home today in 2005, with women doing by far the greater share of the work, it seems that this area is the one feminism found hardest to reach, not least because so much of it is clouded by notions of personal choice, aspiration, lifestyle, and romance. There were more and more women investing their efforts in their careers, but still having to face extremely tough choices if they wanted to succeed. We are reminded of Betty Friedan's picture of the childless professionals in the 1950s, whose lack of family commitments made it possible to give everything to their job, and we realize that in the 1980s and even today it would be easier for any woman with a career to forego the chance to have children or recognize that this will be likely to severely hamper her career.

The term 'career woman' developed clear visual associations in the 1980s, with such women depicted in tailored skirt suits with exaggerated shoulder pads. Their hair, make-up, and shoes reminded us of their essential femininity, but the sharpness of their suits told us they were competing with men on their terms. The career woman *par excellence* at this time would of course be the UK prime minister from 1979–90, Margaret Thatcher. While she herself was at pains to foreground her femininity in her hairstyle (the rather extravagant candyfloss bouffant), her handbag (an accessory she brandished more like an offensive weapon), and her use of metaphors connoting housewifery to running a government, she was nonetheless felt to be unhealthily male, a sense no doubt exaggerated by the fact that she was the first woman to take up this position in this country. Like so many professions before it, the assumption was that its incumbent had to be a man until a woman had successfully discharged the job. Feminists had no reason to be cheered at the election of Mrs Thatcher, given that she had never knowingly supported female advancement either collectively or individually among party colleagues, and in some ways the contempt in which she was held by the liberal and left-leaning press meant that she was mercilessly caricatured in terms of her sex. For instance, in the UK satirical television programme *Spitting Image* she was depicted in a pinstripe suit and tie. Thatcher, in common with all modern political leaders, espoused family values and it suited her to be vague about her own household role when her own two children were young. Her party's embracing of 'Victorian Values' itself suggested that her views of women were retroactive in the extreme and that rather than facilitating an easier path for other women she was, to use more contemporary slang, a 'queen bee', celebrating her own exceptionalism as a personal triumph achieved in spite of her sex.

For other career woman, baffled at how success could be combined with all the messiness of family life and failing to cope with Thatcherite aplomb, there was the new bestseller, Shirley Conran's *Superwoman* (1975), which carried the motto, 'Life is too short to stuff a mushroom'. The book was sold as an updated Mrs Beeton manual of household management and its very existence underlines the fact that housework is still considered to be women's work, since the subject of address is solely female. More than this, Conran insists that the woman of the house '[e]xpect – or rather, exact – no cooperation from your family; it will result in a restful state of nonexpectancy, and consequent non-nagging, non-resentfulness for everyone' (Conran 1977: 2), implying that women should potentially shoulder more of the domestic burden and not less. Conran is, however, emphatic from the opening of this book that its intention is to save its reader time and not to set up expectations that are impossible for a woman to live up to, but it is difficult not to experience that sinking feeling that one gets with any self-help manual that presents an ideal world scenario – theoretically for you to take or leave. It inevitably acts as another yardstick against which one fails to measure up. Worse than this, given that Conran presents this book as stemming partly at least from 'my own home notebooks' (Conran 1977: 2), it offers a view of women as naturally inclined to store up this kind of home folklore. What is most terrifying about Conran is that she presents herself in this book as entirely capable of 'having it all'. Not only does she know how to deal with the rigours of a career, but she also has an encyclopaedic knowledge of stain-removal techniques and similarly assumes that her reader knows what carbon tetra-chloride is and where to purchase it. While the book's virtues might reside in its thoroughness and the way it presents itself as a manual for all occasions, *Superwoman* reads like the most daunting list of chores ever laid out for a lone housewife. Even if this is not Conran's intention, this book again sets standards of perfectionism that would be hard to attain, even if one did nothing but stay at home. Despire Conran's exhortation to 'ignore the impossible, milk and honey standards of the impossible TV housewife' (Conran 1977: 2) and to use her advice to garner more free time for life's pleasures, it is diffi-cult to peruse this book without coming across sections deal-ing with potential chores one never knew existed. Inevitably, books that offer advice on how to do things quickly and effi-ciently create anxiety in women who are genuinely struggling under the weight of their multitudinous commitments; and to be told that it is also their duty to never nag or expect co-operation from their family seems the final insult.

Into this cultural setting where more working women have less time for domestic chores, the emergence of the super-woman in popular women's fiction was the antidote to the guilt inspired by such self-help books. The bonkbuster, or sex and shopping novel as it came to be known, sold dreams, unthinkable riches, and the satisfaction of a good revenge plot. Rita Felski sums up the 1980s bonkbuster thus – '[i]t features a glamorous, ambitious heroine who fights her way to the top of a corporate empire while engaging in conspicuous consump-tion of men and designer labels' (Felski 2000: 100). Usually sexually frank, and often depicting exotic sexual behaviour or lifestyles, these novels seem to reap the benefits of the Sexual

Revolution. Novels such as Shirley Conran's *Lace* (1982), most memorable even to those who haven't read it for the goldfish scene (see Conran 1983: 292), 'could not have been written or widely consumed as morally acceptable if the Women's Liberation Movement had not been in the vanguard of the recent challenging of traditional male views of female sexuality' (Lewallen in Gamman and Marshment 1988: 101). The novels of the 1970s had broken many of the taboos about women's articulating their own sexual needs and desires, and sex, associated in the CR novel with either self-knowledge or self-deceit, becomes in the 1980s bonkbuster an expression of power. As previously discussed, feminists had opposed the notion that the so-called Sexual Revolution provided new freedoms for women on that grounds that sex itself does not equal liberation (even though the liberation from reproduction provided by the Pill has enormous social ramifications). Sex in the bonkbuster is usually further proof of the superwoman's control over her destiny, even one of the perks of her professional success, so that it rarely seems to take place in a more domestic setting, domestic life in general being of little interest in this genre.

Often these narratives are deeply embedded in a sense of the centrality of the family and the need to belong, so that estranged daughters look for their real mothers (as in Shirley Conran's *Lace*) or one individual seeks to gain revenge on behalf of their family against its adversaries (for instance, Barbara Taylor Bradford's *A Woman of Substance*, published in 1979). In all cases their strength derives, tangentially at least, from modern feminism – 'In her aspirations and attempts to acquire power additional to that normally accorded to women, superwoman shares a number of characteristics with the feminists without appropriating the label' (Dudovitz 1990: 16). Emma Harte of *A Woman of Substance* is the definitive superwoman, who observes, '[b]eing underestimated by men is one of the biggest crosses I've had to bear all my life' (Bradford 1993: 20–21), and the fantasy contained in the story of her life and which speaks to her readers is that all the hard work and self-sacrifice will be paid back by real wealth and happiness. The novel opens with Emma as an elderly woman travelling by private jet with her granddaughter, the scene visibly underscoring how she has profited from the fruits of her enormous wealth which is centred on the commercial empire of Harte Enterprises. Emma is repeatedly portrayed as susceptible to the cold, and such symbolism reminds us of her early deprivations as well as pointing to her emotional cold-ness, one of the fatal flaws in her character, 'as if frostbite had crept into her entire being and petrified her very blood' (Bradford 1993: 31). We learn early on that despite her huge business empire and punishing workload, she is, rather improbably, the mother of five children. She had, in her own words, *'given up her youth, her family, her family life, much of her personal happiness, all of her free time, and countless other small, frivolous yet necessary pleasures enjoyed by most women'* (Bradford 1993: 63), and it is understood from the outset of this novel that Emma's sacrifices have been at a huge cost to her personal life – the only area in which she remains unfulfilled. Despite being tales of commercial success and untold wealth, these novels also have a moral core which offers an implicit critique of the superwoman by emphasising her unnatural-ness, and her uniqueness. More rounded 'feminine' women are shown favourably in terms of wholeness and satisfaction (and the superwoman needs an army of such women to main-tain her family for her), whereas the superwoman, if she doesn't compromise her relentless drive for power, will end up like Emma, lonely and vengeful and destined to live her own life vicariously through the lives of her descendents. Readers are thus presented with ambiguous pleasures: they are able to enjoy the aspirational dimensions of the super-woman – her self-belief, professional successes, exquisite taste in consumerables – while being reassured that such a role is impoverished by its incompatibility with family life. Yet the fact that heroines such as Emma Harte can only invest hope for personal satisfaction in the lives of descendents has profound resonances with the way mothers are generally encouraged to invest their energies in their children's potential.

At fifteen Emma becomes pregnant by the youngest son, Edwin, in the Fairley household where she works as a kitchen maid; he betrays her by his helplessness when she tells him of her predicament and when it is clear that he will abandon her completely rather than compromise his own name. She devel-ops a hatred for him and his father (who she suspects dallied with her mother) to such an extent that her desire for revenge becomes the guiding thread of the whole novel, 'a motivating factor, coalescing with her inherent ambition, her drive, her energy, and her shrewdness to propel her to heights not even she, at that moment, dreamed possible' (Bradford 1993: 382). In a further melodramatic twist, her father saves Edwin's life in a fire, only himself to die after the accident, further galvanizing Emma's hunger for revenge. Meanwhile Emma has fled her home and moved to Leeds, where she manages to find work until she has her daughter in secret. She marries for money and advancement, shunning the man she loves because he is a Jew and his mother asks her not to accept his proposal; and in this example alone we can see how Emma is cast as both principled and unscrupulous at the same time. After her first husband's death she marries again to overcome her love for a married man, and her revenge comes full circle when she buys Fairley Hall and its Mill, disenfranchising the whole Fairley family. It is made clear that every decision Emma takes is governed by her determination to build a formidable business empire – 'the most relentless pursuit of money ever embarked on, the most grinding and merciless work schedule ever conceived' (Bradford 1993: 512). When she does fall in love, she rarely gets the opportunity to enjoy stability before tragedy sets in. This is true of Paul, the love of her life and father of her youngest daughter Daisy (the mother of her favourite grandchild, Paula), whom she cohabits with because he is still married, unhappily, to a mentally unstable alcoholic whose Catholicism prevents a divorce and who is described rather quaintly as a 'demented creature' (Bradford 1993: 801), both drunken and promiscuous. Paul, like Mr Rochester, is maimed in an incident which is triggered by his 'mad' wife. Unlike Rochester, who is gradually restored to wholeness by the ministrations of Jane Eyre, Paul, unable to contemplate life in a wheelchair, shoots himself through the heart.

For Bridget Fowler, Emma Harte is 'a modern Moll Flanders – ambitious, quick-thinking, materialistic' (Fowler 1991: 105), and though romance is a key thread throughout the book it is the periods when Emma is alone or estranged and having to rely on her own resources which take up most of the narrative space and interest. She could also have emerged straight from the pages of a naturalist novel in the sense that much of her destiny seems to be prefigured by her own mother's fate. Later in her life she finds out that her mother was Adam Fairley's lover and became pregnant by him, but suffered a miscarriage and went on to marry Jack Harte. This obsession with family lineage is further played out for dramatic effect as all her children come to resemble their various fathers and all except for the last one, Daisy, a child conceived in love, betray their mother. Generational conflict is a popular feature of the bonkbuster, many of which, like Colleen McCulloch's *The Thorn Birds*, take the form of the family saga and span three generations. Emma places her faith in the subsequent generation and past rifts are symbolically healed at the end through the prospective marriage of her granddaughter Paula to Jim Fairley, Edwin's grandson. Unlike the consciousness-raising novel heroine, who embarks on a new life with her new-found knowledge, this novel finds Emma at the end a cold and embittered woman who only finds pleasure vicariously through that of her granddaughter, having succeeded as a business woman but failed as a mother in the eyes of most of her children. Her lust for revenge has brought her enormous wealth and eventually the reconciliation of her hatred, but given the estrangement of most of her children from her it is implied that the cost of her success at a personal level is high. She has often eschewed romance for practical liaisons with men who failed to make her happy and the little sex that is portrayed in this novel is generally unsatisfying, predatory, or perfunctory.

While Bradford's famous blockbuster has elements of Catherine Cookson about it, especially the emphasis on Emma's class and the backdrop of the stark Northern landscape (Yorkshire, rather than Cookson's North-East), there is also the hint of fairytale. In her liaison with Edwin Fairley Emma is repeating history in her mother's own love across the class barriers, and near the end of her life she is given the love token made by Adam Fairley in honour of her mother. Judith Krantz's *Princess Daisy* (1980) contains an even stronger fairytale element in that Daisy is, improbably, the daughter of a Russian aristocrat and Hollywood movie star. Her mother takes her away from her father, Stash Valensky, as a baby when she realizes that while she was suffering from post-natal depression he lied to her and told her that her twin daughter

Dani (born retarded from birth difficulties) was dead. When her mother dies tragically in a car accident, Daisy returns to live with her father and he puts her sister in a home, refusing to acknowledge her existence. As a teenager she comes into contact with her elder half-brother Ram, who treats her with utter disdain until their father dies in a plane crash, and when Daisy is fifteen he has sex with her. It is not uncommon in genre romance fiction to encounter scenes where the young woman's initiation into sexual knowledge seems close to rape, and this scene is equally ambiguous, as Daisy does not antici-pate or desire the liaison – 'In an ecstasy of lust he pried open her thighs and quickly, pouncing, found the opening he had to find and drove himself into her, pounding brutally through the tender flesh because she was a virgin and he had to have her or die of anger and need' (Krantz 1986: 159). By the scene's end her emotions have shifted so that, in the mode of the clas-sic Mills & Boon heroine, she is depicted as being consumed by unacknowledged desire and comes to love Ram deeply. He rapes her again when she refuses to continue sleeping with him and she is scarred by this encounter and also by her sense of guilt that by being born first she was the cause of her sister being starved of oxygen at the moment of birth. After Ram shoots himself in the only moral resolution possible to the plot, Daisy takes up her aristocratic title. Nonetheless, it is significant that in the meantime she has made her own way in the world by working in advertising and portrait-painting, rather than living the life of the idle rich. This is a more straightforwardly aspirational novel than Bradford's, where Emma, who by the end of the novel claims that the secret of life is 'to endure' (Bradford 1993: 878), can scarcely be regarded as living out her dreams. Krantz's novel is much more about location, product placement, and the machina-tions of the rich, allowing the reader the pure escapism of fantasy while enjoying the spectacle of the corruption of the super-rich.

Another style of blockbuster that gripped the bestseller list at this time were those, like Jackie Collins's *Hollywood Wives* (1983), which took the exposé or gossip columnists' view of Hollywood as driven by sex, corruption, and the fetishization of youth. Whereas Krantz and Bradford in particular favour the art of story-telling and dwell on location and all the trappings of wealth, Collins focuses on personalities, drives, emotions, and sexuality. Fifty pages in to the novel and there has already been straight sex, impotence, a lesbian seduction, and the sexually motivated murder of a young man by a group of well-heeled older men. Collins, taking over the mantle of Jacqueline Susann with the glitzy lives of the Hollywood rich, offers an even less rose-tinted view of the rich and famous:

> 'Where have you been all my life?' he gasped, near orgasm, his rigid member clamped firmly between her heaving bosoms.
> 'I don't know;' she gasped, also on the point of divine release. 'But wherever it was, honey, I ain't going back' (Collins 1984: 410).

However, even Collins weaves a fairytale element through her narrative, so that the conclusion is underpinned by the sub-plot of twins separated at birth – one goes on to become a serial killer motivated by the need for revenge against his mother, the other becomes a wannabe movie star, Buddy Hudson. Rather heavy-handedly the novel ends with Buddy's wife giving birth to twin boys, but the previous scene with the heavily pregnant wife Angel, kidnapped and nearly killed by Buddy's serial killer brother, has unpalatable resonances with the killing of Sharon Tate. This sub-plot, both serious and grotesque, jars with the snapshots of Hollywood wives seeking their highs through cosmetic surgery, exercise, and casual lovers. The main intention of the book seems to be to shock and titillate and play up to what we assume is the basic corruption of the Hollywood lifestyle, yet it is also aspirational in that it features locations and products that represent success and glamour even while they seem to take the sheen off the Hollywood dream. While feminism does not get an explicit airing here, it is made clear that women are still largely at the mercy of their men and that their marriages are precariously balanced by their need to keep their men interested and attracted. Children rarely feature at all and the nearest thing to a feminist statement is uttered by top agent Sadie La Salle reprimanding her lover as a chauvinist for calling her breasts 'tits'; generally men are sent up and exposed as idiotically controlled by their sex drive.

In Danielle Steel's *Palomino* (1982) Samantha, while staying at her friend's ranch, can't wait to 'show this rigid chauvinist ranchman what kind of rider she was' (Steel 1982: 54), as Tate Jordan picks out a mild-tempered horse for her first day's riding. But in a sense he is proved right when she has a riding accident and is confined to a wheelchair for the rest of her life. Like all good melodramas, Samantha ironically finds happiness through her accident in that she discovers her life's work at the ranch, converting it into a camp for disabled children, and is even at the end reunited with Tate, who accepts her disability without demur. Most critics agree that the bonkbuster is a politically conservative genre, highly individualized, consumer-driven, and featuring women who are extremely sexually accomplished, as if all their hang-ups have been dispensed with thanks to either feminism or the Sexual Revolution. The chief unexamined contradictions in such texts lie in the fact that 'on the one hand the capitalist ideology that pervades them largely ignores, on a manifest level at least, issues of class, race and gender; but on the other, they problematise and prioritise active sexuality for women in ways that might be regarded as a challenge to the exclusively male gaze of patriarchal structures' (Lewallen in Gamman and Marshment 1988: 88). Their attraction for the reader is clear, in some ways the opposite of the CR novels where the characters' own families are at the foreground of the plot. Here accomplishment is at the forefront, featuring women with a preternatural will to survive. The relegating of the domestic to the background speaks to the aspirations of the CR heroine to move out of the home and to transform the male-identified world of commerce and education.

As in the CR novels, these books are peopled by dysfunctional families and actually nothing is done to rehabilitate them. The central characters, in common with the average Mills & Boon heroine, are either orphaned (particularly motherless) or irrevocably split from their parents, with close friends or associates acting as their only family. They remain focused on the women's point of view and steer a bizarre course between the traditional pulp romance, the fairy story, and the gossip column. In a sense they prefigure the substance of some of the chick lit novels, in that these are women with jobs in advertising, entertainment, or retail, and their appeal is that technically they can lead an autonomous life without a man and the men they do end up with may well be less power-ful or even from a lower social class. The ways in which these novels were marketed and the use of author photographs on the books' covers are themselves worthy of study. The author pictures on the paperbacks by Jackie Collins and Danielle Steel, for example, feature head-and-shoulder shots of both women heavily made up with strongly etched eyebrows, shirt collars tipped up, and severely scraped back hair. Both styled in the overstated glamour of the 1980s, their poses are remark-ably alike – slightly severe, definitely unsmiling, and clearly remote. These are professional authors, the photos say, and for all the publishing hype surrounding some of the more success-ful CR novels there is something more mechanical and calcu-lating in the construction of these author identities. The headier mixture of realism and fairytale, which extends to authorial identity, invites readers to recognize that the super-woman persona of the fictional character is reflected in the writer. The novels suggest that power and wealth are achiev-able and in themselves desirable, while leaving to one side the question of personal happiness or fulfilment. The bonkbusters also seem to say that the lives of the rich and glamorous are as gloriously mundane and fraught with tragedy as our own, with some, such as Bradford's *A Woman of Substance*, champi-oning the possibilities of social mobility – '[t]he message of the fiction of the beginning of the 1980s is that women have now managed to acquire economic independence, that they have "gotten smart" and unlike their counterparts in the 1970s, are no longer afraid to leave unhappy and unsatisfying marriages' (Dudovitz 1990: 148). While this is certainly the case, and the fact that women leave their bad marriages may well suggest a positive rejection of traditional feminine roles, marriage itself is not held up for scrutiny, witnessed by the serial marriages of many of the heroines. Perhaps relationships, like some of the plot-lines, adopt a rather arcane nineteenth-century twist, so that marriage is predominantly defined as a means of cement-ing social status and commercial liaisons.

For Bridget Fowler, '[n]o longer modelled on the Madonna, the heroine in this genre has requisitioned the honorific image of the male entrepreneur as restless Promethean developer. No longer defined by her family identity, she has become the quintessential self-made woman' (Fowler 1991: 104), yet the self-made woman confidently plunders traditional images of femininity rather than starting afresh. Many of the novels, while wanting to junk the family and its retrogressive influence, do seem to be seduced by the naturalist pull of seeing the family as inscribing its mark on each of its members. The most exciting aspect of this genre is the sheer power that some of the women possess, which obviously chimed with a period when self-determination seemed more achievable for women and a means by which they might compete in a man's world on 'male' terms. These novels were fantasies proportionate to the degree that the CR novels were realist and for about a decade they sold dreams of power to female readers of popular fiction – a kind of Mills & Boon with a twist where, more often than not, the men came cap in hand to the woman to celebrate her success rather than persuade her to make sacrifices. Those few children produced by the bonkbuster heroines are very much in the background of the novels and those that are actually brought up by their mothers do not suffer them to be buried in shit and string beans like those memorable moms in *The Women's Room*. As Rita Felski observes, 'women's affinity with the commodity is no longer devalued but triumphantly affirmed as a source of their economic power. This affinity equips them with newfound authority and professional expertise as media magnates and captains of industry in a culture that is increasingly feminized in its preoccupation with image, surface, and style' (Felski 2000: 103). From her point of view, writers like Krantz are simply faithfully reflecting a postmodernist turn in culture and in economic arrangements, although in reality of course the actual position of the majority of women has yet to catch up with the supposed feminization of industry. These novels dramatize the possibilities already inscribed in the enormous social and industrial changes of the past half century, but their status as fantasy strikingly reminds us that these possibilities are not only hampered by whether a woman has the guts to fight to get to the top, but that the ideology of femininity and its twin pulls, even now, between the workplace and the home which serve to exert a powerful counter-influence will be only too familiar to the readers of these texts. As Felski notes, '[t]he money, sex, and power novel is the only popular form that celebrates and rewards the female desire for power and the power of female desire' (Felski 2000: 109). It is true that these novels attempt to be more honest about the realities of female sexual desire and the benefits of mutual response: unlike the CR heroines who combat erratic orgasmic achievements and variably potent men, these women are either experiencing the best sex ever (usually correlative with the love of their life) or suffering brutal rape, sadistic powerplay, or marital neglect. In reproductive terms it is as if we've taken a trip back to the nineteenth century, and of course the novels' historical sweep often takes us back to the earlier part of the twentieth century. This may in part explain a preponderance of illegitimate babies rather than abortions; but it also suggests that frank discussions of abortion, in an era where it was finally possible to obtain an abortion legally in the US and the UK, were becoming strangely unpalatable. Instead, babies are given away at birth, with the plot convenience that they can later turn up and wreck their parents' life at a crucial moment.

I have already said that feminism rarely explicitly rears its head in this genre, although ironically 'the money, sex and power genre would not be possible without feminism' (Felski 2000: 109). In *Lace* Maxine, Judy, Pagan and Kate find solidarity through their own schoolgirl closeness and the later secret they share. Kate, for one, is disappointed by the Women's Liberation Movement – 'the sisters never seemed to talk about practical considerations; discussion was either directed to experience-sharing or else utopian theorizing' (Conran 1983: 495). Kate's solution is to set up her own magazine for the 'new woman', as she sees her. And *VERVE!* declares that 'it's time that women thought more about money – and had more of it for themselves!' (Conran 1983: 499). Though the freedoms feminism wanted for women were never gained in full, these novels continue the story, offering the potential for a much happier ending for women. From Naomi Wolf's point of view, such novels are more in touch with women's lives than Second Wave feminism ever was and she argues, 'these books cannot be seen as mere escapism. In their pages, readers found better psychological preparation for the "real world" than in "victim" feminism, which was withdrawing into increasingly hazy, power-averse utopias' (Wolf 1993: 45–6). Given Naomi Wolf's belief that true feminism is compatible with the individualist competition for power, it is not surprising that she would take more nourishment from the bonkbuster than from the CR novel; but it is this image of the bonkbuster heroine as supremely capable and effortlessly in control – the very model of the power feminist – which the chick litters will write against in the following decade.

While powerful women were cropping up in all popular fictions of the time, from the bonkbuster to television serials like *Dallas* and *Dynasty*, they were also emerging in a more explicitly toxic form in films like *Fatal Attraction* and in moral panics about what power does to women. Even the most powerful women of the day – such as Margaret Thatcher – didn't seem to think that power was good for women and she clearly enjoyed her exceptional status. Nonetheless, in this decade, while feminism steadily crept into the academic institution, a different kind of feminism might be effected through capitalism, which was individualistic and based on competitive choices in spite of social conditions being stacked against women as a whole. As Resa Dudovitz notes, the 'female capitalist tales of Judith Krantz or British-born Barbara Taylor Bradford exemplify bestsellers which present capitalism not only as the natural way of the world but also as the environment which best nurtures women's aspirations' (Dudovitz 1990: 7). This free market feminism, for want of a better phrase, allows women to think that they can change their own lives even if they don't have the mettle to change the world, and it was seductively appealing to a whole new generation of women.

# 7
# Where Have All the Feminists Gone? The Anxiety of Affluence

In Fay Weldon's *Big Women* (1997), a novel about the fortunes of Medusa, a feminist publishing house, and its founder members, Saffron – the daughter of one of the feminist friends of these 'big women' – tries to find out who is responsible for her mother's suicide when she was a child. She wavers between blaming her father, who burned some of her mother's manuscript even though it had been accepted by Medusa (a fact he didn't communicate to his wife), and the feminists at Medusa, whom she regards as having indoctrinated her mother Zoe with theories which made her unable to continue her domestic life at all.

Saffron comes across as the ball-breaking career woman, an editor of a magazine for young women – 'readership profile under thirty, sensualists, A, B and C, forget C, D, E; and our readers would rather have a boyfriend than a promotion any day, though they deny it' (Weldon 1997: 275). She might have added that her readers are assumed to be childless (as she currently is) and that they may want to be married some day, but are still dating as yet. Nonetheless, there are more parallels between the fictional feminist founders of Medusa and Saffron than she'd care to admit. Unlike Zoe, who failed to turn up to regular consciousness-raising sessions because it regularly incurred the wrath of her husband, the Medusa collective grasped their independence and set up their feminist challenge to the literary establishment. Like Saffron, they overturned the traditions and assumptions of a previous generation – their target was patriarchy; Saffron's is feminism itself – and like Saffron they appear intolerant of the weak and passive. Those such as Zoe, who felt the remnants of duty to her husband, bore the brunt of their disgust – partly at her status as a mother, but also because of their outright rejection of any responsibility for the shared upbringing of her child and their resentment of what they see as Zoe's attempted imposition of her problem onto them. The founder members of Medusa generally pursue their ambitions and aim for political credibility, but find that misery, loneliness, and even professional failure confronts them. Their feminism, initially a thing of joy which has them dancing naked together, symbolizing their common bond as women, splits them as the divisions between radical and socialist, cultural and radical feminist become more apparent.

Saffron, reminiscent of a heroine from a 1980s bonkbuster, takes revenge on behalf of her mother by attempting to buy out the majority share in Medusa (and in the process reveals that one of the largest stakeholders is a male sleeping partner). Her mother Zoe achieves her own posthumous revenge as the manuscript of her supposedly destroyed book, *Lost Women*, becomes a bestseller. Zoe has transformed Medusa into a profitable business and makes a fortune for her erstwhile friends. Inevitably, the touch of prosperity throws the company – used to living on a shoestring and publishing to a tiny readership – into disarray. Saffron has done for her mother's book what she has done for her magazine and she subverts the most deeply held principles of the founder members of Medusa by forcing them to be governed by the pursuit of profit and sales, just as much as she is as a high-profile women's magazine editor. Saffron naturally represents the worst excesses of capitalism to the Medusa women, as well as reminding them of their failure to communicate their values or radicalize a new generation. Improbably young for someone so hugely successful, she represents the get-rich-quick ethos of 1980s yuppiedom and the distortions and half-truths of the media, so despised and distrusted by many members of the Women's Movement.

Looking back at the heyday of the Women's Movement, Layla, the prime mover in Medusa, describes feminism as 'the bloodless revolution. The casualty rate was high. Suicides, the collapse of relationships; so many of us alone, because who would put up with us, and how could we put up with them? When every casual word is examined for implication, assessed for correctness, life gets exhausting' (Weldon 1997: 312). Weldon's critique of Second Wave feminism, and her provocatively reductive analysis of its legacy, coalesces with many contemporary views of feminism: that it bled the women for whom it was intended dry; it affirmed their loneliness and sense of isolation; and sent women generally off course. For Weldon, politicizing is mutated into excessive 'political correctness'. Her view of feminism as itself tyrannical and hectoring to women is not a minority view, of course, and this perspective on feminism's Second Wave has endured, perhaps even offering an explanation for the birth of the 'singletons' in contemporary chick lit. Saffron, Weldon's daughter of feminism, is a capitalist, individualist traitor to the Movement. She possesses the confidence and self-belief to succeed in a man's world, takes for granted the social reforms that have eased her passage to success as a woman, and, moreover, she ruthlessly exploits her femininity.

For her, it's not a question of proving herself of equal worth to men, but of playing on her difference from them to expose men's vulnerabilities. She acknowledges the enduring power of patriarchy and its hold upon business and then cuts through it by effectively exposing males and masculinity as weak, flawed by their desire for sexually attractive young women and easy prey to their own egos. Saffron is the avenging angel for women, like her mother, whom she regards as betrayed by the Movement. The reasons for her mother's suicide remain a mystery and by the end of the novel we are left with the symbolic resonances of the fate of these feminists who accidentally profit enormously from the ashes of feminism (in the form of Medusa) and the death of their friend, in a period which seems to have left feminism behind. The name, Medusa, was initially chosen by the women to strike fear into the hearts of men, but it becomes a brand like any other: 'Medusa turns no one to stone; her power is gone; she is thoroughly approved of, upsets nobody and could be any gender at all' (Weldon 1997: 345). Perhaps Weldon is arguing that this is true of modern feminism too?

Weldon's cynicism about the legacy of feminism is clear; her remarks also remind us of feminism's transformation since the late 1960s from the cool label of choice for politically aware women to, in the 1990s, an epithet which suggests you protest too much and are blindly resistant to change. Perhaps it is the destiny of all political outgroups to get sent up as a way of defusing the less palatable elements of their message; but in the case of feminism it veered curiously between becoming branded (for example, the strapline 'women's lib' that appeared on advertisements for sanitary towels and Virginia Slims with their confident slogan, 'You've come a long way, Baby'[1]) to becoming virtually an inappropriate topic to bring up in a political setting in the 1990s. 'Blair's babes', as the 101 women MPs who formed part of the 1997 UK Labour government came to be known, tolerated this media epithet without too much protest; and the subsequent lack of feminist proposals emerging after this historic event suggests a certain fatigue with the term feminism and a degree of acceptance that such an event should be regarded as confirmation that feminism had achieved its major aims and that therefore there was nothing left to lobby for. If feminism has arrived into the mainstream, as was implied by the presentation of such events, then what was the point of carrying on hectoring? By this logic, one might now affirm that one was indeed a feminist, but feel no need to lay claim to this as a significant political identity; rather, it is a statement delivered as part of a common-sense belief in progress. Feminism now, therefore, might be seen as having taken on two identities and there is no way of reconciling them: either you're a feminist in that you subscribe to a general belief in equality and assume that all right-thinking members of the population agree with you or you're a feminist because you stick to your guns and insist on belabouring 'old' causes without due recognition that times change.

It is an interesting but frustrating exercise to try to chart the historical moment when the identity of feminism changed irreversibly. Clearly from the mid-1970s there was a gradual shift away from radicalism and activism. Even while academic acceptance of Women's Studies as an appropriate object of study grew, the groupings that had brought together so many women were becoming riven by disagreements over who feminism could speak for and whether it could ever unite women beyond the barriers of class, race, and sexual orientation. There were noticeable gains for women in material and social terms, but 'by the mid-1980s, women's liberation was everywhere, yet it was nowhere. An era had passed. There would not be another major outburst of rebellion – on the scale of the 1970s – until another generation discovered its own need to re-ignite the fire' (Coote and Campbell 1987: 255). So far that generation has not emerged, and perhaps there is reason to suppose that Second Wave feminism would prove a hard act to follow. It developed from the cracks of a New Left politics that has little or no purchase in the political structures of the millennium, and it eschewed the media, branding, and the cult of the individual – all contemporary essentials if you want to get on in life. But before radical politics went soft, feminism had changed to the point where many women found less easy access for their own exploratory ideas. Whereas once it had been a melting-pot of ideas (though it was never straightforward for black or lesbian women to get themselves heard), by the 1980s some of the priorities of the more public face of feminism had changed and hardened. Crucially, the pornography debate took centre stage in public awareness of gender politics and polarized feminism into two broad wings, the pro-porn one seeing itself as pro-sex and therefore further casting the old radicals, who tended to be constitutionally anti-porn, as resolutely anti-sex and against all forms of pleasure or play because of their core belief that porn causes real acts of violence to be committed against women. Radicals were regarded as puritanical and frighteningly judgemental about other women's life choices; and such harsh divisions within the Movement played into the hands of anti-feminist critics, as this view of radical feminism accorded with their view of feminism as a whole. Writers such as Andrea Dworkin had maintained that there was a direct link between pornography and the abuse of women and her work was an easy target for detractors because she chose to communicate her ideas in the most simple and direct terms possible. Her assertions fuelled protracted discussions about the divisions between porn and art, abuse and freedom of expression, to the point that opposing porn was regarded as correlative with opposing choice and freedom and supporting censorship. In the light of such divisions, there could no longer be any belief that feminism spoke for all women, not only because some of the key issues of the 1980s were peripheral to so many other people but also because that moment of radical utopianism had passed where the problems that united women coming out of a male-dominated political framework seemed larger and more urgent than those which spoke to other aspects of a woman's identity. For others, the media had hijacked and sent up the central tenets of feminism; it was felt that the most prominent spokes-people for feminism were inauthentic, and they were held up to blame for the media's often willing distortions of feminism. The Women's Movement was fracturing even as it was at its height around 1970–72 and, as previously discussed, there was public paranoia about who was making a living off the back of feminism and what the consequences for the Movement might be. For instance Claudia Dreifus, reviewing Germaine Greer's *The Female Eunuch*, asserted, 'the author's insistence that "sexual liberation" is the prerequisite for women's liberation has a lot to do with the fact that she thinks like a man' (Dreifus 1973: 358–61). This casual dismissal of one of the major mouth-pieces for feminism in the 1970s was again playing into the hands of those whose interests were best served by emphasiz-ing the ruptures and lack of direction for feminist politics.

Other icons from another time fare better. Helen Gurley Brown, now in her eighties, has lived to see her *Sex and the Single Girl* relaunched, bizarrely, as a 'cult classic' in the US in 2003, and one wonders what it is about the brains behind *Cosmopolitan* which endures for so long and with the same essential message for women. *Sex and the Single Girl*, as previ-ously discussed, was part self-help manual, part autobiogra-phy: it told us the secrets of Brown's success – secrets which she still embraces and lives by, even at a time when one would imagine she'd earned a quieter life. Brown remains a celebra-tion of material success against all odds and without the aid of feminism: as Susan Douglas observed, 'the bottom line of her message has always been the absolute importance of pleasing men' (Douglas 1994: 68). She is the career girl taken to absur-dity, since she still maintains her association with *Cosmopolitan* – a magazine targeted at young women – and every article about her stresses that she's never gained weight, still wears mini-skirts and fishnet tights, and works out daily, keeping a set of dumb-bells in her office. Strangely, Brown works as both pre- and post-feminist in that her kneejerk position is to place herself as a resolutely individualist feminist, proud of her own successes as a woman and supportive of the right of all young women to strive to realize their own potential; she would be post-feminist in the sense she would hold up her own meteoric rise to power as a reason why there is no need for organized feminism.

Post-feminism of the kind that suggests that feminism is no longer required because women are already finding success in their careers becomes associated in the popular media with self-absorption, summed up by the television successes of *Ally McBeal* and *Sex and the City* and the film versions of *Bridget Jones's Diary*. All these women capitalize on the greater freedoms available to them and are, to varying degrees, successful in the careers they have chosen. However, most of them aren't happy with their lives and there seems to be a huge chasm between the aspirations of their personal lives and those of their professional lives, with the result that their successes are portrayed as contributing to their misery rather than demonstrating that they have moved beyond the constraints under which their foremothers worked. For the first time, perversely, these freedoms of choice are presented either covertly or overtly as burdens to the women in question, as if they are juggling two entirely separate identities: young women today, popular culture implies, suffer the choices set out before them primarily because those choices make their personal lives all the more complex.

Susan Faludi's classic 1992 text *Backlash* popularized the notion that there existed a concerted if not organized backlash against women and the gains they had made through feminism. Her book is particularly powerful in the way that she shows how moral panics can develop around areas about which women are already particularly anxious – for example, the incompatibility of careers and children, the impossibility of getting married after the age of thirty, and so on. Although many later 'new' feminists were more sceptical about her claims, she offered a spirited challenge to some of the ways feminism was perceived to be failing. In subsequent chapters we shall see that maybe these moral panics dug in deeper than some suspected: certainly there is an almost palpable sense of anxiety emanating from many volumes of chick lit.

Naomi Wolf in *Fire With Fire* (1993) believes that women

already have the power for self-definition and simply need to exploit it. Wolf's concept of the 'genderquake' suggests that power is already available to women; they just have to grasp authority from men initially and power will follow. It simply requires us to be confident enough to snatch it away from the kind of feminism she calls victim feminism, because 'if you can no longer square your feminism with your real life experience, then something has gone seriously wrong' (Wolf 1993: 68). Certainly, writers such as Erica Jong would appear to agree with this statement in the attitudes she has her fictional heroines adopt, and however one regards Wolf's anatomy of the victim feminist, she is clearly accurate in her assessment that younger women feel antagonized or disempowered by feminist critiques which fail to speak to their key concerns. Acutely assessing one of Second Wave feminism's central weaknesses as its embattled relationship with the media, Wolf asserts that the media are at the heart of the new 'power' feminism, and that leading power feminists are those men and women such as Madonna, Spike Lee, and Bill Cosby, who might be regarded as manipulating the medium to serve their best interests. Contradicting Audre Lorde, she claims, 'the master's tools can dismantle the master's house' (Wolf 1993: 118), which offers the clearest indication that 'power feminism' advocates working within the *status quo* rather than attempting to overturn current political realities. Power feminism, in this light, seems nothing more than an empty endorsement of a social meritocracy. While claiming that women are antagonized by the more dogmatic elements of feminism, she is quick to point out that there is 'no feminist version of Casaubon's key to all mythologies' (Wolf 1993: 129), yet she implies that it is the idea of rigid orthodoxy that young women are shying away from. What is difficult to negotiate here are the inherent contradictions in the tone of address she adopts. At one point, Wolf is speaking in the first person plural of collective feminism and shows her understanding of the complexities of its multifarious political hues; at others, she is one of the unwilling frightened outcasts. This 'us' and 'them' posturing does not serve her critique of Second Wave feminism well. Ultimately, power feminism seems to be like good old liberal feminism, which has an entirely honourable tradition but offers nothing new to the young, except perhaps the reassurance that in their bid for autonomy nothing needs to get broken. Wolf, according to Suzanne Moore, has had a huge impact on rebranding feminism because she directs it at individual women's quest for power. She argues that for Wolf, 'feminism now becomes such a big tent that any woman who has experienced any kind of horror in her life can enter it without, it seems, having to change anything – except, perhaps, go to a performance of *The Vagina Monologues*' (Moore 2004), implying that declaring one's feminism in Wolf's terms is a simple, painless lifestyle choice about being seen to make the appropriate critical noises. So-called victim feminism – messy, strident, unattractive – is cast to one side as if the memory that it was once deemed urgent to unite and declare resistance to the wholesale oppression of women is rather embarrassing.

Rene Denfeld, in common with Naomi Wolf, seems to be more attracted to the politics of women's suffrage at the turn of the twentieth century than the calls for revolution in the 1960s and 1970s. For Denfeld, organized feminism 'has become bogged down in an extremist moral and spiritual crusade that has little to do with women's lives', which has also drifted into the arcane language of academia, offering 'a worldview that speaks to the very few, while alienating the many' (Denfeld 1995: 5). Radical feminist crusaders Catherine MacKinnon and Andrea Dworkin are cited as the mouthpieces of feminism, with other feminists' objections to their hardline stance on pornography conviently forgotten, and through their perspectives she dubs Second Wave feminists the 'new Victorians'. The pornography debate invited associations of anti-porn activists with the stereotypically staid and prudish Victorian, and this association is exploited for all its implications that feminism's real war was against sex in all its heterosexual manifestations. Katie Roiphe, whose mother had written the bestselling *Up the Sandbox!* in 1970, follows Denfield's lead in her view that young women on US campuses are encouraged to cry rape and have been given a warped sense of heterosexuality as fundamentally destructive by feminists. For Roiphe, 'feminists are closer to the backlash than they'd like to think. The image that emerges from feminist preoccupations with rape and sexual harassment is that of women as victims, offended by a professor's dirty joke, verbally pressured into sex by peers' (Roiphe 1993: 6). If feminists don't get the joke, she seems to be arguing, they characterize women as the frail shrinking violet – an image of women that they supposedly challenged from the outset of Second Wave feminism. Clearly Roiphe, Denfeld, and Wolf are beneficiaries of feminism's pioneering work that for the first time itemized the ways in which women were victims of patriarchal oppression; a generation later, they embraced the opportunity to move beyond victimhood without acknowledging how important it had been for their mothers to understand the processes by which women's secondary social position had been sustained in the first place. Just as I noted earlier how feminists were negligent in charting their own history or understanding the factors that helped improve their visibility in the heyday of activism, so feminism's self-proclaimed new feminist critics would forget how, in a different social and economic climate, early Second Wave feminism had made sense to a huge number of ordinary women. Roiphe sees a developing victim feminism that is counter to the quest for equality; however, equality in this context does not seem to mean ensuring access for all to the scarce resources currently available to the privileged, but simply the possibility of a stake in competing for high-status rewards in existing power hierarchies. Her work is in fact entirely motivated by the conviction that feminism misrepresents reality to women and that feminist militants are simply motivated by their hatred of men: in common with Naomi Wolf she suggests that this incitement to hatred has a profound effect on contemporary heterosexual relationships.

British writer Natasha Walter, in *The New Feminism* (1998), has much in common with Naomi Wolf in her optimism about the existence of female power outside organized feminism. Echoing Harold Macmillan, she asserts, 'we've never had it so good' (Walter 1998: 197), implying that feminists exaggerated the extent of women's oppression and going on to cite examples of women who have achieved fame or success as examples of female empowerment – such as the Spice Girls – in her attempt to depict a feminism which has mainstream appeal and is completely freed from the more damning images and associations of Second Wave feminism. Tellingly, one of the aspects of feminism that she most categorically rejects is its politicizing of the personal, which she bizarrely interprets as nothing short of an invasion of privacy and an attempt by bossy old-style feminists to tell women how to run their lives. She is, in common with many 'new' feminists, more comfortable with the language of rights than of revolution, seeing arguments about images of the power of ideas as detracting from the core of feminist thinking. Her five goals which conclude her book, reminiscent as they are of the original five demands from Women's Liberation in the UK in the early 1970s, have a solid policy foundation and could be revolutionary if implemented (for example, the reorganization of the workplace); however, these goals aren't to be achieved by a women's party or grouping or network, but are uncomfortably left in the hands of the individual woman who reads her book. The image that Walter says feminism has – 'man-hating and [. . .] a rather sullen kind of political correctness or puritanism' (Walter 1998: 36) – is unfortunately perpetuated by these new feminists so that the more potent legacies of feminism lie forgotten and the Second Wave comes instead to be remembered as that of whining victimhood and passivity. New feminists such as Wolf and Walter feel that feminism is in need of a makeover and it is possible that their work is underpinned by a genuine desire to make feminism more relevant and accessible to a new generation; but ultimately their feminism is that of the individual consumer making choices to improve their own life, possibly ethically, but in such a way that the cost to themselves is minimal. Lynne Segal notes that new feminism is emptied of political analysis and really only gauges success by access to powerful jobs and influence, having little idea of how women battle against the new obstacles put in their way – 'although pleasantly symptomatic of many women's goodwill towards a "feminism" they feel free to fashion, it lacks the very thing it hopes to promote: political seriousness' (Segal 1999: 228).

The clearest shift from the point of view of such writers who have done much to popularize feminist debates is the wish to cast the old feminists behind them as rather maudlin characters who simply pleaded sympathy for their victim state and alienated themselves needlessly from men. The new feminism appears to be about learning to love men and disapproves of any hint of criticism of them, even if the criticisms are more abstract and levelled against the ways structures of patriarchy are maintained. Again and again such accounts characterize these pioneering radicals as joyless, puritanical, and fascistic, without troubling to analyse the context from which they were writing and debating their ideas. Rene Denfeld's *New Victorians* (1995) quite categorically positions such feminism as anti-sex and anti-male, taking a voyeuristic delight in its own prudery without really showing any deep understanding of how the sexuality and pornography debates came to the fore. Delilah Campbell, writing in the UK radical feminist magazine *Trouble and Strife*, calls female commentators who berate what they see as victim feminism as 'maverick feminists', who 'think nothing of misrepresenting other feminists; they feel no responsibility to any movement or community. This of course gives them a huge advantage in media terms: they can throw out a soundbite while the rest of us are still collectively and democratically deciding what our position is' (Campbell 1995: 71). It is true that it is hard to defend oneself against the charge of prudery or Puritanism if you adopt anything like a serious and in any way negative response to some aspects of the representation of women in contemporary popular culture; it has become *de rigueur* to celebrate the transgressiveness of popular culture and the freedoms for negotiation it gives the female viewer. All this may be true and undoubtedly the positives of popular culture have been undersold for many a long year. However, there is a palpable risk in asserting that a text's multivalence liberates us from having to make two-dimensional judgements about its sexism, since such dogmatism about the compulsory joys of popular culture is equally oppressive. I'm aware as a teacher and as a writer that many young people are actually looking for guidance on how to articulate the offence they often feel when viewing something on television or listening to the radio, even at the same time as they might be experiencing pleasure in the particular product. Feminists were clearly shortsighted when they kept the mass media at arm's length; but there are dangers in reiterating the sophistication of the young female reader who may feel that sophistication a burden which disallows her the simple satisfactions of anger and offence.

Over the decades since Second Wave feminism emerged, the question of boundaries has recurred on a regular basis. The argument is always returned to the obvious fact that feminism, not allowing for structured movement or membership, is unable to either recruit or exile people from its ranks. In the 1990s and up until the present day, commentators as diverse as Camille Paglia – astutely characterized by Elizabeth Wilson as displaying 'misogyny and feminism combined in one person' (Wilson 2001: 18) – and Natasha Walter would be faddishly embraced by the media as having the next big ideas on feminism. Walter, among others, has done her bit to rehabilitate Margaret Thatcher as a feminist icon, by implying that her legacy to women has a feminist element just by virtue of her holding power for so long. Helen Wilkinson is adamant that the fact of Thatcher's power makes her an enduring role model for women and, in a statement which reinforces Naomi Wolf's championing of 'power feminism', she says, 'we saw a woman who did not shy away from showing how much she loved power, and in turn she made it legitimate for us to love it too. In one stroke, she redrew women's relationship to power, and gave us a road map, a route to follow, a vantage point from which to strike out in a new direction' (Wilkinson in Walter 1999: 31).

What has endured over the last decade is that the tensions between old and new feminists are akin to the tensions one more readily finds between mothers and daughters, and this analogy is often foregrounded to suggest that the generational conflict can be productive as well as inevitable. So young women do not want to heed the wisdom of their elders, but rather they want to point out to these feminist mothers that the world has changed quite considerably since they were young feminists. What is less constructive is the fact that this tension and the nature of the relationship painted as mother and daughter suggests that there is something quite ineluctable about the split. It also plays into the hands of backlash logic, which states that feminism can never operate on any kind of continuum, merely bursting out only to fade again in waves of dynamism and energy.

But what does the new 'feminist' addressed by the media in the 1990s look like? According to Melissa Benn, she

is a young-ish and pleasant-ish, professional woman. If she is not a mother she wonders a lot whether, and how, she will become one [. . .] she is more likely to belong to one of the

new media-related professions than one of the caring
professions [. . .] She goes to the gym, likes sex (probably
more than the men or man she's having it with), and
gossips a lot with her girlfriends. She is interested in
designer clothes, lipstick, the whole 'looks' package and
scorns a slightly mythical older feminism which tells her
she shouldn't be (Benn 1998: 224).

The term Third Wave, first used by Rebecca Walker in 1992
(one of the founders of the US Third Wave Foundation), is a
term with increasing currency on both sides of the Atlantic,
which is used to distinguish a new wave of activism quite
different from the more negative connotations of post-
feminism and which takes on new ground distinct from that
inhabited by feminism's Second Wave. The term is explicitly
embraced by a generation of younger women to announce
that feminism is a space they already inhabit and not a process
they have yet to engage with. For some critics, Third Wave
feminism still suffers from being seen as profoundly individualist and therefore difficult to define as a movement of any
kind; yet, as Astrid Henry implies, there is a new emphasis on
individuality and an active resistance to the group identity
(and all the problems that go with it) of Second Wave feminism (Henry 2000: 217). Third Wave feminists are young
women who are the beneficiaries of a feminist education: they
took their women's studies and gender courses and luxuriated
in an entire, complex, theoretically nuanced language of femi-
nisms (most assuredly in the plural). They profit from a pre-
established discourse of feminism with an embarrassment of
riches, in terms of theoretical and political explorations, and
one of the frustrations they experience is the need to articulate
their own experiences of their postmodern world – arguably
more baffling and contradictory than that inhabited by early
Second Wavers. Over thirty-five years on, Second Wave political writings are bound to look pedestrian and hopelessly
naïve. As Elizabeth Wilson observes:

Western society's attitude towards the position of women is
utterly incoherent, with discourses from Darwinist geneti-
cists competing with deconstruction, and calls for a return
to traditional values competing with paeans of praise for

women's superior ability to survive in the world of glob-
alised markets and touchy-feely management (Wilson 2001:
18).

Third Wavers, generally characterized as those born after the
baby boom (Heywood and Drake in Gillis et al. 2004: 13), are
dealing with such incoherencies on a daily basis, and one of
the things that is said to fundamentally distinguish them from
the Second Wave is that they are likely to identify with their
generation rather than their gender. It is clear that Third Wave
feminism does display critical engagement and commitment
to Second Wave feminism at the same time and claims a different rhetorical space. Rebecca Walker's 1995 collection of
essays, *To Be Real,* was her response to a feeling that her generation were troubled by their relationship to feminism because
of their 'less than perfect histories' (Walker 1995: xxxiii). She
invited contributors to write about how they reconcile less
'correct' aspects of their lives to their politics, and the book
becomes a compelling analysis of the politics of identity, with
many kicking against the old ready-made categories, such as
gender, 'race', sexuality or class. The essays are often intimately confessional and seek to cross (and demolish) the
preceived boundaries of feminist taboos, such as the enjoyment of violence, the pleasures of material success and power,
or the seduction of feminine fripperies. As Catherine Redfern,
writing in her web magazine *The F-Word,* asserts, 'Second
wavers often misunderstand young women's enthusiasm for
the term "Third Wave". They think it's because we don't
respect their achievements or want to disassociate ourselves
from them. In actual fact I think it simply demonstrates a
desire to feel part of a movement with relevance to our own
lives and to claim it for ourselves, to stress that feminism is
active today, *right now*' (Redfern 2002). A number of the
contributors to webzines and contemporary feminist websites
are disarmingly upfront about their own use and affection for
popular cultural products such as magazines and designer
clothing and readily embrace the predominant use of ironic
referencing as a means of offering a more critical response to
their own engagement with the mainstream. They see playful
appropriations of words such as girlie, bitch, and cunt as actually 'a serious part of the third wave's critical negotiations

with the culture industries' (Heywood and Drake in Gillis et al. 2004: 16), and these features of Third Wave feminism have to be addressed as at least part of a political strategy.

Within feminist literary criticism there is an even greater self-consciousness about the dangers of constructing a feminist critical history which attempts to offer a student-friendly and therefore seamless view of how feminist literary criticism came to be and where it is going. Around the mid-1990s, Mary Eagleton, an important figure in the production of surveys of feminist literary criticism, expressed a concern, laudable enough, that her and others' work should not simply reproduce familiar hierarchies and old exclusions in criticism. However, it doesn't take long to become aware, re-reading her 1996 essay 'Who's Who and Where's Where: Constructing Feminist Literary Studies' (Eagleton 1996: 1–23), that beneath the 'canon' of criticism that she is so wary of reproducing as a simplified view of feminist literary history she includes a quite narrowly delineated set of readings of literature. While this is not always clearly articulated, there is still an assumption even in the 1990s and today in 2005 that 'trash' or popular fiction is still not part of the business of feminist literary criticism. Eagleton concentrates so readily on the account of feminist criticism and its growth offered by the dominant critics of the post-Second Wave period – including Mary Jacobus, Susan Gubar and Sandra Gilbert, Cora Kaplan, Toril Moi, Julia Kristeva, and so forth – that one could overlook the relative narrowness of the literary texts such writers have recourse to. Even though feminist criticism has its own wing of critics who look at the production of romance or other genre texts, they tend to be seen as doing something entirely different from those who appraise literary work. For this reason, feminist literary critics were largely unequal to (or uninterested in) the task of analysing the sudden success and accompanying critical furore around a category of writing called, derisively, 'chick lit'. This is a pity, since the epithet is so interesting and provocative. It manages to insult women at the same time as it reminds us that the act of reading is just as gendered now as it ever has been, in addition to alerting us to the fact that having 'women's books' as a category can be positive for women readers as well as continuing to be a useful marketing category in publishing. Because many feminist literary critics have yet to show much interest in the phenomenon of chick lit, there is still little sign that the work done by cultural critics is cross-fertilizing with literary criticism. Flickers of interest in chick lit from a critical perspective have tended to be entirely negative, for example the assertion that British women's fiction is going through the doldrums. This is best summed up by the fact that in 1999 one of the judges of the Orange Prize (a prize awarded only to women writers), Lola Young, commented that such British women's fiction was 'piddling' in scope by comparison to its American counterparts. Chick lit, perhaps, is seen as part of the problem at the popular end of the market and the message seems to be that the domestic, never really the height of fashion, is definitely not worthy of renewed critical appraisal. For critics such as Young, women should be writing on a larger canvas, and this view demon-strates that a focus on the domestic continues to be associated with the trivial, only freely celebrated in the debased genres of romance and melodrama. What is interesting for the purposes of my argument is the evidence that once again women writ-ers of popular fiction should be returning to the domestic to articulate a view of contemporary women's lives as bounded by home and family rather than work and ambition. 'Piddling' or not, this tendency marks a clear link between chick lit and the writings from the Women's Movement.

# 8

# Hooray for the Singletons!

On 19 February 2003, the Radio 4 literary quiz *The Write Stuff* ended with a round where the contestants were asked to produce a pastiche of Virginia Woolf writing chick lit. The fact that the contestants were able to reproduce the 'formula', and that the audience clearly enjoyed the recognition of certain features of both the Woolfian sentence and the chick litters' world as one populated by 'things', suggests that chick lit has arrived, if only on the borders of the literary. Its appearance alongside Virginia Woolf on a literary quiz throws up a lively tension between the high and low in women's writing and is testimony to the massive success of the genre. Though Woolf might not have had such novels in mind when, in *A Room of One's Own* (1929), she urged a new generation of women to write 'all kinds of books, hesitating at no subject however trivial or however vast' (Woolf 1977: 103), chick lit novelists are producing some of the most commercially successful women's writing of the past decade and they do possess the material wealth and the space to write their fiction unhampered. The most successful of these writers and the one who has come to define chick lit is Helen Fielding, whose second novel *Bridget Jones's Diary* became an astonishing publishing success. By the time a film adaptation was made in 2001, the novel had sold in excess of eight million copies and had been translated into over thirty-three languages. Its significance moves far beyond the context of bestselling fiction and Bridget Jones the character is notorious as the definitive single girl, summoned to represent the choices facing young women today.

In *How to Save Your Own Life*, Erica Jong's protagonist Isadora Wing drily observes of her explosive media fame after the publication of her first novel, 'my public insisted on an exact equivalency between her and me – because my heroine, astoundingly enough, had turned out to be amanuensis to the Zeitgeist' (Jong 1978: 20). Erica Jong, writing about Isadora Wing writing about Candida Wong, created a Chinese box of feisty heroines and of course encouraged, along with the resonance of naming, the assumption that Erica Jong was writing her own life. That Isadora characterizes herself as amanuensis to the *Zeitgeist* reminds us that although readers and critics enjoyed the anticipation of a closeness between the lives and loves of Erica and Isadora, it was for reflections of their own experiences and of their times that they also looked to her work. She had captured a moment where people recognized the changes that their culture was undergoing; it wasn't that no one else was writing about modern coupledom, swinging, feminism, and being a writer, but that Jong managed to crystallize, for women in particular, the sense of fragmentation that comes from trying to make sense of one's private life in a wider world that rendered some of the givens of relationships obsolete. Isadora is a character torn by conflicting impulses: her feminism and her drive to realize her ambitions as a writer expose the deep-seated tensions at the heart of her marriage and love affairs, yet her desire for affirmation through romantic love, even at the cost of her sense of self, drives her back to her husband and later to the arms of her next lover.

*Bridget Jones's Diary* has similarly captured the *Zeitgeist* of single life in the 1990s. Published in the same year that the Spice Girls' *Wannabe* went to number one in the UK charts, its protagonist Bridget takes her place in a long line of women behaving badly in a decade where 'girl power' was the most lucid statement of feminist intent available. The key success of the novel was the reader's sense of recognition with Bridget's daily mishaps, where Fielding's keen observational humour deftly seemed to unite contemporary women's experiences in the figure of one young woman and also encouraged readers to speculate about whether Bridget's experiences were actually those of Helen Fielding. What appeals about Bridget is that through the form of the diary we have access to the vulnerabilities of a young woman glorying in the freedoms that contemporary life offers her, yet confessing her own anxieties about the cost of this 'freedom' in the pages of her diary. She speaks to some deep-seated angst at the heart of many a young woman's life, and whatever the true source of that angst its expression gradually starts to crop up, not just in Fielding's chick lit successors but in other areas of popular culture. For instance, in 1998, the year *Bridget Jones's Diary* was published in the US, the UK received the first airing of the US television series *Ally McBeal*. UK viewers saw Ally McBeal through the lens of Bridget Jones and American readers very much saw in Bridget the legacy of both Ally McBeal and Candace Bushnell's newspaper column and later novel, *Sex and the City*.

Chick lit might usefully be compared with its popular fictional predecessors in order to better establish its own distinctiveness, as well as to explore what it borrows from the other forms. The heroines of the CR novels realize that there is something wrong in their lives and the plot of the novel often follows their quest to fix it. Relationships with men are primarily seen as fraught with complexities and unexamined repressive structures, which often prevent the happy resolution of the women's emotional and sexual desires. The burden of the narrative turns on their analysis of these wrongs and the action they propose as a result – leaving the marital home, deliberating on whether to return to an unhealthy marriage on new terms, determining to put their own aspirations first, and so on. Conversely, the heroines of the 1980s sex and shopping blockbusters were out for revenge against some past sin or to uncover a mysterious secret about their childhood or their family's past. Sex and conspicuous consumption figure strongly in the bonkbuster; wealth is fetishized as is class difference; families are generally poisonous, or at the least virtue skips a generation. The new woman of the 1990s and beyond found in *Bridget Jones's Diary* and subsequent chick lit offerings both a warped reflection of the glossy *Cosmo* woman and the rebellious daughter of the bonkbuster heroine.

Whereas the 1980s heroine, perhaps best typified by Emma Harte in Barbara Taylor Bradford's *A Woman of Substance*, is a powerhouse of ambition, drive, and capability, the chick lit heroine is sometimes too anxious to make simple decisions and seems instead to celebrate instances where she fails, as well as resignedly suggesting that character flaws are a part of one's unchangeable personal make-up. Chick lit heroines are loved, warts and all, presumably speaking to a reader's unarticulated desire to have their true nature shine through and be readily apparent to The One. Mark Darcy, for instance, is drawn to Bridget's authenticity, saying that 'all the other girls I know are so lacquered over' (Fielding 1996: 237). Chick lit, in common with the feminist bestsellers, is generally written with self-deprecating humour and even at times physical comedy. Compare this to the tone of the average 1980s bonkbuster, which solemnly narrates events with a seriousness which is sometimes unintentionally comedic and which emphasizes their lead characters' astonishing range of accomplishments. Even though Una Alconbury tries to get Mark Darcy to believe that Bridget is a radical feminist and member of the literati, Bridget is not a high achiever. 'Chicks' like her owe more to Helen Gurley Brown and *Cosmopolitan* on the surface and more to Friedan and Second Wave feminism beneath. They may lack Brown's immense self-discipline and Friedan's macro-level analysis of women's oppression, but their lives are seen as governed by the schizophrenic edicts of glossy magazines and trend-watchers, set against the fact they benefit from more comfortable social and material circumstances thanks, in part, to feminism. While the superwomen of the 1980s blockbusters were driven by the determination to take revenge, clearing their family's name or fulfilling some other entirely focused aim, the chick lit heroine is crippled by the burden of choice – most particularly the freedom to remain single – and suffers indefinable lassitude at the prospect of career advancement. She assumes the successes of feminism without feeling the need to acknowledge the source of these freedoms; in fact, feminism lurks in the background like a guilty conscience.

Despite the fact that chick lit heroines are depicted in a deliberately humorous context, what is striking is the seriousness with which they have been taken by critics. It is not so much about the fairly run-of-the-mill plots they inhabit, but there seems to be a general anxiety about what the fact of their existence in fiction can mean. In a more reflective moment, Helen Fielding (who usually refuses to make anything approaching a serious statement about her book) offers her own take on the woman question – 'these are complicated times for women. Bridget is groping through the complexities of dealing with relationships in a morass of shifting roles, and a bombardment of idealised images of modern womanhood. It seems she's not the only one who's confused' (Fielding 2001). This acknowledgement of some form of identity crisis clearly echoes the feelings of women in the 1960s and 1970s as communicated through popular feminism; and the idea that reading *Bridget Jones's Diary* makes them feel part of a community suggests a longing for an inclusive female sphere of experience.

Chick litters, it seems, are faced with the burden of Having It All. Rather than the opportunities such a position is supposed to promise in Helen Gurley Brown's 1982 bestselling manual of the same name, Having It All in the 1990s comes to mean being torn in two by the twin pulls of career and home life, and these negative connotations underpin all contemporary chick lit. On the face of it, these writers are acknowledging their astonishing good fortune in inheriting the successes of feminist lobbying and finding fewer obstacles to their journey up the career ladder. In addition, they point to a contradiction at the heart of Brown's recipe for having it all which assumed that in the path to success one shouldn't relinquish one's femininity. Because of the failure to interrogate all the baggage which accompanies the notion of femininity at stake here professional identities remain masculine and the home remains feminine, and balancing the two components of one's identity becomes fraught with problems. Feminism's project had been in part to renegotiate femininity and to problematize the boundaries between traditional notions of masculinity and femininity, but the actuality was that women latterly experienced femininity as something essential to them under threat by feminism. Femininity, then, with all its most retrogressive trappings, seemed to experience a mini-revival in the 1990s through to the present day, witnessed by a surge of interest in fashion, lifestyle, and beauty. In academic circles, too, there was a new engagement with popular culture as a complex space in which identities are negotiated. Helen Gurley Brown had promised success through utter self-discipline; and as if in reaction to the unattractiveness of this, chick litters respond by celebrating a clutch of women who consistently fail to achieve the aims they set themselves and lack any kind of discipline at all.

In Maeve Haran's 1992 novel, also called *Having it All*, Liz, a television executive, finds the twin pressures of work and family almost unbearable, but even as she reaches breaking-point, her husband refuses to countenance a stay-at-home wife – 'I want an equal. I want a woman who's her own person with her own life. I don't want to live with my bloody mother' (Haran 1992: 177). In a twist not unusual in later chick lit the key male characters facilitate the heroine's freedom and offer a 'feminist' viewpoint, whereas it is the female character who chooses to retreat from the pressures of high-profile work life and regards feminism as stultifying or alienating. Liz, like her chick lit successors, seeks out the company of women with whom to share her anxieties, and we recognize that women's lives are depicted in these novels as being supported and nurtured by an army of other women, whether it be paid help, mothers, colleagues, or old friends. Once Liz splits up with her husband David and takes her children to the country she finds mothering just as stressful as work and here her friend Ginny acts as the voice of reassurance – '[f]ull-time mothers don't do everything by the book, you know' (Haran 1992: 199). *Having it All* conveys forcefully the message that you can't have it all and is in some degree a paean to motherhood, which contains within it a notion of return to gender ascriptions of old: 'What a crazy world it had become where every woman she knew handed their children over to someone else almost at birth and went back to work!' (Haran 1992: 207) Liz instead discovers that she likes the quiet routine of domestic life – '[t]he biggest revelation over the last few weeks had been in discovering how much pleasure she got from small rituals [. . .] raking dead leaves, hanging clothes on the line, tidying out drawers, making pretty cushions' (Haran 1992: 212). The burden of this plot seems to be that even if you have the most high-powered job, 'none of it meant anything if you loved a man and he didn't want you' (Haran 1992: 221). Novels such as Haran's are testimony to the fact that Fielding did not 'spore a confessional gender' (Fielding 1999: 170), to coin Bridget's self-referential malapropism, but rather that the runaway success of *Bridget Jones's Diary* brought this kind of fiction to a wider consciousness.

*Bridget Jones's Diary* offers us a romance for our age, since Bridget is 'a child of *Cosmopolitan* culture, have been traumatised by supermodels and too many quizzes and know that neither my personality nor my body is up to it if left to its own devices' (Fielding 1996: 59). Her position in a sophisticated world of reflectivity and irony means that she should be able to maintain her scepticism about anything that smacks of simplicity or romance, but what this book portrays so well is that its heroine is on a quest for hidden structures, some mystical arrangement of the universe that makes sense of romance and dating. Bridget and her friends are constantly on the lookout for new wisdoms, usually picked up from glossy magazines and self-help manuals, and the novel exposes how adept women's magazines are at trading on women's anxieties as well as fulfilling their commercial need to produce some 'new' discovery by recycling old features in order to maintain their circulation figures and satisfy their advertisers. Bridget imbibes the cheerful advice and heeds the absurd strictures of each new fad diet, while failing ever to stick to any of them, their ephemerality matched perfectly by her own lack of conviction. Everywhere in contemporary chick lit the heroines seem to be on a quest for rules or commanding logic which clarify the meaning of the dating game, yet in virtually every novel the rulebook is thrown out when The One comes through, and the romance breaks every convention as the narrative draws to a close. This notion that true love breaks all the rules of course returns us to the precepts of classical romance and the message that true love is utterly individual and unique, which Second Wave feminists challenged and dismissed as part of the sugar coating of patriarchy. Having said that real love breaks all the rules, the concern with etiquette and the heroine's general conviction that she would be more successful if only she uncovered the secret rulebook, also suggest that the readers of chick lit are searching for some logic and delimiting structure to their lives which the burden of seemingly free choice has taken away. This searching for the vital answers to the mystery of an effective relationship with a man is sent up in *Bridget Jones: The Edge of Reason*, when Mark Darcy observes, when he has to listen to Bridget counselling her friends about their relationships over the phone, 'it's like war command in the land of gibberish here' (Fielding 1999: 23).

Rules may be found in relationship advice but when it comes to feminism, however, young women assuredly do not want the 'rules' perceived to be handed down from the motherhood – as feminism might more appropriately be dubbed from the vantage point of this generation. As Natasha Walter has written, they 'do not want to learn a set of personal attitudes before being admitted into the club' (Walter 1998: 5). The persona of the Second Wave feminist as rather unpleasant gatekeeper to the secrets of political freedom has been one of the most powerful images to be restated and replicated and held up as the reason that young women, represented in fiction by Bridget Jones, believe that feminism repels men because 'after all, there is nothing so unattractive to a man as strident feminism' (Fielding 1996: 20).

Like Brown in *Sex and the Single Girl*, Bridget celebrates the single life – set against the humdrum world of the smug marrieds – while longing for resolution to her own romance plot. Where Brown's book was aspirational – how many people apart from Brown could live to the strictures she set herself? – Fielding's is a celebration of sloth and inadequacy; a fallible heroine makes her readers feel so much better about their own attempts at self-improvement. From this perspective the book is an ironic treatment of *Cosmo* culture and the pernicious effects of reading such magazines on a monthly basis; but it also becomes the triumph of nature over nurture, since Bridget gets her man despite her haphazard beauty regimen and her dismal attempts at self-improvement. Given that the reader is placed in a privileged position to Bridget and can recognize the way she is repeatedly duped by glossy magazine speak, we are being led to believe that *Cosmopolitan* in the 1990s might just be straining under the wake of its own contradictions in a period when just about everyone can recognize 'spin' when they see it. However one reads the irony and humour central to the content of *Bridget Jones's Diary*, Bridget is anxious about feminism and, perhaps echoing the anxieties of younger women in the 1990s, cannot embrace it without acknowledging its anaphrodisiac qualities.

The confessional tone draws readers in, so that our relationship with Bridget is one of complicity, encouraging agreement with Bridget's world view, even when her utter hopelessness makes us feel so superior to her. *Bridget Jones's Diary* depends on that sense of a shared female discourse; part of the joke is that some of the references should be obscure to the male reader and promulgate the notion that even today in

2005, when it comes to emotional intelligence, the two sexes inhabit vastly different spheres. Chick lit novels mark out a quite different terrain than that which feminist writers in the 1960s and 1970s are trying to claim for their own. In the latter case, the central protagonists are trying to look beyond the space traditionally designated for the female into the worlds of education and creativity which represent the opportunity for self-definition. Conversely, the chick lit heroine is portrayed as located firmly – and lazily – in the home, regardless of her career identity. At some point in the novel she must negotiate the complexities of family and affective bonds as if feminism did not happen. The physical or material constraints suffered by the heroines of the CR novels are readily challenged and often overcome once they recognize the constraints of their own mind and their own perpetuation of the *status quo*. In chick lit, singleness is itself seen as constraining; and this partially identifies the way even contemporary social arrangements militate against singleness, despite the fact that the number of single households has increased exponentially. Single women in particular are still portrayed in much the same way as they have been for the past two centuries, and Bridget Jones and her friends express frustration with this categorization in their coining of the term singleton in an attempt to get away from all the negative meanings of 'spinster'.

What made *Bridget Jones's Diary* particularly successful and different from other examples of young urban women's literature around at the time was its loving homage to Jane Austen in a decade when Austen was receiving a great deal of attention from film and television adaptors in Britain and the US. What Fielding offered us is not only the pleasure of tried-and-trusted plot recognition in borrowing broadly from *Pride and Prejudice*, but also an understanding that the classic heritage adaptations, along with the Richard Curtis-style romantic comedies, are part of the stock of cultural capital of the young urban woman. Bridget and her friends like nothing better than to rewind the scene of Darcy swimming in the lake at Pemberley in the 1995 BBC adaptation of *Pride and Prejudice* and their attraction to the character of Darcy as played by Colin Firth suggests that there is still a lot of mileage in the moody Byronic romantic hero so popular with Mills & Boon.

The attractions of Austen's most famous novel are clear enough: a young woman is impelled towards a seemingly arrogant and moody man, but once all preconceptions and misunderstandings are swept away their love can flourish with emotional and material advantage to the heroine. Were it not for the social conventions of the day, the importance of class and standing, and the restrictions upon women specifically, some of these misunderstandings would not have taken place; other obstacles are not so much misunderstandings, but rather areas where both characters need to recognize their own prejudices and preconceptions about the other. What Fielding skilfully depicted through her representation of Bridget and her friends' serial use of self-help manuals and lifestyle advice was a society saturated with discourse about relationships and personal mental good health to the point where people are rendered mute by the sheer weight of searching analysis available. Logic dictates that women and men should be able to make their feelings about each other perfectly straightforwardly known, but a concern to read the right signals, to know what your partner *isn't* telling you, nearly costs Bridget her relationship. Freedom at this level is depicted as intolerable; perversely, if there aren't enough strictures to prevent people's pursuit of happiness, then they have to invent them.

Bridget Jones is presented as a knowing consumer of culture, though her tastes tend towards mass market television programmes and magazines. She still falls for the seductions of magazines such as *Cosmopolitan*, while acting as testimony to the fact that the flawless *Cosmo* girl simply does not exist; and in this way Bridget and other chick lit heroines represent a resistance to magazine woman. Chick lit, while representing the anxieties women suffer because they don't match up to the ideal femininity on display in popular culture, champions the ordinary and everyday, so it is often the blonde bombshell who comes to grief (as in Jenny Colgan's *Amanda's Wedding*) – and blonde bombshells (Renée Zellweger in her role as the film Bridget is a case in point) are only too pleased to make themselves over as the girl next door. This tendency to revive the image of unattainable femininity while resisting it sets up tensions in reading *Bridget Jones's Diary* and, although I have offered a more positive spin above, there is a feeling that these lives are narrated quite without substance –

reading *Bridget Jones's Diary* is to study the increasing vapid materialism of our daily lives: but the subtext is more inter-esting than this. Bridget and her friends embrace yet are imprisoned by materialist culture; they know (especially Sharon) the language of feminism and in particular the 'new feminist' rhetoric of empowerment through individ-ual choice rather than collective action or political transfor-mation. They can enact empowerment through their career choices and the evidence of a handful of women who really make it, but have also to confront a system of values about sexual difference and relationships which lags desperately behind the progressivism their material advances promise. Ideologically, women are still positioned as the makers of relationships, the people who need marriage and children while men are the dysfunctional breakers of them – the so-called 'emotional fuckwits' who must be deceived into the 'smug married' state (Whelehan 2004: 37).

Bridget, the opposite of Isadora, views her single state with abject fear, predicting that one day she will perish 'all alone, half-eaten by an Alsatian' (Fielding 1996: 33). Even her friend Shazzer's observation that today's men 'have been proved by surveys to be *completely unmarriageable*' (Fielding 1996: 42) fails to reassure Bridget or slow down her fevered search for a suit-able partner.

The new woman that emerges from the pages of chick lit is one who, theoretically, 'tells it like it is' and the readership can be either those who see their lives reflected there or those who look uneasily at the broader social climate that made Bridget what she is. In common with Helen Gurley Brown, the chick lit writers are as much the role models as are their heroines – more so, since their personal success stories give a sense of direction to these otherwise hapless and demotivated female characters. These authors are young women who more often than not have a story to tell of their previous existences in dead-end or unfulfilling jobs until a couple of sample chapters sent off to an agent at the encouragement of a friend result in a six-figure advance and multi-book deals which allow them to enjoy the final joke – that they are nothing like the women they portray. Fielding's success story is a good example, since *Bridget Jones's Diary* first appeared as a column in the

*Independent* newspaper in February 1995. Accompanied by a byline photo of a woman holding a cigarette and a wine glass, many thought Bridget existed and she received fan mail and proposals of marriage as a result. The contemporaneity of many of the references to external events clearly comes from its existence in a broadsheet newspaper. For many readers, Bridget's life was theirs and in the *Diary* they recognized their confusion in their troubled postmodern, post-feminist existence.

Just as Jong spoke to a generation of women who had felt the stirrings of the Women's Liberation Movement even if they were not themselves active in it, Fielding addresses a constituency of women whose politics (if they have any) are played against the increasingly intrusive presence of the media. In this sense, references to women's magazines, self-help manuals, and popular television shows such as *Blind Date* remind us we are in a world in which the mixing of the high- and low-brow has to some extent been achieved (as long as it can be seen to be done with irony) and that popular culture has become the lingua franca of a whole generation. Chick lit itself is a niche market as much as it is a recognizable literary genre; much as some of its writers might deny this, the publishers' decision to put out these books in pastel covers with zany cartoon-style illustrations brands them and tends to homogenize them on the surface, unfair as this may be to the individual writers concerned. I shall look more closely at the work of some of these other writers in the following chapter in order to demonstrate that beneath the chick lit brand these writers are constructing a fairly substantial critique of contemporary women's lives.

No novelist can predict the uses their work will be put to – either at the personal or more public level – and although *Bridget Jones's Diary* is seen as the defining example of chick lit, it really only consolidated a trend in popular fiction which had been brewing since the late 1980s and early 1990s, in novels such as Maeve Haran's, mentioned earlier, and also Kathy Lette's collection of short stories *Girls' Night Out* (1988) and her subsequent novels, including *Foetal Attraction* (1993). Some writers, such as Melissa Nathan, have produced closer imitations than others, in that her novel *Pride, Prejudice and Jasmin Field* also uses the plot of *Pride and Prejudice* to give impetus to its central love story, with Jas landing a role in a celebrity dramatization of Austen's novel while at the same time falling in love with the leading man. *Bridget Jones's Diary* defines chick lit, ironically, by its own liminality. The common thread that it does share with many of these texts is that despite its knowing observational humour it maintains a straightforward romance plot at its core. Just as *Pride and Prejudice* has long been seen as the ur-text for Mills & Boon commercial romantic fiction, so *Bridget Jones's Diary* made it acceptable to import the moody alpha male into urban literature, using ironic self-deprecating humour to deflect the more retroactive implications of this love for Darcy. Interestingly, even Mills & Boon have acknowledged the popularity of this update of the formula romance and have created a chick lit imprint entitled 'Red Dress Ink', launched in the UK in 2002. Although models of courtship are scarcely traditional, the act of courting is central to the narrative. Daniel Cleaver, for example, courts Bridget via the non-traditional means of email, while Bridget pretends to be outraged by his comments about the length of her skirt and her breasts and responds in a parody of so-called political correctness which makes it clear that any budding feminist sympathies Bridget might possess have no place in the office or in her relationship with her boss. It is precisely in the arena of romantic love that sexual politics failed to penetrate in any meaningful or long-lasting way, and what Fielding appears to be sending up here is the absence of a language of sexual desire that went beyond identifying the ways in which heterosexual relationships were imbued by inequalities of power. Clearly on the face of it Daniel is exploiting his position as Bridget's boss, but Bridget is 'v. much enjoying being sexually harassed by Daniel Cleaver' (Fielding 1996: 25). This scene deliberately takes a controversial topic and suggests, implicitly, that feminism can teach Bridget nothing that will get her through the more nuanced, 'ironic', dating practices of the 1990s.

On the face of it at least, femininity is riding a crest of the wave in a new celebration of it as an essential and reassuring space for young successful women to inhabit or even play at, just as Nigella Lawson tells us in her cookery writing how to be a 'domestic goddess', so that we can knock up a cake on a weekend and have all our friends envy our traditional culinary skills. Lawson reassures her reader, 'what I'm talking about is not *being* a domestic goddess exactly, but *feeling* like one' (Lawson 2000: vii): her fulsome sensuous descriptions of the process of cooking and eating all of her recipes evoke nostalgia as the key inspiration. The memory, false or idealized or real, of being served home-baked cakes and pies and their consumption are associated with comfort and maternal protectiveness. As I write this, the hit US series *Desperate Housewives* has just completed its first run in the UK, and Nicole Kidman is set to star in a film adaptation of the 1960s television series, *Bewitched*. *Desperate Housewives* offers us several women who define their domestic roles quite differently; but most powerfully we are presented with a space which, even in 2005, is only 'visited' by men. Interestingly there remains a real romantic attachment to the image of the housewife, even though with that image goes the awareness of the awesome list of chores put before the housewife of the 1950s and 1960s. As demonstrated by the success of Lawson's cookery books, the emphasis is on appearance, rather than wholesale accomplishments, so that she shows the reader how to appear to be a dream housewife, while actually being a sloven.

Chick lit provides a post-feminist narrative of heterosex and romance for those who feel that they're too savvy to be duped by the most conventional romance narrative. It allows for the possibility of promiscuity, illicit sex, ordinariness, loss of dignity, and fallibility, along with all the aspirational features – whether it be clothing, interiors, or food. The humour is always of a self-deprecating kind – things go wrong for the chief characters, wild coincidences happen – but does it actually unseat or subvert the romantic core? The answer is that it uneasily celebrates romance while anatomizing the ways in which romance makes dupes of perfectly rational single women. I will investigate this double register in more detail in the following chapter, where I hope to demonstrate that chick lit has clear links with the tradition of the consciousness-raising novel in seeming to tell it like it is and to raise individual awareness of shared personal concerns through using observational humour and romantic situations. While the mode of confessional address adopted by feminist bestseller writers seems to have fallen out of favour for its rather gloomy view of heterosexual love, chick lit offers another take on the confession by the use of the diary format or the first-person narrative. The activist zeal of Second Wave feminists seemed to wane as they got older and the political upheavals and radical optimism of the 1960s became more distant. Chick lit is a genre of the young, with the eldest among these writers being in their mid-thirties at the time of writing, and the shape of the novels is to some extent dictated by the fact of this youth. The constant focus on the relationship or lack of it as central to the way the heroines define themselves might be explained in part by the age of these writers. In addition, unlike the consciousness-raising novelists whose humour is imbued with earnestness, these women purport to write for fun and for money and in easily digestible, pastel-coloured packages. The return to the confessional means that chick lit will also risk all the criticisms of artlessness which such writing attracts, but on the surface at least those writers who talk about their work seem happy enough not to be taken seriously. In fact some, from Fielding through to Jenny Colgan and Jane Green, practically insist that their work should not be taken seriously even when as a 'phenomenon' it has been taken very seriously indeed. Bridget Jones has risen out of the pages to become a kind of all-purpose folk heroine – or anti-heroine – to be the source of many a moral panic, or otherwise held up as telling us some kind of essential truth about women's lives today. Post-Fielding, these writers are torn between the representation of this genre as modish, lightweight, and 'froth' and making claims for their own work's relevance even while guilelessly accepting its 'trash' status.

Even while feminism is rarely explicitly acknowledged as the motivating force for the characters in such novels, it is acknowledged that such novels address issues of primary interest to women because their experiences of life are still markedly different from men's. Interviewed on the BBC's Bookworm programme, Fielding stated, 'single women today, sort of in their thirties, are perhaps a new type of woman that hasn't really got an identity. And that's all very worrying. Women have said to me: it [*Bridget Jones's Diary*] makes us feel that we're part of a club and we're not the only ones that feel stupid' (Fielding 2001). This acknowledgement of some form of identity crisis clearly echoes the feelings of women in the 1960s and 1970s as communicated through popular feminism;

and the idea that reading the novel will make these women feel part of a community suggests a longing for an inclusive female sphere of experience – this longing seems to be what chick lit can speak to in quite specific ways. Unfortunately, this revival of confessional writing and the acknowledgement of women as a group with shared and specific interests is not likely to prompt a heady renaissance of feminism along the lines of 1970s politics: chick lit seems to be built on an acknowledgement of the 'failure' of feminism and in each case 'empowered' women must find true self-determination through the right kind of men and some form of truce with their own family. It is as if because feminism seemed to support single life as one ideal in its celebration of autonomous identity, that chick lit is committed to showing the obverse – that the only happy ending to aimless singledom is coupledom of the quite traditional kind. Chick lit is, there-fore, an anxious genre. The flickers of recognition it creates in its readers are surely in part at least the shared recognition of the disempowered and disenfranchised, not least in the resent-ful acknowledgement by practically every chick lit heroine that men do not suffer the same relationship agonies as women do. It can only exist in the wake of a powerful wave of feminism and it is written by women who were brought up by those on the chalk face of the Second Wave.

Whereas bonkbusters depict women in control of their destiny and determined to forge their own path with or with-out men, chick lit heroines appear to wish to relinquish control. Like romantic fiction the genre is 'permeated with contradictory phantasies of being powerful and yet powerless, of possessing and not possessing, of having total control and no control whatsoever, of being passive and simultaneously active' (Treacher in Radstone 1988: 83). Overall there is a sense of stagnation around this generation of women, as if their indecisiveness has some common cause. For Susan Faludi, introducing the belief that there has been a backlash against feminism since the 1980s, 'the malaise and enervation that women are feeling today aren't induced by the speed of liber-ation but by its stagnation' (Faludi 1992: 79). For her, the posi-tive strides made by feminism have been diminished by one of the chief strategies of backlash ideology, which is to invent moral panics which halt the march of female equality and 'stir women's private anxieties and break their political wills' (Faludi 1992: 12). The association of 'true' femininity with emotional responsiveness, obsessiveness about the body and physical appearance, and charming flakiness seems hard to shake, and some women seem to be retreating to a celebration of these characteristics as a solution to this state of stagnation, which is terrifying because it reminds us of the deep associations between femininity and nature. The naturalness of the impulse to associate with the domestic and with the arena of feeling is explored again and again in chick lit, and its self-deprecating humour allows for a certain deflection of these impulses from feminist scrutiny and from the writer's own ambivalence about female identity today. As Elizabeth Wilson remarks, 'jokiness is a way of warding off anxiety' (Wilson 2001: 24), and it is interesting to speculate whether this is the most powerful motivation for the mixture of humour with romance in chick lit.

The reason *Bridget Jones's Diary* made such a powerful impact in wider cultural terms is that it is a book that constantly comments on itself. The diary possesses destabilizing meta-narratives found in the fact of its appropriation of the *Pride and Prejudice* plot and the celebration of its misuse of the conventions of the fictional diary format. This simultaneously allows for those who wish to see the truth about their lives reflected in Bridget unhampered to do so and for others to sense the unease of what 'being Bridget' means in broader social terms. I am not trying to say that readers who wholeheartedly identify with the character are hapless and naïve dupes – one of the most powerful features of chick lit as a genre is that it seeks that identification which doesn't simply come from empathy with the central female characters – but rather in understanding the world they inhabit, readers actually have to accept that women's lives are governed by quite different realities. While in the 1970s CR novel this realization allowed the reader to assess and critically appraise their own life and perhaps politicize their gendered identity, in chick lit the use of humour suggests that an appropriate response is a shoulder shrug of resignation, accompanied by the thrill of fantasizing that romance seeks out those who have given up on it.

Critics are torn between dismissing chick lit as pure comedy and fantasy and reflecting on women's lives today; equally, the readers of chick lit may be torn between a celebration of its disposability and the pleasures of knowing the genre will deliver the goods, set against a nagging feeling that something else reverberates within the huge success of these writings and their intertextual exchanges with chick flicks, television series, and even product placements (for example, in 2003 an advertisement for a detox kit marketed by the British company Boots featured a young woman using the same mode of telegrammatic speech adopted in Bridget's diary entries). As an academic and a feminist I find myself taking this stuff very seriously indeed and I'd like to think there's more to this than mere perversity or a spot of elegant slumming. When I first wrote about *Bridget Jones's Diary* in *Overloaded* I emphasized the means by which the celebration of Bridget as a character with a shelf-life far beyond the pages of the book foregrounds the power of 'post-feminist' discourses that situate feminism as the chief oppressor of women. I concluded, '*Bridget Jones* became a bestseller because women recognised within its irony their own experiences of popular culture, and especially the tensions between the lure of feminist politics and fear of losing one's femininity. This perception of the incompatibility of feminism with having a meaningful heterosexual relationship has unfortunately been perpetuated beyond reason to its current status as self-evident "truth"' (Whelehan 2000: 151). In the following chapter I would like to further explore the tensions raised by chick lit as it moves into the twenty-first century and consider its possible future mutations.

# 9

# Urban Sex

In the previous chapter, my main aim was to propose that while *Bridget Jones's Diary* came to be regarded as the defining chick lit novel, there were precursors which demonstrated that Fielding had merely tapped a nerve with her own writing which already existed. What emerged from Fielding's success was a more general tendency for young women to write popular fiction which stuck very closely to the conditions of their own lives and adopted a confessional tone of narration – first person, diaries, emails, or a mixture of all of these. Links to Bridget Jones remain in the work of chick litters moving into the millennium, but their work has also grown up and diversified, suggesting that if in the reception of *Bridget Jones's Diary* a 'genre' was identified, newer writers coming into the marketplace sought to expand it and incorporate wider aspects of female (and male) experience. In addition, whereas original chick lit writers (and readers) were in their twenties and thirties during the mid-1990s, many are now creeping into their thirties and forties, and the generational specificity of original chick lit is starting to broaden and blur.

In 2001, Beryl Bainbridge famously dubbed chick lit 'froth' and generated a small flurry of renewed interest in the genre. Here she is intent on making some distinction between the domain of the middle- and the lowbrow and in doing so implicitly suggests that writers such as herself have some claim to literariness, but that chick lit writers' work should simply be consigned to the trash can. Responses to Bainbridge range from the media's trying to get other women writers to say something provocative about chick lit (Jeanette Winterson was reported as saying that she loved *Bridget Jones*, while Doris Lessing hated it – see Ezard 2001) and featuring articles by chick lit writers mounting some kind of defence of their writings. Successful and media-savvy chick lit writer Jenny Colgan issued her own riposte to Beryl Bainbridge, basing her response on her suspicion that Bainbridge as a woman from an older generation simply had no understanding of what it is like to be a young woman in today's society – 'We really are the first generation who have grown up with education as a right; with financial independence; with living on our own and having far too many choices about getting married [. . .] having children [. . .] and hauling ourselves up through the glass ceiling' (Colgan 2001). This, taken with Fielding's more reflective comments, quoted in the previous chapter, about her work allowing readers to recognize shared female experiences, suggests that chick lit writers are aware that in writing about young women's lives they are usefully reflecting on the material context in which their actual readers feel they live. In addition to this chick lit, for Colgan, represents progress for aspiring women writers in signifying an increasing democratization of literature. She is aware that the epithet is seen as synonymous with trashy disposable fiction and that the writers suffer some pressure from publishers, driving them towards a degree of homogeneity in their desire to produce more of the same that sells. Nonetheless, some of the best-known novelists, such as Jane Green, Lisa Jewell, Marian Keyes, Adele Parks, and of course Jenny Colgan have capitalized on their own success as individual authors to experiment to some degree. In some cases this has been effected not only by the inclusion of topics that would have previously been seen as anathema to the genre, but also by the themes so central to the form having become darker and more reflective (Neustatter 2002).

Chick lit has even started referring to itself. In Marian Keyes's *The Other Side of the Story* (2004), of the three central characters two women write bestselling works of fiction and the other is a high-flying literary agent. The story is divided between their three points of view and, given that two are ex-best friends and the other is their literary agent, there is an opportunity to tell the same stories from parallel points of view and reflect on how the ego interpolates motivations and emotions that are simply not apparent to other participants in life's dramas. Lily Wright's book *Mimi's Remedies* becomes an immediate success, despite the fact that some critics are repelled by its sugary sweetness and the magical element which has a woman miraculously curing people's relationship problems. As Lily says of the book, which she wrote while pregnant and after she had been mugged, 'I was going to write a story where everyone lived happily ever after, in a fictional world where good things happened and people were kind' (Keyes 2004: 24). An early review of Lily's book allows Keyes further playful intertexuality – 'Jonesin'? Bum too Big? Tattoo gone septic? Then Doctor Flash! Recommends that you sling on your Jimmy Choos, get down to your nearest bookstore and treat yourself to *Mimi's Remedies*' (Keyes 2004: 276). This review comprises references to some of the stock features of chick lit/flicks as a kind of product placement, but Keyes's novel also acts as a defence against accusations about the homogenization of chick lit, given that the three authors who are featured in the novel (one subsidiary character is also an author) are shown to have quite different strengths. It is only Lily who endures (to be nominated for the Orange Prize for her more 'serious' second novel), while Gemma's novel is seen very much as parasitic on her experiences of her parents splitting up for a time, suggesting that in the case of chick lit fiction only imitates life; and once Gemma's life takes a turn for the better, her creative ambitions dry up.

What is particularly striking in this latest offering of Keyes is how much detail is spent on showing the domestic strife each woman has to endure while maintaining her professional identity. Gemma has to effectively move in with her mother when her father leaves her for another woman. She faces enormous difficulty getting her mum to become more independent while she continues her job as an events organizer, as well as trying to conduct a relationship of her own. Lily has a young child and her partner Anton is unsuccessful in his attempt to pitch new television shows, so that she feels the pressure to maintain her breadwinning role by writing a follow-up novel as profitable as her first. However, she fails to get sales and loses her house, which ultimately jeopardizes her relationship. Jojo, the literary agent, is conducting an affair with her married boss, and this relationship eventually comes into conflict with her professional ambitions when she is a candidate for partnership – not least because her lover, Mark, votes against her candidature. Even where men like Anton are depicted sympathetically as supportive and caring, they are also portrayed as having simpler life choices than women. Jojo's lover remains with his wife after she ends their affair and although he claims to still be in love with Jojo he seems to be unable to leave the comfort of his marriage and children, or indeed to understand his wife's pain at the discovery of his infidelity. Women in these books produced in a mature phase of chick lit aren't necessarily dippy or feckless: they're efficient and directed and even when they're positioned as antagonists to other women, it is clear that they understand them.

There has been some discussion that chick has 'grown up', mainly because of the arrival of so-called 'mumlit' – effectively the natural sequel to chick lit where the singleton grows up, settles down, and has her babies. While mumlit has a clear precursor in Maeve Haran's *Having it All*, discussed earlier, it is usually the case that the stories of women having babies are mixed with narratives about single women so that the narrative works on a continuum of young female experiences. In mumlit, instead of the skirts tucked into underwear or numerous culinary disasters, there is the toy in the handbag or the mad taxi dash to a nativity play in the middle of a key executive meeting. The self-deprecating humour remains a consistent feature and the long descriptions of the schizophrenia of having a child and a job are told with a weary fondness, as if to attach too much seriousness would be to enter into a more chaotic and dangerous realm of human experience. But mumlit inevitably beckons to more serious topics through the depiction of the ways in which women suddenly have little choice about their destinies when the realities of childcare set in. Some seem to tend towards a conservative view of working motherhood: Katharine Reddy in *I Don't Know How She Does It* (2002), like Liz Ward from *Having it All*, gives up her high-powered job to save her relationship and salve her sense of guilt about the lack of time she has for her kids. She moves to Derbyshire, like Liz exchanging the city for the country, and offers wisdoms on motherhood that would bring grief to any single-minded career woman. Remembering her carefully orchestrated quality time with her daughter, she reflects, '[y]ou just have to be around when it happens' (Pearson 2002: 350) and while she is tempted to go back into business by her sister, who works at a doll's house manufacturer that is being repossessed, the ending is suitably open about whether or not she takes this on. The suspicion is that she does, but that this time she works around her home life and on her own terms in a utopian moment where the job fits itself snugly around the life. Katharine's equally high-flying friend Candy, who accidentally falls pregnant, ends up giving up her career and starting up a mail-order sex toys business at home. The possibility of working from home to one's own timetable seems to be the nearest these women can get to mounting a challenge to the crippling work schedules of the professions and the expectation that children come second.

The fact that almost all of these women drop out of the rat race despite their clear talents in their professions suggests the weary acknowledgement that feminism would never succeed in socializing the workplace or in implicating men in childcare responsibilities as fully as women. Kate's idyllic life in the country and Candy's efficient home mail-order business are reminiscent of the mommy convert Diane Keaton in her role in *Baby Boom* (1987), but what is more memorable about the film is the way that Keaton's character is unsympathetically portrayed until she accepts her motherly responsibilities and starts to consider the child first. It seems that in chick lit, like Hollywood, there is no benign way to present the career woman, since all these texts, conservative or otherwise, vividly depict the incompatibility of motherhood and work; yet the novels seem to offer implicit critiques of the system that treats women who reproduce with contempt. The Epilogue to *I Don't Know How She Does It* offers a mildly politicized reading of this conflict, recognizing the sheer waste of female talent and drive where jobs are inflexible enough to not be able to incorporate individual demands. Much as Kate is seen to celebrate the pleasures of time at a slower pace with her kids, she also notes that after one coffee morning too many she is 'bored to the point of manslaughter' (Pearson 2002: 351). These conditional endings successfully demonstrate the frustrations of the career woman and the ways in which guilt effectively ends their commitment to their own self-advancement, while showing that characters like Kate simply can't stop striving beyond the confines of the domestic and the inference is that they never will. Such novels show, depressingly, that there is no solution to the work/motherhood dilemma. At least for the singleton there is the gloss of the romance, however ironically narrated; mumlit presents problems less easy to shrug off with a little whimsical humour, and the fact that these mums never do stop thinking about work as effectively denaturalizes the link between female destiny and full-time motherhood as does Marilyn French's vivid portrayal of suburban women awash with dirty nappies and squalling kids.

If mumlit has a different tone to chick lit, it is a more anguished one where the actualities of long-term relationships and the transition to parenthood pose thorny problems and necessary sacrifices. Partnered and settled, these women find that men are now part of the problem and that monogamy, which implicitly underpins the chick lit narrative, is hard work. Kate Reddy always regrets she didn't sleep with an American business associate, teasingly named Jack Ablehammer, and characterizes her drunken flirtatious evening with him as 'the best sex I never had' (Pearson 2002: 349). There are moments when the sentiments expressed in these books collide with those of the feminist bestsellers, not least because, in many cases, the narrative journey is primarily emotional. Through it, she comes to understand the limits placed upon her as a woman. The contemporary answer to encountering such obstacles is to find a very individual way round them, rather than rail against the system, but what is the reader to make of these new kinds of open ending? The ending to I Don't Know How She Does It allows the possibility of a dual reading, but is ultimately conservative. Talking about a mother's relationship to her children, Kate remarks, '[t]heir need for me is like the need for water or light: it has a devastating simplicity. It doesn't fit any of the theories about what women are supposed to do with their lives: theories written in books by women who never had children, or had children but brought them up as I mostly bring up mine – by Remote Access' (Pearson 2002: 165). This intimate connection that is so tied to notions of biological ineffability was a connection that feminism problematized but could not sever – to be the mother and therefore the most needed was to be in a position of power even when it contributed to women's powerlessness; and men's capacity to take over all of women's roles is humorously debated, but dismissed with a semi-essentialist finality –

'women carry the puzzle of family life in their heads, they just do' (Pearson 2002: 190).

More and more of these novels have a fundamental moral or ethical question positioned at their centre and despite the whimsy of the endings and the inevitable humour, sometimes this very contemporaneity remains with the reader. Adele Parks's *Game Over* (2001) is fascinating in this respect, because although it combines the stock features of chick lit – successful young woman working in the media, close friends, family ties – it also does something interesting with the formula in the way it depicts the heroine forced to take a hard look at the lifestyle she adopts, and in particular her involvement in the production of reality-style television shows which depend on humiliation of members of the public. Interestingly, Cas (Jocasta) Perry's idea is to produce a programme which actually encourages people on the verge of marriage to be unfaithful with an old flame. *Sex with an Ex* recruits people who suspect that their future partner still harbours feelings for an ex and engineers situations where the partner and the ex are thrown together for the specific purpose of tempting the partner into having sex. The thrust of the show is that the fact of his or her infidelity can then be broadcast on television while each of the three protagonists – suspicious person, their partner, and the ex – looks on in a *Jerry Springer*-style set-up. Cas is portrayed as someone who, unlike her friend Issie, is uninterested in marriage or indeed in relationships, and oper- ates on the principle that given the chance people will be unfaithful to their partner. At another level this programme is her revenge on her father, who left her and her mother when she was seven. It is readily embraced by her production company and becomes an instant ratings success, but because of it she suffers huge disapprobation at the hands of her family and friends. The movement of the novel towards its conclu- sion is to some degree the progression of Cas from scepticism towards to belief in love and monogamy. The novel gradually challenges and questions whether Cas is really happy being serially promiscuous and avoiding relationships, with the key challenge in the form of Darren, an 'ex' who refuses to partic- ipate in the programme by tempting his former girlfriend away from her fiancé.

The inevitable romance between Darren and Cas is

hampered by Cas's refusal to believe in relationships and finally by a decision to marry her best friend as insulation against her feelings for Darren. Her own idea is thrown back at her when she unwittingly stars in the final programme of *Sex with an Ex* as her colleagues set up a meeting with Darren. The usual chick lit triangle of heroine, Mr Right, and Mr Maybe is replayed, with Cas in danger of losing both men and having to come to terms with the consequences of her own lack of belief in true love and marriage. In addition, the assumed glamour of the media, so often exploited in chick lit as shorthand for excitement and success, is here exposed as cut-throat, superficial, and immoral. To be thoroughly morally cleansed, Cas must move on from this world and her departure from this job becomes symbolic of her growing moral maturity. Stripped of her career and down among the dinosaurs in the Natural History Museum, Cas encounters Darren:

> Over the last few days I've lost everything: both my fiancés – one my love, the other my best friend, my job, my privacy and now my reason. I've been cheated, deceived and humiliated. I've felt despair and loneliness and regret.
> I take stock.
> All that and I still believe in love (Parks 2001: 373).

Darren has come to represent the functional family in the form of his large working-class Northern family, who are shown to be supportive, intrusive, but fundamentally loving. With them he is shown to be entirely himself, and the experience of 'real' family life begins to heal the scars of Cas's early experiences of a broken home. The journey of the narrative, in common with Mills & Boon romances where the heroine takes stock by experiencing the life of the man she loves, is that a glimpse into his life makes her look askance at her own. He provides the moral education and she must make the leap and the sacrifice, which she does, and this allows her to forge a compromise between their two viewpoints – which is effectively a full professional sacrifice on her part.

In common with most other works of chick lit, *Game Over* seems on the surface to provide a refreshing antidote to the sugary coating of the classic romance narrative in an exposé of the truth behind the myths of ideal femininity. In Cas's evaluation of her body, she observes,

> I'm very thin and fit. Whenever anyone asks me how I manage this I smile and say it's genetic and effortless. This is, of course, bollocks, but I know that if there is anything more annoying than a thin woman, it's a thin woman who professes that she never diets (Parks 2001: 83).

Here, this deliberate fallacy is presented as a conspiracy among women: we know how difficult it is to achieve and maintain the 'ideal' figure and therefore we present excuses for ourselves and contribute to the mythification of the feminine ideal. It is only in the novels which explore pregnancy and childbirth that women's bodies can be legitimately let go and where physical deterioration is discussed with a perverse relish – 'it was a depressing day when I could no longer button my jeans all the way to the top, but it was nothing on today. Today I couldn't tug them past my knees' (Parks 2002: 103).

Lisa Jewell experiments with exploring male points of view in both *Ralph's Party* (2001) and *A Friend of the Family* (2003), and this means that for substantial parts of the novel women are positioned as to be scrutinized, admired, but rarely understood. In *A Friend of the Family* this predominance of the male viewpoint also takes place in a very family-centred environment, with the mum Bernie and her husband Gerry and three grown-up sons – Tony (a businessman), Ned (the youngest, who has gone to live in Australia then comes back early on during the narrative), and Sean (middle son and a bestselling writer). Bernie meets Gervase in a pub where she sings and he becomes part of the family, much to the annoyance of the sons; however, he reveals himself to be some kind of seer who addresses individual's dissatisfactions and poses solutions to their problems. While Marian Keyes's depiction of Lily writing the magical *Mimi's Remedies* seems a far cry from what we have come to understand as chick lit, there seems to be even a more persistent strand where magic and wish-fulfillment come to be central features. This is a novel where the parents are happy, but the children need some relationship guidance. The characters themselves make intertextual references to stock chick lit features in casual utterances, so that Sean's girlfriend Millie, newly pregnant, refers to her old self as, 'Classic singleton. I've been preparing myself with all the essential accoutrements for my inevitable lonely destiny. Even had a gay best friend lined up . . .' (Jewell 2003: 169).

Sean's second novel proves to be the novel of his recent life, as he rails against the unexpected pregnancy of his new partner –

It was going to be a paean to men the world over in thrall to the power of woman's ability to reproduce and hence make the most important decisions in the world . . . Western women, the very women who complained most about male oppression, about equal rights, about "fairness", were also the most strident in their right to decide whether or not to bring a child into a relationship and into the world (Jewell 2003: 196).

If this is a work of lad lit contained within the pages of a chick lit novel, it speaks of a yawning gap between the way women and men understand their lives and motivations; but the radical potential of such a searing critique of women, with its suggestion that women have some kind of power over men and that men might be experiencing some kind of crisis, is not pursued here. The men generally prove themselves to be just as committed to relationships and romance as the women and the novel ends in predictable chick lit style, which doesn't just offer a happy resolution to the lovers but ends with traditional social events such as weddings or christenings. In this case it is with the 40th anniversary of Gerry and Bernie's first date, celebrated with all the family around them.

In light of Lola Young's observation that British women's writing only aired the most 'piddling' matters, it seems appropriate to affirm that chick lit is indeed quite narrow and might be construed as dwelling on the trivial and the quotidian. But this very mundanity is also what in part recalls the legacy of earlier feminist novels such as *The Women's Room*, which makes the repetition of the women's lives an organic part of the structure of the novel. This focus on the ordinary is also reminiscent of the substance of early feminist criticism, which asked for authentic images of women to counter the perniciousness of those which were blazoned across billboards and magazines. These images in chick lit are held to be authentic because they provoke in the reader a response of recognition; but are there times when we are duped into 'recognizing' as authentic something which is entirely manufactured? Perhaps our recognition is of the images, trends, and valued behaviours which we are accustomed to prizing and internalizing, rather than those which give us access to truths about women's lives. Undoubtedly the latter aspiration is unobtainable, and yet we still seek authenticity to tell us something more searching about ourselves. The aspirational elements of these novels also expose their limited commitment to realism and mean that the introduction of fate, magic, or other means of arriving at wish-fulfilment are extraordinarily compatible with the form. This balance between empathetic realism and aspirational glamour is achieved in different ways depending on the author, but essentially we revisit the anxieties about how we match up to these other 'normal' women depicted. The body looms large in all of this and sometimes the body *is* large, at least to begin with – for example, Daisy in Louise Bagshawe's *The Devil You Know*, 'started to lose more weight, without noticing it. She was too busy to think about eating and quite often she'd grab a Boots Shapers sandwich for lunch, not because it was lo-cal, but just because it was there. And fast. The last few pounds of puppy fat were melting from her thighs [. . .] As she dropped the weight and started to like herself a little, Daisy found she was making more money' (Bagshawe 2003: 203). Here Daisy's weight loss is intimately tied to her developing success: she is only rewarded when she is thin. There is no space for large girls in chick lit except at the beginning of novels waiting for their makeover, as in this novel or in Jane Green's *Jemima J*. There's a cynicism in Bagshawe's novel, an awareness of the injustice that pretty girls make more money waitressing, but the novel's capacity to reward or punish types of behaviour manifested by different characters gives us an insight into the real moral core of the text.

The endings themselves turn against the more eccentric features of the novels by seeming to endorse the most conventional values even when the characters have up to that point seemed unconventional or challenging. It's not that one expects anything but the pairing-off of at least one romantic lead, but it is the means by which this has to be achieved which can frustrate. At the end of Marian Keyes's *Sushi for Beginners*, Lisa the classic career woman has to return to her working-class roots and learn to value her family before she can remarry her ex-husband – 'No sneaking away to Vegas this time – no, they do it properly' (Keyes 2001: 562). Ashling the 'ordinary' one is rewarded by the love of her charismatic boss, who encourages her to cast off all her anxieties by tossing her handbag into the sea (after removing her credit cards and on his promise he'd buy her a new one because this one was 'old and mank'); Clodagh the beautiful perfect married mother loses her husband after she has an affair with Ashling's boyfriend and ends up with neither friend nor husband in punishment for disobeying the 'rules'. At the end of Jane Green's *Babyville*, meanwhile, one of the main characters Julia announces her pregnancy to Samantha who then agrees to be 'the best godmother the world has ever seen!' (Green 2002: 456); Mel in Colgan's *Amanda's Wedding* gets her man on the verge of his wedding to her controlling friend Amanda; Clara Hutt in Knight's *My Life on a Plate* (2000) cements her new relationship at the fourth wedding of her mother. Weddings, birthings, and returns to the bosom of the family are all too often the substance of the endings of such novels, even when the implication of the rest of the novel has been that for young women with means and style there is an infinite number of possibilities beyond marital felicity and the nuclear family. Within the tight constraints of this kind of resolved ending there are much wider and more challenging concerns, with issues such as gender politics in the workplace, female rivalry/friendship, homelessness, poverty, eating disorders, mental illnesses, marital breakup and stress. Although at times these issues threaten to take over the centre of the novel they are generally defused by the humour and the momentum of the central romance plot, instead painted as part of the trials of everyday life – just as we have become accustomed to all manner of relationship, family, and emotional dysfunction being paraded in front of us on daytime television.

Jenny Colgan's oft-quoted defence of chick lit suggests that contemporary women needed a new form to encapsulate the very specific life experiences of their generation. Writing in response to Beryl Bainbridge's assertion that all of chick lit is 'froth', her rejoinder is, '[g]rowing up in the 1980s all we had to read if we wanted commercial fiction were these thick, shiny brick novels covered in gold foil in which women with long blonde hair built up business empires from harsh beginnings using only their extraordinary beauty and occasionally some goldfish. Is it really any wonder we fell on Helen Fielding so desperately?' (Colgan 2001) If chick lit is really a reaction to the bonkbuster, which was itself a movement away from the disarmingly confessional feminist novel of the 1970s, it isn't really clear from this what Colgan thinks chick litters are railing against, though I suspect what she voices is an utter weariness with the myth of competence displayed by the classic bonkbuster career woman and a more cynical refusal to accept that women can have it all. As Katharine Viner muses, 'maybe women feel a bit useless themselves, or perhaps because we're not offered anything else' (Viner in Walter 1999: 24). Certainly there is some substance to the idea that chick lit is a celebration of uselessness and even now it's known more for its shared ingredients rather than for the individual quirks of its authors, so that for most people it means, 'a "fun" pastel-covered novel with a young, female, city-based protagonist, who has a kooky best friend, an evil boss, romantic troubles and a desire to find the One – the apparently unavailable man who is good-looking, can cook and is both passionate and considerate in bed' (Thomas 2002). These protagonists are, it is true, often hapless and lacking personal direction, but more than this chick lit celebrates the fact that in spite of their hopelessness they are swept up in the resurgence of good, honest romance narratives. As Lillian Robinson remarked in her celebration of 'trash' nearly thirty years ago, 'female readers do not seek out trashy novels in order to escape or to experience life vicariously, but rather to receive confirmation, and, eventually, affirmation, that love really is what motivates and justifies a woman's life' (Robinson 1978: 222).

Of course, feminism never killed off the tendency to romance narrative in writing by women and, as John Sutherland has pointed out, the Women's Movement and its novels arguably gave way to an increased appetite for 'romance' – particularly the more explicit and masochistic bodice rippers which 'exploited the new permissiveness'

(Sutherland 1981: 85). Romance in the CR novel is fused with sexual desire and yet these novels simultaneously expose romance as the destroyer of female sexual pleasures: so often the narration of the young woman's adolescence shows how she comes to accept her desires as secondary to men's in exchange for the promise of romantic love. The CR novels of the 1970s saw this period in a woman's life as essential to the narrative shape of the *Bildungsroman* and intrinsic to the ways in which her life since that point is moulded; the concern most centrally is with how the girl becomes a woman and how the processes of socialization, beyond the individual choices the woman makes, dictate the direction of her future life. Chick lit, on the other hand seems more intent on showing how the girl remains inside the woman, to some extent only partly formed and wary of decisions which could change lives. We come to her in her mid-twenties or thirties with little idea of her adolescent sexual experience, though perhaps being introduced to her childhood girlfriends. With reason, this perspective, which focuses so much on the travails of the single woman's life, is often seen as vacuous and self-centred and even absurdly inward-looking; but then this is what it takes from the tradition of romantic fiction, which depicts women as only half-formed until they acknowledge their love for the man. As Modleski and others have observed, the quest for love in the romance narrative acts as a symbolic return to the moment of unconditional love associated with the bond between infant and mother, and crucially at some point in the Mills & Boon novel the hero will be seen to perform some 'maternal' duty for the heroine, confirming his love. Although such features may also be present in chick lit, the mother herself also often takes centre stage in an apparent acknowledgement that the mother's continuing role in the life of the heroine is as crucial as the romance itself.

Underneath the quest narrative of many feminist protagonists in the 1970s CR novels there also remains a thirst for romance – and this goes very much against the grain of the feminist writings of the time. As Katherine Payant observes, 'despite the debunking of romantic love found in feminist non-fiction, most of the heterosexual protagonists of the 1970s never give up on the possibility of love between the sexes' (Payant 1993: 32). In the most successful novels of the 1970s, such as *Fear of Flying* and *Kinflicks*, it is the mother who emerges as the most powerful (though not always most positive) force in the heroine's life – often in the face of romantic failure. Chick litters may not want to 'have it all' in the style of the bonkbuster heroine, but they do want it all in emotional terms – the romance with the candid observational truthtelling, the reflections on the trials and tribulations of a woman's life with the desire to believe that there is something more than this around the corner. There are links here with the popular feminist fiction of the 1970s, which usually ended with the women on the verge of a new quest armed with selfbelief, but whereas such women are left assuredly alone, the chick litters are laughing all the way down the aisle or its equivalent. Both genres are testament to the fact that the woman question continues to be asked. The worst that can be said of chick lit (and I've said this myself) is that it excises feminism for the empty promises of free-market capitalism; more interestingly, we can look to this million-selling genre in order to reflect back to the questions Second Wave feminism became unable to answer around relationships, sexuality, and romantic love. Ultimately, chick lit is a celebration of stasis on the grounds that for each of their heroines 'things can only get better'. As singletons they rail against the politics of dating etiquette, but end up paired off in a constant re-enactment of the myth that true love seeks you out.

Desire is also at the heart of these texts, but it moves beyond that of sexual desire to a wider desire to have all one's cravings fulfilled: thus the novels are redolent with conspicuous consumption, whether it be of male bodies or of designer goods. For Deborah Philips, '[t]hese are novels written for young women who are skilled and experienced in contemporary discourses of consumption; their design suggests that they are clearly targeted at the readers of such consumer and lifestyle publications as *Elle* and *Marie Claire*' (Philips 2000: 240). The desire for things as well as for The One become hopelessly muddled together, so that too often the central protagonist is so busy itemizing the qualities of the ideal man, as if he were the perfect product, that she fails to see him lurking under her nose. The way men are depicted in chick lit speaks to one of Second Wave feminism's gaping conceptual gaps and one only addressed in the CR novels: how do you square your feminism with your desire for men? The men in CR novels were variously demonized, pilloried, and picked at, but they were also men in transition baffled by the swift changes in sexual politics. Sex in CR novels is often unfulfilling or abortive (remembering particularly Adrian Goodlove's inability to achieve a full erection with Isadora Wing). Chick lit, however, is notably coy about sex, yet men seem to experience no problems performing or satisfying their women, suggesting another unheralded legacy of feminism as well as the 'sexual revolution' – they now know their way around women's bodies. However, this coyness becomes suspicious, ultimately – are women so completely satisfied with the sex they're getting or would the depiction of troubled sex be too strident, too feminist?

While for the most part you can separate chick lit from bonkbusters by the inertia of the heroines of the former, novels such as Candace Bushnell's *Sex and the City* (1996) present more obviously high-achieving women, 'who have as much money and power as men' (Bushnell 1997: 41) and whose lives are supremely well organized. Instead, New York is itself presented as the obstacle to romance –

When it comes to finding a marriage partner, New York has its own particularly cruel mating rituals, as complicated and sophisticated as those in an Edith Wharton novel. Everyone knows the rules – but no one wants to talk about them. The result is that New York has bred a particular type of single woman – smart, attractive, successful, and . . . never married. She is in her later thirties or early forties, and, if empirical knowledge is good for anything, she probably never will get married (Bushnell 1997: 25).

The novel is episodic and fragmentary, partly due to its origins as a weekly newspaper column in the *New York Observer* between 1994 and 1996, and the point of the ending is not to draw threads together, but to represent the New York dating scene as cyclical, with the same clutch of bachelors circulating around the same venues with the same lines in seduction. Carrie, Miranda, Charlotte, and Samantha all feature, but not in the tight friendship network they have in the television adaptation. In reality, this work of fiction has very little in common with any contemporary British chick lit, except that subtextually the women are all shown to be desperate to have a meaningful relationship. Men are represented as types, sometimes to the point of having no proper name at all, like Mr Big and Mr Marvellous, and are to a large extent grotesques, whom the women, when they meet together, bitch about and show open contempt for.

It is of course the television series, started in 1998, which has invited the link with *Bridget Jones's Diary* and *Ally McBeal* and which marks off the most eminent singleton triumvirate while representing the cross-fertilization of popular culture from newspaper column, to novel, to popular television. But, as Deborah Siegal notes, although the actors of *Sex and the City* are fêted as female role models, they are at pains to distance themselves from the lifestyles of these characters, often emphasizing their own settled relationships, featuring husbands and homes. She notes the link between this seeming celebration of the single life on screen and the denial, by the real life status of the actors, of it as a viable reality. Just as I identified earlier that the power of Helen Gurley Brown's book on singleness is the power of her assertion that she managed to marry well against all the odds, Siegel also concludes, '[t]oday, as in Brown's day, the liberated Single Girl remains larger than, and somehow outside of, life as we know it' (Siegel 2002). The excitement generated by the television series *Sex and the City* in its first couple of seasons was located in the way these women seemed to value their jobs and their friendships as well as enjoying all the social aspects of being single, even when they were sporadically dating. But by the last series the darker side of 'real' life has kicked in, having Sam battling cancer, Charlotte infertility, Miranda the pressures of a young child, and for Carrie the desperate need to make it happen with Mr Big. Carrie gets her romantic resolution, but all in all the women are portrayed as careworn and a little too old to be out on the circuit any more. Bushnell, in the novel, similarly points out the absurd lives that some of the single women she depicts lead, portraying them as trapped or at the whim of serially monogamous men. For all the novel's queer politics, it comes over finally as a straight endorsement of the classic romance.

The chick lit authors more often than not now include in

their biographical notes the fact that they are married and/or have children and this somehow contributes to the sense that singleness 'after the age of thirty is not pleasant and when you're tipping thirty-five it is distinctly uncomfortable' (Parks 2002: 68), unless you confidently know it to be a fun interlude before settling down. The chick litters and the mum-litters are beginning to take themselves more seriously, and 'darker' themes are beginning to pervade the genre. Beyond the humour and calamitous events which befall the heroine, there are few chick novels narrated free of any sense of emotional pain. In the work of writers such as Marian Keyes, for instance, there is mental illness, alcoholism, and marital breakups, and many writers depict the need for some kind of resolution of family tensions. This might well lead us to conclude that chick lit, for all its 'frothiness', teaches us about life. Writers like Jong and French offered scenarios to their readers for them to respond to by recognizing the closeness of some of the issues to the problems in their own lives. They were intended to generate discussion and they aroused strong negative feelings in some feminist commentators for their acceptance that their emotional life was going to be the toughest to straighten out in feminist terms. More than thirty-five years later chick lit generates discussion, but this time because on the surface it refuses to take itself seriously. There is no political intent as there was at the heart of the consciousness-raising novels – even those that were disowned by the Women's Movement because their writers were seen as limelight-seeking self-publicists. Here, feminist politics is the merest ghostly presence, haunting discussions which touch on equal opportunities or the distribution of domestic chores between the sexes; it anxiously and vociferously marks out its difference from sexual politics by its greedy embracing of the classic romance narrative.

In the 1970s novels, femininity was a burdensome construct, fetishized by men but often denied any essence by the chief female protagonists. By the 1980s and the bonkbuster, femininity is in crisis, presented in ways that make it its own parody – in the popular television serial *Dynasty*, a form of bonkbuster for the small screen, actors like Joan Collins are so exaggeratedly costumed in female attire that they appear to be to all intents and purposes in 'drag'. Femininity was exaggerated to neutralize the overt masculinity of the roles that such high-achieving businesswomen occupied and some of this anxiety about displaying femininity has been appropriated within chick lit and popular culture to the point where feminine trappings have again become fetishized and naturalized as common objects of desire – for example, Carrie's love affair with shoes and bras in *Sex and the City*; chick lit protagonists boasting about the uncomfortableness of their shoes or the general impracticality of their clothing. In the chick lit universe where women no longer cook or keep house, they are still curiously self-aware of sexual difference and summon the most stereotypical and conflictual qualities supposedly displayed by women: so they're shown as dizzy and chaotic in their personal lives, yet highly organized and responsible in their professional careers. These books are asking for a feminist appraisal not just because they have, unusually for popular fiction, raised a significant number of critics' hackles, but because nowadays feminist criticism of fiction is more ready to turn its gaze to all aspects of popular culture in ways that allow us to explore further why there is a new upsurge of interest in the romance narrative across media. Is chick lit a sign of the new democratization of the literary and publishing world, as Jenny Colgan asserts? Either way, it isn't that we choose to take chick lit more seriously than it allegedly intends, but that modern feminism is still a recent enough event to nudge us into questioning why so many young women seem to feel its central precepts are worthless to them. This is why it is important that feminist criticism concern itself with popular manifestations of women's lives, in order to challenge a common acceptance that these depictions get to the heart of women's real feelings; or that their lives could not be otherwise.

The focus on the everyday and mundane in chick lit and the sweetly achieveable ambitions to take oneself in hand are perhaps less a recognition of ourselves and more a recognition of cultural trends which we are accustomed to seeing prized. Weddings, birthings, and returns to the blood family are a feature of chick lit endings and no degree of ironic knowingness on the narrator's part detracts from the fact that, in common with Helen Gurley Brown, this celebration of single life can only be comfortably done from the safe vantage point of the comfortably coupled. We can be heartened that the harsh criticisms of contemporary chick lit are not new to women's writing and as far back as 1974 Rosalind Miles was lamenting the 'colour supplement superficiality and meaningless behaviour' of heroines populating novels by the likes of A. S. Byatt and Margaret Drabble, commenting, '[t]he increasing use of the world of communications – television, journalism, advertising – as something attractive and desirable, has become a thumping cliché of the modern novel' (Miles 1974: 193). Certainly chick lit is populated by women working in the media or PR and the very fact of holding such a job, rather than any detailed description about what they actually do in it, is signposted as shorthand for glamour and achievements so that their disastrous personal lives don't make us write them off as dismally pathetic. Miles disliked what she saw as the focus on the minutiae of women's lives because she felt that women writers should look outwards beyond the constraints of the 'I'; presumably, she would find much of chick lit equally self-regarding and unimaginative in its naïve use of the first-person narrative as a means of forging the necessary intimacy for the reader to act as confidante.

The romance dimension to these texts is equally important because romance fiction 'speaks to, and satiates, conscious and unconscious needs of love and relationships to be simple, clear and yet passionate' (Treacher in Radstone 1988: 78), and chick litters seem to envy a previous generation for what they see as simplicity in a context where women had fewer choices. Certainly the reprise of the Mills & Boon style romance narrative suggests a huge degree of nostalgia for romance enacted against the backdrop of retrogressive gender identities. Romance is framed, with mothers and families looming in the background, representing nothing more than the knowledge that their daughters are reassuringly identical to them in a celebration of continuity and stasis quite opposed to the perceived need in the CR novels for the women to break with their mothers altogether.

In 1963 Betty Friedan observed, with some bafflement,

It is more than a strange paradox that as all professions are finally open to women in America, 'career woman' has become a dirty word; that as higher education becomes available to any woman with the capacity for it, education for women has become so suspect that more and more drop out of high school and college to marry and have babies [. . .] why with the removal of all the legal, political, economic, and educational barriers that once kept woman from being man's equal, a person in her own right, an individual free to develop her own potential, should she accept this new image which insists she is not a person but a 'woman', by definition barred from the freedom of human existence and voice in human destiny?' (Friedan 1982: 60)

Friedan is here specifically referring to the magazine soft-sell that encourages highly educated women to believe that the performance of femininity and life within the home took precedence over any kind of self-definition. A whole generation of women were inspired enough by Friedan's observations to take part in more or less active ways in a feminist swell that would shake some pretty tenacious patriarchal foundations. Forty years on, chick litters lament the fact that in spite of the control of their fertility and a multitude of reproductive choices and despite a real grasp of their independence in material terms, they are still not happy. Presumably, change has not happened in the way women thought it should, in that it has happened despite the great reluctance of institutions to change and despite the fact that domestic arrangements have still to be managed by women. There is instead accompanying guilt and often sheer fatigue, depicted so well in mumlit.

So how does one write cheerfully of women's successes in moving forward in the public sphere while showing any kind of progress in the private? Writing about the Mills & Boon Temptation series launched in 1985 to provide more sexually explicit romance stories and also those more in tune with the 1980s career woman, Nickianne Moody observes, 'texts that appear to be about a new level of sexual permissiveness for women are actually concerned with the "seductions" of marriage and domesticity. Romantic fantasy is thus purposefully incorporated into *domestic fantasy* and readers are shown a "new" sequence of sexual, professional and family negotiations' (Moody in Pearce and Wisker 1998: 154). But beyond the chick lit ending, where one man is able to make our heroine happy and to accept the fact she can't cook, buys too many shoes, or is in denial about her humble origins, there is a palpable dissatisfaction with heterosex and male relationship attitudes. Rather than come to the radical feminist conclusion that romance is dead and sex a power struggle, these writers makeshift a tolerable ending which tries to be ironic about the inevitability of marriage at the end. Of course, they're too savvy to be duped by the most conventional romance narrative, so this must be the 'post-feminist' reflection on love. As a result, these books celebrate a woman's difference from all other women, even though the success of the chick lit market is to take infinite repetitions of the same broad plot and therefore suggest, as feminists did for different reasons, that women's lives are fundamentally the same. The genre is, of course, a dynamic one, as genres always 'represent a set of conventions whose parameters are redrawn with each new book and each new reader' (Carr 1989: 7); but so far the sentiments expressed at the conclusion of these books have yet to explicitly voice these dissatisfactions with men so palpable elsewhere within the novel.

# Conclusion

Jenny Colgan, one of the most vocal defenders of chick lit and its writers, argued at the 2003 Edinburgh Book Festival that the term chick lit is being used as a catch-all category to embrace a certain kind of popular literature which can then be casually dismissed. She is particularly caustic about 'hairy legged' critics, whom she sees as leading the vanguard of this trivialization of the fiction (Gibbons 2003), while she seems to ignore the machinations of publishers who brand and homogenize such work by the use of packaging and marketing. It is fascinating that a young woman so conscious of the negative effects of over-generalized categorization should resort to one of the most well-known put-downs against feminism – second only to 'bra-burner' – used over the past thirty-five years. She need not use the word feminism in her riposte: it is enough to call these critics 'hairy legged' for every general reader to be aware that Colgan is talking about feminism and that, furthermore, feminists represent a legion of women devoid of true femininity and hostile to ordinary young women who want to live their own lives. It may be that chick lit is used frequently as a term for dismissing any possible literary worth in a text which deals with the intimate life of a young urban professional single woman, but it is also the case that Colgan herself was all for willingly embracing this term on the grounds that the writers sold under this category knew what they were writing, who they were writing for, and what the genre's limitations were in cultural terms. The colourful covers featuring line drawings of a martini glass, a shoe, or a handbag are as recognizable in identifying this clutch of novels as is the Mills & Boon rose.

Colgan argues that it is 'time we reclaimed the name' but, judging by the success of websites such as http://www.chicklit.us/ and http://www.chicklit.co.uk, there are many readers doing just that and happily bending it and stretching it to accommodate all their favourite contemporary books by women writers. What all these constituencies agree upon is that the main requirement to qualify as chick lit is that the books are about *young* women (usually no older than their mid-thirties) and that this period of a woman's life be treated as a special category of concern. This emphasis on youth and the difference between this and a previous generation of women is at the centre of all chick lit writings: chick lit is built on a tacit acknowledgement that feminism has failed to speak to 'ordinary' women and that they wanted some other forum to address their concerns. In the majority of chick lit writings, already 'empowered' women must find true self-determination through the right kind of men and some form of truce with their own family. I used to think this quite simply evoked some elemental nostalgia for a past untroubled by the difficult questions posed by feminism and for the comforts of unconditional love repeatedly played out in formula romances, but now I regard it as proof that chick lit is an anxious genre which, rather than playing out the age-old battle of the sexes, itemizes the casual privileges of maleness; but, having catalogued them, does not know what to do with them. As in some of the CR novels written in the 1970s, there is always a tension between the self-deprecating humour used in the novels and the more serious implications of some of the issues raised. The narrative voice allows these flickers of recognition to be intimately communicated with the reader in recognition of the shared experiences of the disempowered and disenfranchised – not least in the resentful acknowledgement by practically every chick lit heroine that men do not suffer the same relationship agonies as women.

I hope that readers have not reached this point to find themselves frustrated for lack of the kind of conclusion that ties all the threads of the argument together seamlessly. This book has travelled a long way and is as much about the ups and downs of modern feminism as it is about the changing face of women's popular fiction. These shifts aren't always easy to chart and there's so much material which tells the story of feminism that it is pretty difficult to recount the same tale twice. There's no real agreement about what went wrong or right with Second Wave feminism, or whether there was a necessary relationship between the political writings and the others which had a more peripheral link, writings such as fiction and popular journalism. I would assert that the link lies in attempting to discover how feminism struck the consciousness of the woman reader who perhaps only ever had access to feminist ideas through the fiction and popular journalism. Exciting and dynamic as the writings from the Second Wave were, most of them were destined for a small readership, except those essays and pieces which were anthologized in some of the wider circulation collections or the work of those very few women who became minor celebrities either because of their views or because they displayed the requisite amount of media-friendliness.

Today in 2005, it is those writings that endure most visibly that can be further anthologized and circulated for the purposes of academic study and there will always, therefore, be a tension between what the 'real' Women's Movement might have looked like from the inside and what it came to be portrayed as by the best-known figureheads as perceived from the outside – this is particularly true in the under-representation of writers of colour or from the working class. There is a great deal to be got from going back to original documents and reconstructing feminism's history,[1] but equally there is something to be achieved by evaluating feminism through seeking understanding of what the majority of women would have known about it and by what means they would have received their information. This book has set out to evaluate what women came to know about themselves through and after Second Wave feminism. The intention has been to place women's popular fiction in a context which allows us to trace it as a reaction to contemporary political and cultural experiences. In looking back at the novels which shocked from the 1940s onwards, and more particularly scrutinizing the way in which popular fiction responded to the growing Women's Movement in the 1970s, I wanted to show that the confessional form has been perennially popular among women writers and that it is especially suited to the desire to expose the underside of women's lives and to explore the realities of what had been too often dismissed as trivial and unremarkable.

Whereas the CR novels of the 1970s specialized in the portrayal of the minutiae of women's domestic lives to catalogue the ways in which they were trapped by the association of women with home life and the maintenance of children and husbands, for chick lit women's domestic circumstances are makeshift and give the impression of being temporary. Where these women are depicted in flatshares, the implication is that they are existing in a grey area between young adulthood and 'growing up' and that they do not enter full maturity until their future with The One is sealed. While Fielding might have engendered a whole host of novels that railed against the baggage linked with spinsterhood, singletons still endorse the view that to be without a man is to fail to reach full maturity. The numerous moral panics engendered by *Bridget Jones's Diary* reinforced how powerfully this novel had affected people, to the point where it had them reflecting on real young women as well as fictional ones, and sometimes this could show how poor an opinion such panic-mongerers had of young women or how much they depended on villainizing them in order not to scrutinize the behaviour of young men. As Resa Dudovitz reminds us, '[w]omen's popular fiction may incite rebellion at home, but it will never cause social upheaval because of its emphasis on the personal' (Dudovitz 1990: 5–6), but both at the height of feminism's popularity and at the end of the last century, such fiction struck a chord deep enough to cause a significant flurry of excitement among the media.

If feminism has been scrutinised and found wanting by chick lit writers, one possible conclusion is that it contains some pretty powerfully unpalatable truths for a younger generation of women, truths that are carefully evacuated from their novels. As I have discussed in the previous chapter, feminism is a shadowy presence in much chick lit and openly feminist characters are often a source of discomfort for the others –

> Liz is an ardent feminist, even though she knows it isn't fashionable any more. To be fair, she's a really interesting woman, full of thoughts, ideas, facts and viewpoints. She can be very pleasant and informative company.
> As long as you are not a man.
> And you don't like men.
> Men are the enemy and women who like men are traitors (Parks 2000: 126).

Feminists are sent up in this fashion with surprising regularity, leading one to suspect that it suits these writers to perpetuate the idea that feminist ideas are totally unsympathetic to young women and show a complete lack of understanding about their lives. Chick lit, I am sure, knows the power of radical feminist rhetoric but, in the years that it has been increasingly sent up, has forgotten the authentic message beneath the fabulous media monsters; or perhaps the message is so scary that it is easier to laugh at oneself, to depict the trivialities of daily feminine navel-gazing rather than grasp the nettle of political motivation which is so incendiary to comforts of the 'personal', which are so lovingly restored in the world of chick lit. Chick lit takes us inevitably from the alienations of single life in interminable London flatshares to partnership and the hope of double income bliss. Coyly, the writers often pause before marriage or any formal partnership arrangement and therefore the acid test – the real trials of the post-feminist heterosexual relationship – is constantly deferred, just as it was by feminists before them.

But at the same time that chick lit exerts a powerful influence on women as readers of popular fiction, as well as on the shape of romantic comedy films and television drama aimed at women, Third Wave feminism has gone beyond its subcultural origins to offer a political dimension to the scrutiny of young women's lives and ambitions. Third Wave feminism, seen by some to mark a rejection of Second Wave feminism in such a way that writers such as Naomi Wolf and Natasha Walter suggested that it no longer had any relevance, actually seems to take further the spirit of Second Wave feminist activism, though wanting to remodel it to suit its own time. Third Wave feminism has more in common with Second Wave feminism than is obvious at first sight: both are young movements dominated by women under thirty-five years old, and the concept of 'everyone doing their own thing' (Freeman 1971) espoused in early Second Wave writings has re-emerged in the Third Wave notion of DIY feminism, which includes the appropriation of popular cultural images of women, music, style, and anything else, to new effects which allow some distanciation from the intended meaning of the image or artefact. The DIY ethos reaches its peak in the manufacturing of zines and webzines which are often freely available to a wider constituency and, while not mimicking the small communities represented by consciousness-raising groupings and radical groups in Second Wave feminism, 'It is a truly democratic form of media, everyone who reads a zine can create one.'[2] While I'm not convinced that Third Wave riot grrrls would 'read against the grain' of current chick lit to produce something more radical, on their websites and in their zines they express frustration with similar issues and choose to write on the 'margins' to express their dissatisfaction with the limits of popular culture. I suppose, more negatively, they too provide only individualist answers to problems rather than foregrounding the need for societal change; yet cyberspace, like fiction, can be an effective 'global consciousness raising tool' (Gillis in Gillis et al. 2004: 185). After all, young women owe nothing to Second Wave feminism, except to not fall for the line that feminism is the source of all their problems and anxieties and, given that Second Wave feminism could not solve some of the most intimate problems for women – how to conduct heterosexual relationships, how to negotiate self-identity, and how to deal with 'power' – it is not really surprising that these themes crop up again and again in the writings of young women, whether or not they are explicitly engaging with feminism. As Lynne Segal remarks, '[p]art of the ongoing project of feminism should be the attempt to map out and assess which different pieces in the jigsaw of feminism get picked up and why; it should also be asking, at any given time and place, who is selecting the fragments, and however unintendedly – whose particular interests their delivery serves' (Segal 1999: 231). I believe that this is an important project to continue, particularly as feminism has been going through another important transition in recent years

I remain in two minds about chick lit and this uncertainty might be discerned at the points I waver on both sides of the argument in this book. I never tried to claim it has radical potential; merely that its resolute conservatism is interesting and perhaps itself telling. If feminism is in demise or young women have moved beyond a need for such a gender-specific politics, then why does it emerge so frequently with these writers, so often embracing the confessional form, feeling the need to defend themselves against some invisible critic?

Erica Jong noted, 'in the beginning of the "second wave" of the women's movement [. . .] there was so *much* blood and guts in women's writing that one wondered if women writers did anything but menstruate and rage' (Jong 1999: 4). In chapters 3 to 5 I explored some of that rage and many of the physical inconveniences of being a woman, and that physical discomfort was echoed in the uneasiness many of these heroines felt if they occupied space in male 'territory'. In an era where menstruation has its own merchandising machine and sanitary towels are advertised during prime-time television, it is the more surprising that one thing women in chick lit novels never do is menstruate. While pregnancy scares (and now more frequently pregnancies) abound, periods, like bad sex, abortions, and sexually transmitted diseases, remain absent. Bridget Jones has her pregnancy scare while sleeping with Daniel Cleaver but it is resolved by the use of an over-the-counter pregnancy test rather than the joyous celebration of her period, as might have been the case in a novel by Erica Jong or Marge Piercy. It seems that chick lit heroines simply aren't troubled by periods or that their power as the symbol of essential femaleness, the reminder of the link between sexual pleasure and reproduction, has faded. Neither do chick lit heroines rage. Rage, it seems, belongs with the po-faced humourlessness deemed to typify Second Wave feminism, while self-deprecating humour has taken over as the dominant register of chick lit. Could it be, as I have tried to suggest earlier in this book, that the laughter is rather more disturbingly the anxious laugh at one's own expense; the humour that now rather ineffectively disguises the blood and the rage underpinning it?

# Notes

## Introduction

1. This became *Modern Feminist Thought*, Edinburgh: Edinburgh University Press, 1995.
2. Both popular British television situation comedies in the 1970s which played interestingly on the notion of the war between the sexes.
3. It is commonly the case that genre romance fiction depicts the heroine as distanced from her family and friends, work, or any other interests dissolve into the background upon the entrance of the romantic hero.
4. 'We live at home, quiet, confined, and our feelings prey upon us.' (Austen 1965: 236)

## Chapter 2   Burnt Offerings: The Emergence of Radical Feminism

1. This newsletter, published in Chicago, produced seven issues before its demise in June 1969. See Echols 1989: 53.
2. It expired in 1993.
3. Anon., 'Consciousness Raising' (Koedt et al. 1973: 280–1); see also The Women's Collective (undated). Less accessible examples include Anon. 1985: 2–6.

## Chapter 4   Women's Spaces: Marilyn French, Erica Jong, and Marge Piercy

1. Maurice Charney, *Sexual Fiction*, London: Methuen, 1981, p.113. But Charney seems to misread Jong while claiming she misreads Mrs Portnoy, asserting for instance that Isadora refuses 'a much-desired bout of fellatio with her Arabic brother-in-law' (123), which actually misses the point of this scene (which might be criticized for other reasons, such as its overly vigorous stereotype of the Arabic husband as predatorily polygamous).

2. See http://www.ericajong.com/abouterica.htm, accessed on 30 May 2004.

## Chapter 5   Forbidden Fruit: Sexuality

1. As declared in *Women's Report*, 1978 (no page numbers). They regarded 'Penguin's marketing strategy [as] obscene'.
2. They 'pass through a phase of very intense but short-lived fixation to a woman (usually their mother) [. . .] preceeding from a basis of narcissism, they look for a young man who resembles themselves and whom *they* may love as their mother loved *them*' Sigmund Freud, *On Sexuality: Three Essays on the Theory of Sexuality and other works*, trans. and ed. Angela Richards, Harmondsworth: Penguin, 1977, 56.

## Chapter 7   Where Have All the Feminists Gone? The Anxiety of Affluence

1. As discussed briefly in chapter 2.

## Conclusion

1. Books such as Alice Echols's *Daring to be Bad* (1989) are invaluable in this respect.
2. Grrrlzine Network, http://www.grrrlzines.net/about.htm, accessed 18 November 2004.

# Bibliography

## Primary Reading

Alther, Lisa, *Kinflicks* (1976), Harmondsworth: Penguin, 1977.

——, *Original Sins*, Harmondsworth: Penguin, 1981.

Bagshawe, Louise, *The Devil You Know*, London: Orion Books, 2003.

Ballantyne, Sheila, *Norma Jean the Termite Queen* (1975), Harmondsworth: Penguin, 1983.

Bradford, Barbara Taylor, *A Woman of Substance* (1979), London: HarperCollins, 1993.

Brown, Helen Gurley, *Sex and the Single Girl*, New York: Bernard Geis Associates, 1962.

——, *Having it all: Love, Success, Sex, Money . . . Even if you're Starting with Nothing* (1982), London: Sidgwick and Jackson, 1983.

Brown, Rita Mae, *Rubyfruit Jungle* (1973), New York: Bantam Books, 1977.

Bryant, Dorothy, *Ella Price's Journal* (1972), New York: The Feminist Press, 1997.

Bushnell, Candace, *Sex and the City* (1996), London: Abacus, 1997.

Colgan, Jenny, *Amanda's Wedding*, London: HarperCollins, 2000.

Collins, Jackie, *Hollywood Wives* (1983), London: Pan, 1984.

Conran, Shirley, *Superwoman: Everywoman's Book of Household Management* (1975), Harmondsworth: Penguin, 1977

——, *Lace* (1982), Harmondsworth: Penguin, 1983.

Davidson, Sara, *Loose Change: Three Women of the Sixties* (1977), Berkeley: University of California Press, 1997.

Fielding, Helen, *Bridget Jones's Diary*, London: Picador, 1996.

——, *Bridget Jones: The Edge of Reason*, London: Picador, 1999.

French, Marilyn, *The Women's Room* (1977), London: Abacus, 1986.

Friedan, Betty, *The Feminine Mystique* (1963), Harmondsworth: Penguin, 1982.

Gould, Lois, *Such Good Friends* (1970), London: Corgi, 1972.

Green, Jane, *Mr Maybe*, Harmondsworth: Penguin, 1999.

——, *Babyville*, London: Penguin Books, 2002.

Haran, Maeve, *Having it All*, London: Signet, 1992.

Jewell, Lisa, *Ralph's Party*, Harmondsworth: Penguin, 2001.

——, *A Friend of the Family*, London: Michael Joseph, 2003.

Jong, Erica, *Fear of Flying* (1973), London: Grafton Books, 1974.

——, *How to Save Your Own Life* (1977), London: Grafton Books, 1978.

——, *Parachutes and Kisses*, London: Granada, 1984.

Kaufman, Sue, *Diary of a Mad Housewife* (1967), London: Michael Joseph, 1968.

Keyes, Marian, *Sushi For Beginners*, Harmondsworth: Penguin, 2001.

——, *The Other Side of the Story*, London: Michael Joseph, 2004.

Knight, India, *My Life on a Plate*, Harmondsworth: Penguin, 2000.

Koomson, Dorothy, *The Cupid Effect*, London: Piatkus, 2002.

Krantz, Judith, *Princess Daisy* (1980), London: Bantam, 1986.

Lessing, Doris, *The Golden Notebook* (1962), London: Flamingo, 1993.

Lurie, Alison, *The War Between the Tates* (1974), London: Minerva 1994.

McCarthy, Mary, *The Group* (1963), Harmondsworth: Penguin, 1966.

Metalious, Grace, *Peyton Place* (1956), London: Virago, 2002.

Millett, Kate, *Flying* (1974), London: Paladin, 1976.

Parks, Adele, *Playing Away*, Harmondsworth: Penguin Books, 2000.

——, *Game Over*, Harmondsworth: Penguin Books, 2001.

——, *Larger than Life*, Harmondsworth: Penguin, 2002.

Pearson, Allison, *I Don't Know How She Does It*, London: Chatto & Windus, 2002.

Piercy, Marge, *Braided Lives*, Harmondsworth: Allen Lane, 1982.

Plath, Sylvia, *The Bell Jar* (1963), London: Faber, 1967.

Roiphe, Anne Richardson, *Up the Sandbox!*, New York: Simon and Schuster, 1970.

Rule, Jane, *Desert of the Heart* (1964), Vancouver: Talonbooks, 1991.

Shulman, Alix Kates, *Memoirs of an Ex-prom Queen* (1969), Chicago: Academy Chicago Publishers, 1985.

Shulman, Alix Kates, *Burning Questions* (1978), New York: Thunder's Mouth Press, 1990.

Steel, Danielle, *Palomino* (1981), London: Sphere, 1982.

Susann, Jacqueline, *Valley of the Dolls* (1966), London: Corgi, 1982.

Weir, Arabella, *Does My Bum Look Big in This?*, London: Hodder and Stoughton, 1997.

Weldon, Fay, *Big Women*, London: Flamingo, 1997.

Winsor, Kathleen, *Forever Amber* (1944), London: Futura, 1991.

## Secondary Reading

Akass, Kim and Janet McCabe, *Reading Sex and the City*, London: I.B. Tauris, 2004.

Allen, Sandra, Lee Sanders and Jan Wallis (eds), *Conditions of Illusion:*

*Papers from the Women's Movement*, Leeds: Feminist Books Ltd, 1974.

Allison, Dorothy, *Skin: Talking About Sex, Class and Literature*, London: Pandora, 1995.

Anon. ('written by the women who took part in the demonstrations against Miss World Contest in 1970 and were arrested'), 'Miss World', in Michelene Wandor (ed.), *The Body Politic: Women's Liberation in Britain 1969–1972*, London: Stage 1, 1972, pp. 249–60.

——, 'Male Chauvinist Pigs: How to recognise them and how to deal with them', *Honey*, May 1972, 55.

——, ('by some of the Women's Liberation Movement's Conference Organisers'), 'Such Devoted Sisters', *Red Rag*, 1978 (no month, volume or no. given), 18–19.

——, 'Consciousness Raising for Beginners', *Edinburgh Women's Liberation Newsletter*, 28 June 1985, 2–6.

Austen, Jane, *Persuasion* (1818), Harmondsworth: Penguin, 1965.

Bedell, Geraldine, 'Sex and the silicone girl', *Observer*, 17 February 2002.

Benn, Melissa, *Madonna and Child: Towards a New Politics of Motherhood*, London: Jonathan Cape, 1998.

Bowles, Tina, 'The Very Beginnings of a Women's Action Group', *Honey*, May 1975, 87–90.

Brownmiller, Susan, *In Our Time: Memoir of a Revolution*, London: Aurum Press, 2000.

Campbell, Delilah, 'With friends like these . . . the media, the mavericks and the movement', *Trouble and Strife*, 31, Summer 1995, 65–72.

Carr, Helen (ed.), *From My Guy to Sci Fi*, London: Pandora Press, 1989.

Charney, Maurice, *Sexual Fiction*, London: Methuen, 1981.

Clarke, Norma, 'Feminism and the Popular Novel of the 1890s: A Brief Consideration of a Forgotten Feminist Novelist', *Feminist Review*, 20, Summer 1985, 91–104.

Cohen, Marcia, *The Sisterhood: The True Story of the Women who Changed the World*, New York: Simon and Schuster, 1988.

Colgan, Jenny, 'We know the difference between foie gras and Hula Hoops, Beryl, but sometimes we just want Hula Hoops', *The Guardian*, 24 August 2001.

Coote, Anna and Beatrix Campbell, *Sweet Freedom* (new updated edition), Oxford: Blackwell, 1987.

Coward, Rosalind, '"This Novel Changes Lives": Are Women's Novels Feminist Novels?', *Feminist Review*, 5, 1980, 53–64.

——, *Female Desire: Women's Sexuality Today* London: Paladin, 1984.

Cowie, Elizabeth, Claire Johnston, Cora Kaplan, Mary Kelly,

Jacqueline Rose and Marie Yates, 'Representation vs. Communication' in Feminist Anthology Collective, *No Turning Back: Writings from the Women's Liberation Movement 1975–80*, London: The Women's Press, 1981, pp. 238–45.

Crain, Jane Larkin, 'Feminist Fiction', *Commentary*, 58: 6, December 1974, 58–62.

de Bertodano, Helena, 'Sex and the Octogenarian', The *Telegraph*, 26 June 2003.

Denfeld, Rene, *The New Victorians: A Young Woman's Challenge to the Old Feminist Order*, New York: Warner Books, 1995.

Densmore, Dana, 'On Celibacy', *No More Fun and Games: A Journal of Female Liberation*, Cell 16, 1:1, October 1968 (no page number), http://scriptorium.lib.duke.edu/wlm/fun-games1 accessed on 3 June 2001.

Douglas, Susan J., *Where the Girls Are: Growing up Female with the Mass Media*, New York: Times Books, 1994.

Dreifus, Claudia, 'The Selling of a Feminist', in Anne Koedt et al. (eds), *Radical Feminism*, New York: Quadrangle Books, 1973, pp. 358–61.

Dudovitz, Resa L., *The Myth of the Superwoman: Women's Bestsellers in France and the United States*, London: Routledge, 1990.

Duffett, Judith, 'WLM vs Miss America', *Voice of the Women's Liberation Movement*, October 1968, http://www.cwluherstory.com/CWLUArchive/voices/voices4-1html, 5, accessed 7 October 2004.

Duncker, Patricia, 'Writing and Roaring', *Trouble and Strife*, 6, Summer 1985, 41–6.

——, *Sisters and Strangers: An Introduction to Contemporary Feminist Fiction*, Oxford: Blackwell, 1992.

Dundee Women's Liberation Group, 'Manifesto for the Liberation of Women', papers from the 6th National Women's Liberation Movement Conference, Edinburgh, 28–30 June 1974 (held at the Feminist Library, London).

Du Plessis, Rachel Blau and Ann Snitow (eds), *The Feminist Memoir Project: Voices from the Women's Liberation Movement*, New York: Three Rivers Press, 1998.

Eagleton, Mary, 'Who's Who and Where's Where: Constructing Feminist Literary Studies', *Feminist Review*, 53, Summer 1996, 1–23.

Echols, Alice, *Daring to Be Bad: Radical Feminism in America 1967–1975*, Minneapolis: University of Minnesota Press, 1989.

*Edinburgh Women's Liberation Newsletter*, June 1985, 28.

Ehrenreich, Barbara, Elizabeth Hess and Gloria Jacobs, *Re-making Love: The Feminization of Sex*, London: Fontana, 1987.

Eriksson, Helena, Husbands, Lovers, and Dreamlovers: Masculinity and Female Desire in Women's Novels of the 1970s, published doctoral thesis, Uppsala, Sweden: Uppsala University, 1997.

Evans, Mary, *Introducing Contemporary Feminist Thought*, London: Polity Press, 1997.

Evans, Sara, *Personal Politics: The Roots of Women's Liberation in the Civil Rights Movement and the New Left*, New York: Alfred A. Knopf, 1979.

Ezard, John, 'Bainbridge Tilts at "Chick Lit" Cult', *The Guardian*, 24 August 2001.

Fairbairns, Zoë, 'On Writing *Benefits*', in Feminist Anthology Collective (eds), No Turning Back: Writings from the Women's Liberation Movement 1975–80, London: The Women's Press, 1981, pp. 256–7.

——, 'Saying What We Want: Women's Liberation and the Seven Demands', in Helen Graham, Ann Kaloski, Ali Neilson and Emma Robertson (eds), *The Feminist Seventies*, York: Raw Nerve Books, 2003, pp. 93–103.

Faludi, Susan, *Backlash: The Undeclared War Against Women*, London: Chatto & Windus, 1992.

Felski, Rita, *Beyond Feminist Aesthetic: Feminist Literature and Social Change*, London: Hutchinson Radius, 1989.

——, *Doing Time: Feminist Theory and Postmodern Culture*, New York: New York University Press, 2000.

Feminist Anthology Collective (eds), *No Turning Back: Writings from the Women's Liberation Movement 1975–80*, London: The Women's Press, 1981.

Fielding, Helen, interview, *Bookworm*, BBC Radio Four 2001, programme 4, http://www.bbc.co.uk/education/archive/bookworm/tran4.html, accessed on 10 November 2001.

Fowler, Bridget, *The Alienated Reader: Women and Popular Romantic Literature in the Twentieth Century*, Hemel Hempstead: Harvester Wheatsheaf, 1991.

Freeman, Jo (writing as Joreen), 'What in the Hell is Women's Liberation Anyway?', *Voice of the Women's Liberation Movement*, 1:1, March 1968, http://www.cwluherstory.com/CWLUArchive/voices/voices4-1.html, accessed on 7 October 2004.

——, 'The Women's Liberation Movement: Its Origins, Structures and Ideas' (1971), http://scriptorium.lib.duke.edu/wlm/womlib/, accessed on 25 February 2002.

——, *The Politics of Women's Liberation*, London: Longman, 1975.

—— (writing as 'Joreen'), 'Trashing: The Dark Side of Sisterhood', *Ms*, April 1976, 49–51; 92–8.

French, Marilyn, *The War Against Women*, London: Hamish Hamilton, 1992.

Gamman, Lorraine and Margaret Marshment, *The Female Gaze: Women as Viewers of Popular Culture*, London: The Women's Press, 1988.

Gerrard, Nicci, *Into the Mainstream: How Feminism has Changed Women's Writing*, London: Pandora, 1989.

Gibbons, Fiachra, 'Stop Rubbishing Chick-lit Demands Novelist', *The Guardian*, 21 August 2003.

Gillis, Stacy Gillian Howie and Rebecca Munford (eds), *Third Wave Feminism: A Critical Exploration*, Basingstoke: Palgrave, 2004.

Gilman, Charlotte Perkins, *The Home: Its Work and Influence*, London: William Heinemann, 1904.

Greene, Gayle, *Changing the Story: Feminist Fiction and the Tradition*, Bloomington: Indiana University Press, 1991.

Greer, Germaine, *The Female Eunuch* (1970), London: Paladin, 1971.

——, *The Whole Woman*, London: Doubleday, 1999.

Grrrlzine Network, http://www.grrrlzines.net/about.htm, accessed on 18 November 2004.

Henry, Astrid, 'Biting the Hand that Feeds You: Feminism as the "Bad Mother"', in Andrea O'Reilly and Sharon Abbey (eds), *Mothers and Daughters: Connection, Empowerment, and Transformation*, Lanham, MD: Rowman & Littlefield Publishers Inc., 2000.

Hogeland, Lisa Maria, *Feminism and its Fictions*, Philadelphia: University of Pennsylvania Press, 1998.

Hole, Judith and Ellen Levine, *Rebirth of Feminism*, New York: Quadrangle Books, 1971.

*Honey*, May 1972.

Joannou, Maroula, *Contemporary Women's Writing: From The Golden Notebook to The Color Purple*, Manchester: Manchester University Press, 2000.

Johnston, Jill, *Lesbian Nation: The Feminist Solution*, New York: Touchstone Books, 1973.

Jong, Erica, 'Writing a First Novel', *Twentieth Century Literature*, 20:4, October 1974, 262–9.

——, *What do Women Want: Power, Sex, Bread and Roses*, London: Bloomsbury, 1999.

Koedt, Anne, Ellen Levine and Anita Rapone (eds), *Radical Feminism*, New York: Quadrangle Books, 1973.

Lauret, Maria, 'Seizing Time and Making New: Feminist Criticism, Politics and Contemporary Feminist Fiction', *Feminist Review*, 31, Spring 1989, 94–106.

——, *Liberating Literature: Feminist Fiction in America*, London: Routledge, 1994.

Lawson, Nigella, *How to be a Domestic Goddess: Baking and the Art of Comfort Cooking*, London: Chatto & Windus, 2000.

Malos, Ellen (ed.), *The Politics of Housework*, London: Allison & Busby, 1980.

Miles, Rosalind, *The Fiction of Sex*, London: Vision Press, 1974.

Millett, Kate, *Sexual Politics* (1970), London: Virago, 1977.

Milsom, Nicola, 'What Women Want', http://www.bbc.co.uk/arts/books/genre/women/pg2.shtml, accessed on 7 June 2004.

Moore, Suzanne, profile of Naomi Wolf, *The New Statesman*, 1 March 2004, http://newstatesman.com/site.php3?newTemplate= NS Article_Peopel&newDisplayURN=200, accessed on 6 December 2004.

Morgan, Robin, *Sisterhood is Powerful: An Anthology of Writings from the Women's Liberation Movement*, New York: Vintage Books, 1970.

Neustatter, Angela, 'How chick-lit grew up', The *Guardian*, 26 March 2002.

Oakley, Ann, *Housewife* (1974), Harmondsworth: Penguin Books, 1976.

O'Faolain, Nuala, 'You've come a long way, baby', *The Guardian*, 13 September 2003.

O'Rourke, Rebecca, 'Summer Reading', *Feminist Review*, 2, 1979, 1–17.

Palmer, Miriam, 'Reviews' (Marge Piercy's *Small Changes*), *The Second Wave*, 3:1, 1973, 44–45.

Parker, Rozsika and Eleanor Stephens, interview with Erica Jong, *Spare Rib*, 60, July 1977, 15–17.

—— and Amanda Sebestyen, 'A Literature of Our Own', interview with Elaine Showalter, *Spare Rib*, 78, January 1979, 29.

Payant, Katherine B., *Becoming and Bonding: Contemporary Feminism and Popular Fiction by American Women Writers*, Westport, CT: Greenwood Press, 1993.

Payne, Carol Williams, 'Consciousness Raising: A Dead End?', in Anne Koedt et al. (eds), *Radical Feminism*, New York: Quadrangle Books, 1973, pp. 282–4.

Pearce, Lynne and Gina Wisker (eds), *Fatal Attractions: Rescripting Romance in Contemporary Literature and Film*, London: Pluto, 1998.

Philips, Deborah, 'Shopping for Men: The Single Woman Narrative', *Women: A Cultural Review*, 11:3, 2000.

Piercy, Marge, book reviews, *The Second Wave*, 2:1, 1972, 46.

Plimpton, George (ed.), *Women Writers at Work: The Paris Review Interviews*, Harmondsworth: Penguin, 1989.

Radford, Jean, 'Women Writing', an interview with Sara Maitland and Michele Roberts, *Spare Rib*, November 1978, No. 76, p. 16.

Radstone, Susannah (ed.), *Sweet Dreams: Sexuality, Gender and Popular Fiction*, London: Lawrence and Wishart, 1988.

Redfern, Catherine, 'I Love the 70s', *The F-Word*, October 2002, http://www.thefword.org.uk/features/2002/10/i_love_the_70s, accessed on 6 May 2005.

Rich, Adrienne, *Blood, Bread and Poetry: Selected Prose 1979–1985*, London: Virago, 1986.

Robinson, Lillian S., *Sex, Class, and Culture*, Bloomington: Indiana University Press, 1978.

Roiphe, Katie, *The Morning After: Sex, Fear, and Feminism*, London: Hamish Hamilton, 1993.

Rowbotham, Sheila, *The Past is Before Us: Feminism in Action since the 1960s*, London: Pandora Press, 1989.

Sage, Lorna, *Women in the House of Fiction: Post-War Women Novelists*, London: Macmillan, 1992.

Schuch, Beverly, transcript of interview with Helen Gurley Brown, aired 18 January 1998, http://cnn.com/TRANSCRIPTS/9801/18/pin.00.html, accessed on 19 July 1999.

Seaman, Barbara, *Lovely Me: The Life of Jacqueline Susann*, New York: Seven Stories Press, 1996.

Segal, Lynne, *Why Feminism? Gender, Psychology, Politics*, Oxford: Polity Press, 1999.

*Shrew*, March 1971.

Siegel, Deborah, 'Sexing the Single Girl', April 2002 (14 pages), paper lodged online by the Center for the Education of Women, University of Michigan, accessed on 25 September 2004.

Skinner, Beverly, 'Unity is Vital', *Enough* (Journal of the Bristol Women's Liberation Group, UK), 2, June 1970, 33–5.

*Spare Rib*, 60, July 1977.

Sutherland, John, *Bestsellers: Popular Fiction of the 1970s*, London: Routledge Kegan & Paul, 1981.

Templin, Charlotte, *Feminism and the Politics of Literary Reputation: The Example of Erica Jong*, Lawrence, KN: University Press of Kansas, 1995.

Theroux, Paul, review of *Fear of Flying*, *The New Statesman*, 19 April 1974, 554.

Thomas, Scarlett, 'The Great Chick Lit Conspiracy', *The Independent*, 4 August 2002.

Toth, Emily, 'Fatherless and Dispossessed: Grace Metalious as a French-Canadian Writer', *Journal of Popular Culture*, 15: 3, Winter, 1981, 28–38.

Tufnell Park Women's Liberation Group, untitled article, *Shrew*, April 1970, 1–4.

Updike, John, *Picked-Up Pieces*, London: André Deutsch, 1976.

*Voice of the Women's Liberation Movement*, 1:1 (March 1968), http://www.cwluherstory.com/CWLUArchive/voices/voices1-1.html, accessed on 7 October 2004.

*Voice of the Women's Liberation Movement*, October 1968 (no vol. or no.), http://www.cwluherstory.com/CWLUArchive/voices/voices4-1.html, accessed 7 October 2004.

Walker, Nancy A., *Feminist Alternatives: Irony and Fantasy in the Contemporary Novel by Women*, Jackson, MI: University Press of Mississippi, 1990.

Walker, Rebecca, *To Be Real: Telling the Truth and Changing the Face of Feminism*, New York: Doubleday, 1995.

Walter, Natasha, *The New Feminism*, London: Little, Brown and Company, 1998.

——, (ed.), *On the Move: Feminism for a New Generation*, London: Virago, 1999.

Wandor, Michelene (ed.), *The Body Politic: Women's Liberation in Britain, 1969–1972*, London: Stage 1, 1972.

Weisstein, Naomi and Heather Booth, 'Will the Women's Movement Survive?', *Catcall*, 8, June 1978, 16–27.

Whelehan, Imelda, *Modern Feminist Thought*, Edinburgh: Edinburgh University Press, 1995.

——, *Overloaded: Popular Culture and the Future of Feminism*, London: the Women's Press, 2000.

——, 'Sex and the Single Girl: Helen Fielding, Erica Jong and Helen Gurley Brown', in E. Parker (ed.), *Contemporary British Women Writers (Essays and Studies 2004)*, Cambridge: D.S. Brewer, 2004, pp. 28–40.

——, 'A Space of My Own: Feminine/Feminist Spaces in Contemporary Popular Culture', in S. Villegas-López and B. Domínguez-Garcia (eds), *Literature, Gender, Space*, Huelva: Universidad de Huelva Publicaciones, 2004, pp. 23–33.

—— and Maroula Joannou, 'This Book Changes Lives: The "Consciousness- Raising Novel" and its Legacy', in Helen Graham, Ann Kaloski, Ali Neilson and Emma Robertson (eds), *The Feminist Seventies*, York: Raw Nerve Books, 2003, pp. 125–40.

Wilson, Elizabeth, *The Contradictions of Culture: Cities, Culture, Women*, London: Sage, 2001.

Wisker, Gina (ed.), *It's My Party: Reading Twentieth Century Women's Writing*, London: Pluto Press, 1994.

Wolf, Naomi, *Fire with Fire: The New Female Power and How it will change the 21st Century*, London: Chatto & Windus, 1993.

The Women's Collective, 'Consciousness-Raising' (undated), http://www.cwluherstory.com/CWLUArchive/crguidelines.html, accessed on 20 April 2005.

*Women's Report*, 6:2, February–March 1978.

*Women's Report*, June–July 1979.

Woolf, Virginia, *A Room of One's Own* (1929), London: Grafton Books, 1977.

# Index